Essentials of U.S. Foreign Policy Making

Essentials of U.S. Foreign Policy Making

Ralph G. Carter

Texas Christian University

Boston Columbus Indianapolis New York San Francisco Upper Saddle River
Amsterdam Cape Town Dubai London Madrid Milan Munich Paris Montréal Toronto
Delhi Mexico City São Paulo Sydney Hong Kong Seoul Singapore Taipei Tokyo

Editor in Chief: Ashley Dodge
Senior Acquisitions Editor: Melissa Mashburn
Editorial Assistant: Courtney Turcotte
Managing Editor: Denise Forlow
Program Manager: Maggie Brobeck/
   Kathy Sleys
Senior Operations Supervisor: Mary Fischer
Operations Specialist: Mary Ann Gloriande
Manager, Central Design: Jayne Conte
Cover Designer: Suzanne Behnke
Cover Image: The Protected Art Archive/Alamy

Director of Digital Media: Brian Hyland
Digital Media Project Management: Learning
   Mate Solutions, Ltd.
Digital Media Project Manager: Tina
   Gagliostro
*Full-Service Project Management and
   Composition:* Murugesh Namasivayam/
   PreMediaGlobal
Printer/Binder: Courier Companies
Cover Printer: Courier Companies
Text Font: Sabon LT Std 10/12

Credits and acknowledgments borrowed from other sources and reproduced, with permission, in this textbook appear on appropriate page within text.

Many of the designations by manufacturers and sellers to distinguish their products are claimed as trademarks. Where those designations appear in this book, and the publisher was aware of a trademark claim, the designations have been printed in initial caps or all caps.

Library of Congress Control Number: 2014934444

10 9 8 7 6 5 4 3 2 1

Student Edition
ISBN 10: 0-205-64439-2
ISBN 13: 978-0-205-64439-1

BRIEF CONTENTS

CONTENTS

PREFACE

The purpose of any textbook seems clear: to inform and guide students in a particular area of study. But such a simple statement hides a complex reality. What is the best way to approach such tasks? What should be emphasized? What should be left out? Good answers to these questions are not always obvious.

There are various ways of teaching a U.S. foreign policy course. Should one take a historical approach to U.S. foreign policy? What about emphasizing the procedures and politics that characterize the policy-making process? Should a current events/contemporary problems approach be used? Some authors seek to combine all of these approaches into one book, which is, of course, very lengthy and expensive for students.

My goal is to produce a short, relatively inexpensive foreign policy-making textbook that provides maximum flexibility to instructors to pair it with other resources. With a length of no more than 250 pages, this book could be paired with other works that allow instructors to use historical approaches, primary documents, edited readings, case studies, current events and contemporary problems, and so on. This text is available in a variety of formats—digital and print. To learn more about Pearson programs, pricing and customization options, please visit www.pearsonhighered.com.

Ralph G. Carter

Texas Christian University

Essentials of U.S. Foreign Policy Making

CHAPTER 1

Introduction: The Foreign Policy–Making Process in the Post-9/11 Era

After the 9/11 attacks, U.S. citizens could not ignore the fact that U.S. foreign policy choices affected them as well as others.
Source: dpa picture alliance/Alamy

LEARNING OBJECTIVES

- Define "foreign policy."

- Describe the five stages of the foreign policy input–output process.

- Explain the formal foreign policy powers of the three

main branches of the U.S. government.

- Differentiate between the concentric circles of foreign policy–making approach and the shifting constellations approach.

Introduction

The September 11, 2001, terrorist attacks on New York City's World Trade Center and the Pentagon headquarters, Washington, DC, did more than kill nearly 3,000 people from over 90 different countries.[1] The attacks also changed the mind-sets of most Americans. Many no longer felt safe at home, something most had taken for granted for their entire lives. In trying to understand why a coalition of **Takfiri terrorists** would launch such attacks, many Americans were rudely reminded that they were all affected by (1) the policies of the U.S. government in international affairs, (2) how those policies were made and implemented, and (3) how those policies and subsequent actions were perceived by others beyond U.S. borders.[2] Perhaps not since the Cuban Missile Crisis in 1962 had these realities been brought home so forcefully to so many Americans.

Recently, the United States withdrew its troops from Iraq, launched air-strikes to protect civilians from their repressive government in Libya, encouraged other repressive regimes to modify their rule or step aside, and called on its allies to do more to help in these regards. It also began the process of disengaging troops currently posted in Afghanistan. The United States initiated steps to try to organize a coordinated multinational effort to recover from the Great Recession of 2008–2010, sought to improve the health care of millions of people suffering from HIV/AIDS, and tried to empower women in places where their essential human rights have not been respected. In all these ways, the U.S. government addressed its own national interests and the interests of others in the international system, and the consequences of those actions continued to affect the lives of Americans—both at home and abroad.

Yet it has always been that way. From the earliest days of the republic, international events and U.S. responses to them impacted where Americans could travel, the safety risks to which they were exposed, the availability and prices of goods, and the quality of life Americans could expect. Like other countries, the United States had to adapt to events beyond its borders, as these events present either problems to be solved or opportunities to be exploited. That adaptation process involved making foreign policy.

Simply defined, **foreign policy** refers to the goals and actions of the U.S. government in the international system. Thus foreign policy may be what the U.S. government wants to achieve, and the steps taken in that regard, toward other international actors (e.g., China, the World Trade Organization, or al Qaeda) or issues (e.g., foreign trade, genocide, or global climate change). The overarching thesis of this book is *how policies are made and by whom affects the substance of the resulting policies.* That means the actors (the individuals, groups, or organizations) involved in making the policies, their motivations, their differing amounts of power or influence, and the processes by which they make foreign policy decisions combine to shape the resulting policy outputs and ultimately their outcomes. These actors, motivations, processes, outputs, and outcomes are the focus of this book.

How Is Foreign Policy Made and by Whom?

Foreign policy making is very much like domestic policy making in the United States. While there are some differences between the two basic processes, overall the similarities found outweigh these differences. At its most fundamental level, policy making is a five-stage process. As shown in Figure 1.1, it starts with **inputs**—things that stimulate potential policy makers to act. Such inputs could be international events that seem to require or invite a response, or they could be domestic pressures by those who seek a foreign policy change. In the second stage, policy makers make decisions about whether and how to address these inputs. This is the decision-making stage. There are many different ways

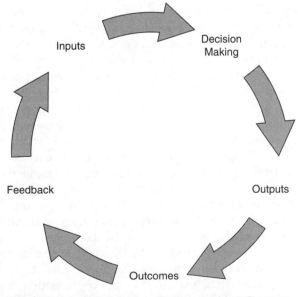

FIGURE 1.1 The Foreign Policy–making Process

to make such decisions; we will discuss many of them in the pages to follow. The result of the decision is the foreign policy **output**. It is the response by the foreign policy makers to those inputs. Sometimes outputs are words—signals of what the United States is willing to do—or broader policy declarations; other times they are more assertive actions on the part of the government. These outputs have results called **outcomes** that answer the "so what?" question; policy makers chose a course of action, so what happened then? The "what happened then" is the outcome. Finally, outcomes can create a feedback loop: Based on those outcomes, what new inputs arise?

Some foreign policies are the results of decisions made in the executive branch; others are the result of interactions between a number of interested governmental and nongovernmental actors—like presidents, other administration officials, formal and informal presidential advisers, individual members of Congress, representatives of relevant interest groups, the broader public, foreign leaders concerned, and at times the federal courts. All these interactions are reported by the various elements of the national news media, which may also become a factor in determining whether policies get made and how. Compared to many other countries, the United States has foreign policy–making processes that are extremely open to numerous participants who may become significantly involved.

In the crucial decision-making phase of any foreign policy process, the amount of influence these actors wield is a unique blend of the intersection of the nature of the issue, the political context involved, the timing, the actors' position in government or politics, and so on. However, presidents and members of Congress have important foreign policy advantages in terms of powers granted to them by the Constitution, and we should note that from the outset.

Let's begin with the president. The constitutional powers presidents have in foreign policy making are significant. Presidents serve as the commander in chief of the nation's military. This power allows them to order troops into conflict and determine military strategies. Presidents also have other constitutional roles that allow them to serve essentially as the nation's chief diplomat. For example, the role of sending and receiving ambassadors gives presidents the sole power to diplomatically recognize other regimes. Presidents have the power to make treaties with other countries, but the Senate must approve them by a two-thirds vote of those present. Presidents also can make personal commitments in the form of executive agreements with other world leaders that do not require Senate approval. The Supreme Court recognizes executive agreements as essentially the same as treaties, at least for the presidents who make them.[3]

As the nation's chief executive, presidents appoint (with Senate approval) a number of other foreign policy officials. These officials range from Cabinet officers (e.g., secretaries of state, defense, treasury, or homeland security and a few others like U.S. trade representatives) to the directors of national intelligence and central intelligence and to the different ambassadors who represent the United States in foreign capitals. Presidents also appoint some other influential foreign policy officials without Senate confirmation. A good example is the post of national security adviser. The Constitution also gives presidents the power to see that the nation's laws are faithfully executed, a power that provides presidents with considerable authority to conduct the nation's foreign affairs. Finally because presidents, along with their vice presidents, are the only nationally elected officials in the country, they are uniquely situated to speak for the entire nation when dealing with other international actors or issues.[4]

Congress—the legislative branch—actually has more enumerated constitutional foreign policy powers than do presidents. These include the specific powers to:

- declare war;
- raise, support, and regulate the nation's military;
- make rules regarding piracy and its punishment;
- regulate international commerce;
- regulate immigration; and
- make any other laws "necessary and proper" for carrying out the above powers.

Not willing to wait around for an administration to act, some individual members of Congress will take these powers and push and prod the U.S. government into making new policies; these legislators will use whatever political leverage they can to put their imprint on foreign policy.

More generally, as a collective body, Congress has the power to pass whatever legislation its members desire—prohibiting any cooperation with the International Criminal Court or calling for the overthrow of the Iranian government, just to name two examples. Presidents have the right to veto such legislation, but Congress can override presidential vetoes by a two-thirds vote of each chamber. Finally, virtually everything done by the U.S. government requires money, and the Constitution provides Congress the sole power to authorize and appropriate funds. Put another way, every part of a presidential administration is dependent on Congress for its annual budget. Just like parents dealing with their children's allowances, Congress can provide or withhold funds to reward or punish the administration for its policy actions.

Long ago these overlapping foreign policy powers were described as an "invitation ... to struggle," and that depiction remains an appropriate one.[5] When their policy preferences diverge, the presidential administration and Congress struggle for control of the policy-making process, because *the actor who controls the process will have the best chance to decide the resulting policy output.* Some situations favor presidential control, such as decisions to send U.S. troops into harm's way, recognize a foreign regime, undertake a covert operation abroad, or make an executive agreement with another country's leadership. In such instances of **presidential preeminence**, the foreign policy process can be seen as a series of concentric circles as illustrated in Figure 1.2. The innermost and most important circle is dominated by presidents and their advisers and top political appointees. Executive branch departments and agencies play a secondary role and are therefore in the second circle. Finally, the least significant actors are in the outermost circle of influence. These include Congress, interest groups, public opinion, and the mass media.[6]

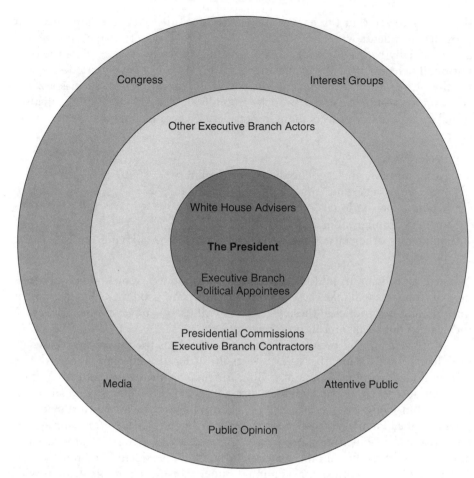

FIGURE 1.2 Concentric Circles of Foreign Policy Making

Source: Based on Roger Hilsman, To Move a Nation (Garden City, NY: Doubleday and Company, 1967), pp. 541–544.

The fact that presidents are undoubtedly the single most important foreign policy makers in most cases does not mean other actors are without significant influence. At times, foreign policy bureaucracies or Congress dominates foreign policy making. Therefore, a more accurate depiction of ongoing interbranch foreign policy interactions is captured by the idea of "**shifting constellations**" of power.[7] In a triangular relationship, presidents (along with other White House actors), Congress, and the foreign policy bureaucracies interact to make foreign policy. However, instead of executive branch actors being central to policy making regardless of the issues involved, each of these three groups has the potential to play a dominant role vis-à-vis the others for some foreign policy issues but not others. The president and other White House actors may dominate some issues, Congress may dominate others, and various foreign policy bureaucracies may dominate still others. All three of these major sets of actors are impacted by societal forces in the public arena like interest groups, public opinion, and the media, and all are also impacted by forces from the international arena.

Regardless of the nature of these actors' interactions, the foreign policy outputs they produce have outcomes—not just in the international arena but also on the United States itself (as the 9/11 attacks dramatically showed). These outcomes may have limited or no impact on others, or they may fundamentally change the dynamics of international politics. Either way, the nature of these outcomes and their magnitude can often produce feedback that leads to new inputs to the foreign policy–making system. Thus foreign policy making can be seen as a virtually never-ending process of adapting to external challenges and opportunities.

The Plan of the Book

In our effort to understand how and why U.S. foreign policy is made, we will follow the general framework provided by the model of the foreign policy–making process. In the first part of the book, we will look at inputs. Perhaps the most important inputs are the ones in our minds—how we think the political world works, how it should work, and why. Chapter 2 will focus on these interpretive ideas, which lead to a discussion of four major theories of international relations. Next we will look at the inputs that come from the external political environment of the international arena, the internal political environment within U.S. borders, and the environment of conditioning ideas that shape U.S. behavior. These environmental inputs are the focus of Chapter 3.

In the second part of the book, we will examine various decision-making processes. That's right—processes plural. There are many ways decisions get made, and oftentimes the process used depends on who is in the decision-making group. So Chapter 4 will focus on the major governmental foreign policy–making actors, Chapter 5 will look at how individuals and small groups make decisions, Chapter 6 will examine bureaucratic politics and policy making, and Chapter 7 will focus on how Congress participates in foreign policy making. Beyond these governmental actors, other societal groups—like interest groups, think tanks, the media, and individual opinion leaders—also get involved in foreign policy making. These nongovernmental actors and their influence on policy making will be the focus of Chapter 8, and other societal factors like political culture and public opinion will be examined as well. Chapter 9 examines how foreign actors—individuals, groups, or organizations—also get involved in the making of U.S. foreign policy. As you will see, many different actors and their diverging viewpoints combine to shape U.S. foreign policy decisions.

In the third part of the book, we will wrap up our examination of the U.S. foreign policy–making process. In Chapter 10, we will take a brief look at the types of foreign policy outputs that are the product of this process and the kinds of outcomes that they generate. In Chapter 11, we will suggest some concluding thoughts by looking toward the future. We will offer suggestions about the changing nature of future foreign policy priorities, possible changes in the mix of actors who make U.S. foreign policy, ideas about how the processes by which foreign policy is made might change, and how foreign policy outputs may shift in the future.

Our goal in this book is to help you understand the people and politics involved in making U.S. foreign policy. To assist in that effort, we will offer learning objectives at the start of each chapter. Keep them in mind as you read the chapter; they can prove useful in guiding you through the reading. Also periodically, we will have boxes inserted in the chapters. The material in these boxes provides more in-depth, real-life illustrations of the theories, concepts, and relationships we are trying to convey. Important terms and concepts will be presented in **boldface**. These are defined in the chapters and also included in the glossary at the end of the book.

Finally, we hope by the end of the book you better understand certain things. These include the following:

- Who makes foreign policy matters.
- What motivates these actors can vary tremendously.
- Policy making is shaped by both international and domestic inputs.
- There are many different ways to reach foreign policy decisions.
- Those resulting decisions have impacts on others.

Once you have a firm grasp of these points, you will know far more about U.S. foreign policy making than do most Americans and will be poised to act on that understanding for the rest of your life!

Glossary Terms

Foreign policy   the goals and actions of the U.S. government in the international system.

Inputs   the stimuli that cause potential foreign policy makers to act.

Outcomes   the consequences of foreign policy outputs.

Outputs   the actions taken by foreign policy makers in response to the inputs they receive.

Presidential preeminence model   the idea that presidents dominate foreign policy making for the issues they care most about.

Shifting constellations model   the idea that presidents and their White House advisers, elements of the foreign policy bureaucracies, and Congress compete for policy-making influence and who dominates the process can change as foreign policy issues change.

Takfiri terrorists   Muslims who believe in Takfirism, the notion that any Muslim who does not believe as they do is an infidel and must be killed.

Endnotes

1. Carolee Walker, "Five-Year Remembrance Honors Victims from 90 Countries: Nations United Will Win War on Terror, Officials Say," *Washington File*, September 11, 2006, available online at http://www.america.gov/st/washfile-english /2006/September/20060911141954bcreklaw0.9791071.html.

2. For more on Takfiri terrorists and Takfirism, see David Kilcullen, *The Acciden-tal Guerrilla: Fighting Small Wars in the Midst of a Big One* (New York: Oxford University Press, 2009), pp. xviii–xix.
3. The most relevant Supreme Court cases are *U.S. v. Belmont* (1937) and *U.S. v. Pink* (1942). For more information, see Jean E. Smith, *The Constitution and American Foreign Policy* (St. Paul, MN: West Publishing Company, 1989), particularly Chapter 3.
4. The Supreme Court agreed by noting that foreign affairs called for the nation to speak with one voice and that the president was the "sole organ of the nation in its external relations" in the 1936 *U.S. v. Curtiss-Wright Export Corporation* case. See Smith, *The Constitution and American Foreign Policy*, pp. 6–10.
5. See Edwin S. Corwin, *The President: Office and Powers* (New York: New York University Press, 1957), p. 171.
6. Roger Hilsman, *To Move a Nation* (Garden City, NY: Doubleday, 1967), pp. 541–544.
7. See James M. Scott, *Deciding to Intervene: The Reagan Doctrine and American Foreign Policy* (Durham, NC: Duke University Press, 1996).

CHAPTER 2

Interpretive Ideas: The Impact of Foreign Policy Theories

What motivates the leader of the world's greatest military power to call for nuclear disarmament, as President Barack Obama did in Prague in 2009?
Source: SAUL LOEB/AFP/Getty Images

LEARNING OBJECTIVES

- Define a theory.

- Identify the roles played by theories in foreign policy making.

- Differentiate among realism, liberalism, idealism, and constructivism.

- Apply each of these four theories to a case of foreign policy making.

Introduction

Since the mid-1970s, the U.S. presidency has been occupied by Jimmy Carter, Ronald Reagan, George H. W. Bush, Bill Clinton, George W. Bush, and now Barack Obama. When it comes to their foreign policy agendas, these leaders stressed some similar and some different goals, as well as different means to achieve them. As we will see in Chapter 3, some of these decisions were driven by factors arising in the contexts in which these leaders found themselves. However, these decisions were also the result of the basic ideas each leader had about what was really important and how the political world works. Such concerns lie in the realm of theories of foreign policy. In this chapter, we will discuss the importance of theories, outline the four major ones often applied to U.S. foreign policy, and then illustrate them with real-life examples.

Theories and International Politics

Theories are sets of interrelated ideas that explain some reality. Often thought of as cognitive maps, theories simplify reality by telling us what matters—and what does not—and what the relationships are regarding the topics that interest us. Like lenses, they bring certain things into focus. You and I use theories every day. We rely on theories of nutrition and how the body works to tell us what to eat and what not to eat, how and when to exercise, what personal habits are associated with long life, and so on. If our car doesn't start, we don't have to be expert auto mechanics to check whether the battery is dead. We understand some basic relationships about how things are or how they work, and why some things are good and other things are bad. Theories are no more than these bundles of interrelated ideas that help us interpret things.

Further, theories of foreign policy tell us what policy makers care about and why, and they often prescribe actions to achieve foreign policy goals. Theories help foreign policy makers organize facts and determine appropriate actions in the international arena. Four major theories can be identified that help us understand foreign policy behavior: realism, liberalism, idealism, and constructivism.[1]

Realism

"Political realism" is the name given to a bundle of ideas that have their roots in the observations of writers like ancient Greece's Thucydides or the Italian Renaissance's Machiavelli. However, world events in the 1930s and 1940s led writers like E. H. Carr, Reinhold Niebuhr, and Hans Morgenthau to emphasize how they thought the international system *really was* rather than on how they wished it to be.[2] Their concerns revolved around the **security dilemma**—how states protected their security in a system marked by **anarchy** without alarming other states, which would then respond by enhancing their security measures. The result could be an arms race that could erupt into violence.

To these thinkers, the most important essence of how the international system worked, and thus the essence of what they chose to call **realism**, was that (1) humans banded together and interacted as groups, (2) such groups were motivated primarily by self-interest and the greatest self-interest was survival, and (3) survival depended on the possession of power.[3] Thus in the 20th century, realism meant states sought to maintain or increase their military power so they could gain or protect their national interests. For example, a realist explanation of the origins of World War II would stress that Germany and Japan were states on the rise that wanted to ensure their survival and needed to increase their material resources. To do so required them to expand their territory at the expense of others. Thus Japan attacked China in 1931 and again in 1937, and Germany attacked Poland in 1939 and France the next year. When Japan attacked U.S. forces at Hawaii's Pearl Harbor naval base in 1941 and Germany backed its ally by declaring war on the United States shortly thereafter, the United States was thrust into a global war that had grown far beyond its East Asian and European origins.

Of course, reducing the most meaningful aspects of foreign policy to the ideas that societies are greedy and power-seeking means other aspects are minimized, and not all would agree that these points capture all the most meaningful aspects of how the international system works. So-called neorealists reject the idea that states are greedy seekers of power for their own sake. Instead, neorealists argue that in an international system marked by anarchy and without any coercive authority to which one can turn for protection, it is only prudent to seek, maintain, and increase one's own power resources. In essence, when there is no law enforcement agency, one has to protect oneself. Thus **neorealism** sees this inadequacy of the international system itself as the reason states to act as they do—not as a result of their inherent bad nature.[4]

Realists also generally share the assumption that states are rational, unitary actors. To them, it doesn't really matter who the country's leaders are at any given point in time, because national interests objectively exist independent of personalities. States face situations in the international system to which they need to respond, and that is what concerns realists—not who the leaders are. For example, policy makers might think that the most dangerous time is when states are undergoing power transitions relative to each other. A challenger state may be eager to start a war to demonstrate its growing power, or war could be more likely when the challenger reaches power parity and is dissatisfied with the status quo.[5] Therefore, it is little wonder that U.S. policy makers pay careful attention to states like Iran that may be developing nuclear weapons and states that did like North Korea to offset their already significant regional military assets. Thus U.S. foreign policy makers may often think in such realist terms, and they focus on the power resources of the United States and how they compare with the power resources of others.

However, an oft-heard criticism about realism and its variants is that, by accepting the premise that only military power and national interests really matter, the same old international system is maintained, and wars and other violent conflicts remain the norm. Those who think more positive changes in the international system can be achieved tend to see the world differently. If they think "what states want is the primary determinant of what they do," then those foreign policy makers wishing for a more peaceful international system can act to create such a system.[6] We next turn our attention to those thinkers.

Liberalism

Classic **liberalism** is marked by an emphasis on the rights of an individual person over the rights of the collective state. If individual liberty matters most, then individuals should not only be free from undue state control, they should also have the rights to pursue their own economic opportunities and have a say in their own governance. Consequently, classic liberals stress individual freedom, free-market capitalism, and democracy.[7] Classic liberals also assume that humans are cooperative by nature, and such cooperation is just as possible in international as well as domestic politics. By the way, we are using the term "classic liberalism" here to distinguish it from the way the term "liberal" is more commonly used in U.S. political discourse. Most Americans who use the term "liberal" are generally referring to "welfare liberalism"—a preference for state action on behalf of endangered groups in society—and that's not exactly what we are discussing here.

When applied to foreign policy, classic liberalism produces a pronounced preference for states with some form of democratic or representative regimes that respect the individual liberties of their citizens and allow capitalism to operate as freely as possible. Not only are such liberal political and economic systems thought to be best for their own citizens, they also produce a **liberal** or **democratic peace**. The historical record shows that well-established liberal democracies do not go to war with other well-established liberal democracies. A variant of this idea is that advanced capitalist systems do not go to war against each other. Such a **capitalist peace** is based on the idea that these advanced capitalist economies are often highly intertwined and wars are therefore bad for business.[8]

The idea that liberal regimes avoid war with each other and foster cooperation is not new. Enlightenment writers like Montesquieu and Kant were saying similar things in the 18th century.[9] So as the number of liberal democratic regimes increases, an enlarging zone of peace emerges in the international system.[10] Many liberals are thus quite optimistic about the future.

Still the international system is not quite at that stage, and the idea of the liberal peace does not mean liberal states do not engage in warfare. They are quite willing to go to war against **illiberal regimes**—those that do not share the values of individual liberty, capitalism, and democracy.[11] Whether such conflicts are motivated by the basic incompatibility of their respective values or the desire of liberal societies to convert illiberal ones, the results are the same—warfare. Thus the zone of peace idea only means peace within that group of liberal regimes, not necessarily in the broader international system.

How can wars be discouraged and greater international cooperation advanced? Advocates of neoliberal institutionalism (or simply **neoliberalism**) think they have the answer. Even under conditions of system anarchy, they argue that international cooperation is far more common than confrontation, as states find cooperation advances their national interests.[12] The creation of regional and global international institutions designed to foster cooperation reduces the chances of conflict and war. Whether based on their membership in regional organizations like the **Asia-Pacific Economic Cooperation (APEC)** forum or the **European Union (EU)** or global institutions like the **United Nations (UN)** or **International Monetary Fund (IMF)**, as states create more cooperative linkages, they gain more benefits from a peaceful status quo.[13]

A number of observers over the years have used the terms "liberalism" and "idealism" interchangeably. However, there is an important distinction to idealism that leads us to consider it separately.

Idealism

While realists stress the likelihood of conflict and the need for self-protection and liberals stress the possibilities of international cooperation to achieve national goals, idealists stress the notion of remaking the world into a better place—by whatever means necessary. Since President Woodrow Wilson brought the United States into World War I to "make the world safe for democracy" and stressed the principles of international cooperation in the creation of the League of Nations and its support for national self-determination for all peoples, some foreign policy makers have been motivated to spread what they saw as universal values—particularly liberalism's emphasis on democracy, capitalism, and individual freedom—to new areas of the world. So **idealism** refers to the use of U.S. power and influence to spread a system of Western values throughout the world and, by doing so, to make the world a better place.

We should note that it was Woodrow Wilson's idealism that realists reacted against in the interwar years of the 1920s and 1930s, saying that events in those two decades proved that the United States had neither the will nor the means to go around acting like a world policeman. They counseled instead that the United States should deal with the world as it really was and save scarce U.S.

resources (in terms of both blood and treasure) to pursue more narrow national interests that could actually be achieved.

Realist thinking dominated the Cold War period beginning in the late 1940s, but toward the end of the Cold War, idealism made a bit of a comeback. In his brief time as president, Gerald Ford tried to make human rights a more important aspect of what the United States was trying to promote internationally. His successor, Jimmy Carter, largely abandoned anticommunism as the guiding force in U.S. foreign policy and instead made the promotion and protection of human rights the guiding force behind how the U.S. government evaluated and reacted to other governments.

Most recently, George W. Bush sought to take advantage of the U.S. role as the lone remaining superpower to impose democracy and regime change in the Middle East by force, beginning with Iraq in 2003. The idea was that a democratic Middle East, free of authoritarian regimes, would help solve many international problems arising from this conflict-ridden region. Further, one might assume that former president Bush would see the popular revolts in the "Arab Spring" of 2011—where the people rebelled against authoritarian regimes in Tunisia, Egypt, Bahrain, Syria, and Libya—as proof that his ideas were correct.

Realism, liberalism, and idealism have something in common. Each of these labels denotes what its adherents see as objective beliefs about how the international system works or should work. Another way of understanding international politics is more instrumental in nature. Foreign policy is typically made by groups, and members of groups often agree among themselves about what is important and why, and then they act on the basis of these socially constructed realities. To understand this more subjective phenomenon, we must consider another theoretical approach.

Constructivism

Unlike the theories discussed to this point, **constructivism** involves a subjective set of ideas about *how* we understand reality, not necessarily about what that reality is. Constructivists believe reality is socially constructed.[14] To the extent that members of a group share a set of ideas about how things are and reinforce that set of beliefs in their repeated communications with each other, they assume that their ideas are accurate and act on the basis of that socially constructed reality as if it was an objective reality.

For example, during much of the Cold War between the United States and Soviet Union, most Americans thought communism was an evil menace seeking to destroy them. Given how widespread that societal agreement was, U.S. leaders typically interpreted Soviet actions as threats even when the Soviets did not mean to be threatening. Moving to the present, there is little question that Israel possesses nuclear weapons and in fact has far more nuclear weapons than does North Korea or even Iran, but U.S. leaders worry a lot more about North Korea's nuclear weapons and Iran's nuclear program than about those of Israel. The difference here is primarily "social." Israel is seen as a friend and de facto ally, and North Korea and Iran are typically seen in much less-friendly terms and with a great deal of wariness.

The idea that reality is "constructed" is not hard to understand either. If those with whom we interact regularly keep framing something in positive terms, we typically react to it on that basis. In keeping with the Israel example, Israel is generally described in the U.S. media and by policy makers as a close friend and a bastion of democracy in a region filled with autocratic regimes. Thus Americans tend to give Israelis the benefit of the doubt when the interests of the two countries conflict, which occurs from time to time. So when Israeli forces attacked a U.S. naval vessel (the USS *Liberty*) during the 1967 Six-Day War, U.S. policy makers accepted the Israeli explanation that it was a mistake and accepted Israel's apology and financial compensation for the 34 Americans dead, 170 Americans wounded, and the extensive damage to the ship. One wonders: how would U.S. policy makers have reacted if such an attack had come during the Cold War from Soviet instead of Israeli forces? Might the result have risked World War III?

The impact of collective identities is another emphasis of many constructivists. For example, the years shortly after the end of World War II witnessed the birth of a number of new international organizations, and the most important of these was the UN. The United States was instrumental in helping create the UN. So as an actor that saw itself as one of the creators of the UN, a natural leader in the postwar world, a state that embraced the rule of law, and a state with an overwhelming majority of support from the friendly nations that made up the majority of the UN's membership in its first decade, it is not surprising that U.S. policy makers turned often to the UN as a forum to achieve U.S. national interests. In later years, the majority of the UN's membership was composed of states that sought to be nonaligned or were friendlier to the Soviet Union than to the United States, and so U.S. leaders relied on the UN less as a tool of foreign policy making. As far as the American public was concerned, the collective identity of Americans had not changed, but instead the collective identity of the UN changed from being pro-U.S. to anti-U.S. Thus the U.S. orientation toward and participation in the UN changed.

Some constructivists also focus on how we use language to construct or mediate social reality. For example, from the mid-1960s until the early 1990s, most references to Arabs came in U.S. media when acts of violence were being conducted against Israelis, Western aircraft were being hijacked and their passengers and crews were being held, airports were being attacked, Israeli Olympic athletes were being killed, and so on. Thus the word "Arab" was usually followed by the word "terrorist." Soon many Americans seemed to think all Arabs were terrorists, which made dealing diplomatically with Arab regimes difficult and made dealing with Palestinian representatives politically prohibited.

Regardless of the approach used, most constructivists would agree on the following: (1) objective or material facts have little meaning until observers assign them a meaning and (2) those socially constructed meanings are then treated as "facts."[15] These two observations can help us understand differing responses to the problems posed by Saddam Hussein's regime in Iraq. Based on the success of the European Coal and Steel Community evolving eventually into the

EU, Western European leaders typically showed considerable respect for in-ternational organizations and multilateral approaches to solving problems. Further, states like France and Russia had a history of doing business with Saddam Hussein's Iraqi regime. Thus, when inspectors of the International Atomic Energy Agency (IAEA) failed to find stockpiles of banned chemical weapons in Iraq in the 1990s, a typical European viewpoint was that—given the considerable ex-pertise of those inspectors and the perception that Saddam Hussein's regime no longer represented a military threat—the weapons must no longer exist.

However, the same material fact—that chemical weapons seemed to be missing from Iraq—generated a very different response from top members of the George W. Bush administration. President Bush, Vice President Dick Cheney, Defense Secretary Donald Rumsfeld, and Deputy Defense Secretary Paul Wolfowitz seemed to have somewhat less respect for the UN and its as-sociated member organizations like the IAEA. When such organizations acted contrary to U.S. interests, they were often ignored or circumvented, and these decisions were usually justified by stressing that policy makers were protecting U.S. national sovereignty. Further, Bush, Cheney, Rumsfeld, and Wolfowitz per-ceived Saddam Hussein as an evil person and his Iraqi regime a threat to both the region and U.S. national interests. Sharing their distrust of Hussein's regime, these officials could not accept the fact that the weapons were no longer there. In this social construction featuring an evil leader (and possibly less respect for international agencies), top members of the administration constructed a reality that said these chemical weapons must still exist (after all, an evil regime would not just get rid of them) and they must have been hidden away for future use, and this "fact" made the Iraqi regime even more dangerous.[16] In each case the material facts were the same, but differing social constructions led to very dif-ferent interpretations of the meaning of such facts.

Now that the main ideas of these four theoretical approaches have been outlined, a more detailed illustration can be provided of how they offer differ-ent lenses through which to view, interpret, and understand foreign policy. The expansion of the NATO military alliance provides a nice example.

The Theories Applied: NATO Expansion

How do these differing theories help us understand who makes U.S. foreign policy and why such policy is made? U.S. support for NATO expansion to the east provides a good example of these theories in action.

The refusal of the Soviet Union to remove its troops from Eastern Europe in the late 1940s, along with its instigation of the first Berlin Crisis in 1948, led to the signing of the North Atlantic Treaty in April 1949. The 12 original sig-natories—Belgium, Canada, Denmark, France, Iceland, Italy, Luxembourg, the Netherlands, Norway, Portugal, the United Kingdom, and the United States—vowed to come to each other's aid if attacked. The surprise invasion of South Ko-rea by communist North Korean forces in the summer of 1950 created a greater sense of urgency, and the **North Atlantic Treaty Organization (NATO)** was cre-ated to serve as an ongoing military structure ready for use on short notice if needed. West Germany then joined NATO in 1955, and the Soviet Union responded by creating the Warsaw Pact, a corresponding anti-Western military alliance in Europe. Besides the Soviet Union, the Warsaw Pact initially included the communist-bloc states of Eastern Europe: Albania, Bulgaria, Czechoslovakia, East Germany, Hungary, Poland, and Romania. Albania pulled away in 1961 and formally quit the alliance in 1968. Over the course of the Cold War, Greece, Turkey, and Spain joined NATO, but as Western European states already friendly to the United States, their inclusion did not provoke a strong Soviet reaction.

As the Cold War was ending, the Soviet Union dissolved the Warsaw Pact in 1991, and the Soviet Union broke up into 15 independent states—the largest of which was Russia. *President Boris Yeltsin and other Russian leaders expected NATO to be dissolved as well, but it was not.*[17] Instead, NATO expanded steadily eastward toward Russia through the inclusions of the Czech Republic, Hungary, and Poland in 1999; Bulgaria, Estonia, Latvia, Lithuania, Romania, Slovakia, and Slovenia in 2004; and Albania and Croatia in 2009. NATO's expansion eastward caused great alarm among Russian leaders who perceived NATO as an inherently anti-Russian military alliance. To them, NATO's encroachment into Russia's traditional sphere of influence in Eastern Europe was a highly provocative act. Given such Russian perceptions, why did the United States support it? Our four theories provide different answers to this question.

Realism and NATO Expansion

Based on realism, U.S. support for NATO expansion is simple and straightforward. Even after its old nemesis the Soviet Union dissolved into 15 newly independent states, the Russian Federation was still a potential threat to the United States or U.S. interests. Russia had been a great power before the 1917 Bolshevik Revolution, and in the 1990s it still possessed significant military capabilities, not to mention thousands of nuclear warheads.

Given the lack of any overarching authority to constrain Russian expansion, neorealism would suggest that the United States look out for its own interests vis-à-vis Russia. By increasing its number of members, NATO could present a stronger united front against possible Russian actions in the future. Such a stronger united front should deter Russia from undertaking risky or provocative actions. Expanding NATO's membership deeper into the old Soviet sphere of influence and closer to Russian borders would make it easier to project U.S. power against the Russian Federation should that become necessary at some future point.

Liberalism and NATO Expansion

Liberalism sees increasing international cooperation as a positive for the international system. States are either naturally cooperative (as per liberalism), or they recognize that cooperation serves their national interests (as per neoliberalism). In the context of the post–Cold War era, admitting former Soviet client states (e.g., the Czech Republic, Hungary, Poland, Slovakia,

Bulgaria, and Romania) and states that were formerly part of the Soviet Union itself (Latvia, Lithuania, and Estonia) would help bind them tighter to the liberal West, making it more likely that their regimes would continue to respect individual freedom and embrace both capitalism and democracy. NATO membership for such former communist states would thereby increase their chances of becoming liberal regimes and decrease their chances of lapsing back into illiberal regime status. As the number of liberal regimes in Central and Eastern Europe increased, the chances of war in that region decreased. Strengthening an organization like NATO also satisfied neoliberal institutionalism's goal of adding to an international architecture supportive of peace.

Another neoliberal factor explaining this expansion is the fact that Europe's NATO members had become accustomed to NATO and its institutions over time, seeing them as part of a fabric that held liberal democracies in Europe together for nearly half a century. Thus when seen as part of the existing architecture of a cooperative European landscape, it becomes easier to see why adding more members to NATO just seemed like the natural thing to do—particularly when the hegemonic power in the international system (the United States) supported the idea of expansion.

Idealism and NATO Expansion

In this case, an idealist interpretation of U.S. support for NATO expansion starts with the liberal interpretation discussed earlier and takes those ideas a bit farther. To idealists, democracy, respect for individual rights and freedoms, and a belief in capitalism are universal values the United States should actively promote. Making these former communist states members of NATO—an organization composed of Western democracies—would help cement these values in the recipient nations. NATO could and would require that these values be respected by its new members, and these former communist states were so eager to be under the protection of NATO that they would readily agree to any conditions asked of them. Thus idealists could stress that Central and Eastern European fears of being the target of Russian expansionism at some point in the future could be exploited to force these societies to make the domestic changes necessary to become better places for their people to live. In short, NATO expansion could improve the daily lives of millions of people. How could that be a bad thing?

Constructivism and NATO Expansion

A constructivist explanation for U.S. foreign policy makers' support of NATO expansion begins with the socially constructed fact that NATO had long been the most important and popular military alliance to which the United States belonged. Secretary of State Hillary Clinton voiced what many U.S. foreign policy makers have long thought when she described NATO as "the greatest military alliance in history."[18] The major conclusions of a 1997 State Department report to Congress on NATO expansion are worth quoting, as they illustrate official U.S. thinking on NATO expansion:

- NATO enlargement contributes to the broader goal of a peaceful, undivided, and democratic Europe.
- Enlargement will yield benefits for the United States, NATO, and Europe.
- NATO enlargement carries costs.
- Costs to the United States will be modest.
- There are greater costs and risks to *not* enlarging NATO on the current schedule.
- The United States and NATO are committed to constructive relations with Russia.[19]

Regarding Russia's opposition, the report says:

> The United States and its NATO Allies are committed to building a strategic partnership with a democratic Russia; indeed, that effort and NATO enlargement are both part of the same enterprise of building a peaceful, undivided and democratic Europe. While many Russian leaders have expressed opposition to NATO enlargement, this initiative can serve Russia's own long-term security interests by fostering stability to its west.[20]

Thus a constructivist interpretation would be that U.S. leaders agreed among themselves that NATO expansion was a good thing, as it strengthened the U.S. identity as a peace-loving society by making Europe safer. In this way, NATO expansion furthered U.S. interests in a peaceful world and improved the future for Central and East Europeans at the same time. Russian fears could be dismissed because, as a defensive alliance, NATO represented no offensive threat to Russia, and NATO expansion was in Russia's long-term interest.

This societal construction of reality was widely held in the West. Virtually all the elites of Central and Eastern Europe were in favor of NATO expansion, the existing NATO members in Western Europe were in favor of it, and U.S. elites were in favor as well.[21] Among the U.S. public in 1997, a strong majority was supportive of NATO, a slight plurality favored NATO expansion, but a strong majority was found favoring NATO expansion among those who said they followed the issue carefully.[22] Thus, foreign policy makers and the members of the attentive public were united in their support of NATO expansion.

As noted earlier, NATO had been socially constructing its identity for nearly half a century as *a defensive entity that saw itself as nonthreatening to others.* As NATO members saw it, the Soviet Union had been a threat to NATO, not the other way around. Thus the fears of NATO as a threat to Russia seemed unfounded among NATO members. On the other hand, the norms of NATO cooperation had become an important part of the military and political culture of NATO members—particularly of Germany. These norms were reinforced over time with joint training missions and multinational military assignments. With no one other than the Russians arguing the opposite viewpoint, NATO expansion was socially constructed as an absolute good, and the "goodness" or value of NATO expansion became a political fact to which U.S. foreign policy makers responded.

More recent illustrations of these four theories can also be found. One involving some of these same players is suggested in Box 2.1 on President Barack Obama's declaration in favor of a nuclear-free world.

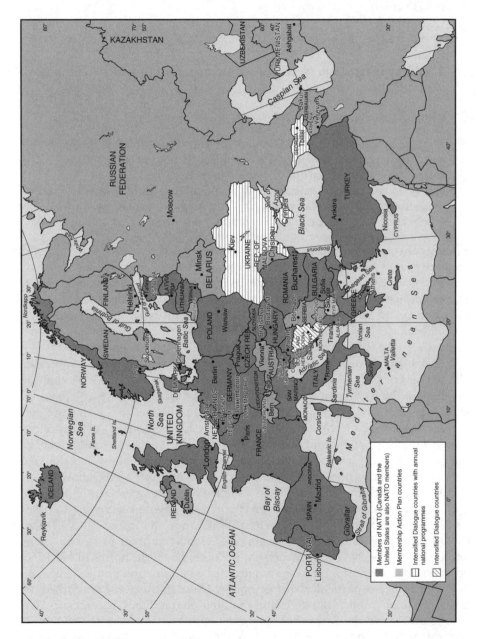

BOX 2.1

The Search for a Nuclear-Free World:
The View through Four Lenses

As shown in the chapter-opening photo, on April 5, 2009, President Barack Obama made a much-heralded speech in Prague, Czech Republic, in which he called for a world free of nuclear weapons. Not since the 1950s when President Dwight Eisenhower called for sharing nuclear technologies in a program called "Atoms for Peace" had a U.S. president gone so far in calling for nuclear disarmament. How do our four theories account for this policy declaration?

The Realist View

For some realists, endorsing nuclear disarmament as a U.S. foreign policy goal may have seemed like a foolish idea. Why would any nuclear weapons state willingly give up such a powerful set of weapons? However, a realist argument can be made for this idea.

In the early 21st century, it was clear that the United States had the most powerful conventional military force in the world. Its naval and air forces were unparalleled in the world. The United States had more ships, combat aircraft, smart and unmanned weapons, and logistical support than any other country in the world. While Russia and India had about the same numbers of troops as the United States, only China had significantly more active duty military personnel, and none of these others had military forces that could perform the missions that U.S. forces routinely did. From this point of view, the primary way a rival could offset the U.S. military advantage would be through possession of nuclear weapons. If all gave them up, then the U.S. qualitative conventional

military advantage over others would be even more enhanced. So the policy declaration makes sense from a realist perspective.

The Liberal View

The case to be made here is very straightforward. Liberals emphasize a world system based on peaceful cooperation. Nothing could be a more significant step toward world peace than removing the most devastating weapons humankind has ever devised. If nuclear weapons states like Russia, China, the United Kingdom, France, India, Pakistan, North Korea, and even Israel (which can be considered a nondeclared nuclear power) joined the United States in this endeavor, the world would be safer from horrific destruction on either a regional or global scale. Thus liberals would see this policy declaration as an important initiative that could pay off for humankind.

The Idealist View

For idealists, this was an easy call. When one considers the way the world should ideally be, nuclear weapons should have no place in it. After all, these are called weapons of mass destruction for a very good reason. If targeted against major urban centers, the blast and firestorm effects would kill hundreds of thousands, if not millions, of people, depending on the population of the area. Further, exposure to radiation from nuclear weapons would contaminate the physical area for decades to come, thereby making it unsafe for human habitation. Finally, the use of nuclear weapons is generally considered so horrendous that most nuclear weapons states would reply with a vengeance to such an attack, launching a nuclear counterstrike at the aggressor. The result of such a nuclear war would be multiple societies that were devastated, if not totally destroyed.

From the idealist point of view, ridding the world of such weapons could only make the world a safer place. Moreover, these weapons cost a tremendous amount of money to develop, test, maintain, and deploy. From the idealist perspective, couldn't those millions or billions of dollars be better spent improving the quality of life for one's citizens, rather than being spent on weapons no rational person hopes will ever be used?

The Constructivist View

Constructivists would emphasize this policy declaration as a major step in the ongoing social construction of a new reality regarding such weapons. Since the early 1960s, significant international steps have been taken to rein in the threat of nuclear weapons. A series of nuclear weapons treaties have been found to be in the interest of most actors in the international system, and the outliers who do not abide by the rules of the **nuclear nonproliferation regime** are a very small minority.

Thus Obama's call for nuclear disarmament did not just put more pressure on those who seek nuclear weapons, it also helped bolster a collective sense among most nuclear-capable states that nuclear weapons are dangerous—or even evil. The more the international community demonizes such weapons in its rhetoric and works to limit their possession, the harder it is for outliers like Iran and North Korea to justify their possession of nuclear weapons in the face of this international climate of opinion. So Obama's policy declaration, while just a set of words, could be seen by constructivists as a major step toward the construction of a more peaceful world in the long run.

What's your view? Which of these explanations makes the most sense to you? Was this policy declaration a shrewd move to actually enhance U.S. military power relative to others (a realist view), part of a global commitment to cooperation in everyone's best interest (a liberal view), a step toward ending the 20th century's most significant threat to all humankind and gaining all the benefits that step could bring (an idealist view), or a significant step in the creation of a like-minded community where possession of such weapons violates widely shared norms and cannot be justified (a constructivist view)?

Conclusion: The Importance of Theories

Foreign policy is made by individuals, either acting alone or more commonly in groups. As individuals, they are guided by fundamental notions of how the political world works and their own ideas of right and wrong; these value premises come from political theories. If policy makers consistently act in terms of U.S. national interests perceived largely in terms of military power, they are relying primarily on realist views. If instead they prefer more often to promote international peace and cooperation by encouraging the protection and expansion of individual liberties, capitalism, and democracy abroad, they are relying primarily on liberalism to guide their actions. If they want to use persuasion or even force to make the rest of the world a better place by making it more like the United States, idealism is motivating their choices. If none of these theoretical lenses seems to capture the thinking of individual policy makers, constructivism may be used to identify how foreign policy makers and those with whom they interact construct the meaning of the facts they perceive and then act accordingly on those meanings at the time. Again, none of us react randomly to events; we react based upon what we interpret to be important.

Glossary Terms

Anarchy   the idea that no supranational governing entity controls what states may do, thus there is no cop on the corner. It doesn't mean "chaos," because the international system is surprisingly orderly in most of its operations.

Asia-Pacific Economic Cooperation (APEC) forum—a group of 21 Asian/Pacific Rim economies that represent approximately 40% of the world's population, over half of the world's GDP, and nearly half of the world's trade.

Capitalist peace   the idea that advanced capitalist societies do not choose to go to war against each other.

Constructivism   the theory based on the premise that the world is socially constructed by agents interacting with the structures in their environment. Thus material facts are less important than how they are socially interpreted.

Democratic peace   the idea that well-established liberal democracies do not typically go to war against each other. Also known as the **liberal peace**.

European Union (EU)   a group of 28 democratic European states that are bound together economically and, to a slightly lesser extent, politically.

Idealism   the desire to make the world a better place by using U.S. power and influence to spread a system of Western values throughout the world—primarily values like the protection of individual rights and freedoms and the promotion of democracy and capitalism.

Illiberal regimes   those that fall short on at least one of liberalism's criteria: the protection of individual liberties, free-market capitalism, and democratic rule.

International Monetary Fund (IMF)   an organization of 186 member states that provides short-term loans to protect the value of its members' currency.

Liberal peace   the idea that well-established liberal democracies do not typically go to war against each other. Also known as the **democratic peace**.

Liberalism   the theory of politics that emphasizes the importance of individual freedom from state control, free-market capitalism, and democracy. People are seen as essentially good, and cooperation is seen as the normal method of interacting with others.

Neoliberalism   the idea that international institutions can be created to provide incentives for states to cooperate with each other. Thus states cooperate not necessarily out of any inherent goodness on their part, but rather because cooperation advances their national interests.

Neorealism   the idea that the structure of the international system forces states to act as they do. The most important aspect of system structure is anarchy; there is no overarching coercive authority present to enforce system rules. In such an anarchical system, prudence forces states to seek to maintain and increase their power resources and to pursue their own national interests.

North Atlantic Treaty Organization (NATO)   a military alliance linking the United States, Canada, and a number of primarily Western European states to oppose communist expansion in the 1950s; it evolved to include more central and eastern European members after the breakup of the Soviet Union.

Nuclear Nonproliferation Regime   a global set of rules and institutions (e.g., the International Atomic Energy Agency) that seek to limit the spread of nuclear weapons and to ensure their control by prudent governments.

Realism   the theory of international politics that sees states as the most important actors, and those states seek to achieve their national interests primarily through the threat or use of military power. States are seen as unitary actors interacting in the international system. Sometimes called "classical realism."

Security dilemma   how states protect their security in a system marked by anarchy without alarming other states to enhance their security measures as a result.

Theory   a set of interrelated ideas that explains reality. Theories of international politics help us understand what international actors consider important and how to achieve their goals.

United Nations (UN)   a global organization of 193 member states that was created after World War II to enhance peace and security.

Endnotes

1. For a good, brief introduction to international relations theory, see Yale H. Ferguson and Richard W. Mansbach, *The Elusive Quest Continues: Theory and Global Politics* (Upper Saddle River, NJ: Prentice Hall, 2003).
2. See Thucydides, *The History of the Peloponnesian War: Revised Edition* (Translated by Rex Warner, M.I. Finley, ed.) (Baltimore, MD: Penguin Classics, 1954); Niccolo Machiavelli, *The Prince and the Discourses* (Introduction by Max Lerner) (New York: Random House, 1950); Edward Hallett Carr, *The Twenty Years' Crisis, 1919–1939: An Introduction to the Study of International Relations* (New York: St. Martin's Press, 1946); Reinhold Niebuhr, *Moral Man and Immoral Society: A Study of Ethics and Politics* (Introduction by Landon Gilkey) (Louisville, KY: Westminster John Knox Press, 2002); Hans J. Morgenthau, *Politics among Nations: The Struggle for Power and Peace* (5th ed., rev.) (New York: Knopf, 1978).
3. See William C. Wohlforth, "Realism and Foreign Policy," in Steve Smith, Amelia Hadfield, and Tim Dunne (eds.), *Foreign Policy: Theories, Actors, Cases* (New York: Oxford University Press, 2008).
4. See Kenneth Waltz, *Theory of International Politics* (Reading, MA: Addison Wesley, 1979), and Robert O. Keohane (ed.), *Neorealism and Its Critics* (New York: Columbia University Press, 1986).
5. For more on the power transition notion, see A. F. K. Organski and Jacek Kugler, *The War Ledger* (Chicago: University of Chicago Press, 1980).
6. Andrew Moravcsik, "Taking Preferences Seriously: A Liberal Theory of International Politics," *International Organization* 51 (Number 4, 1997), 521.
7. See Michael W. Doyle, *Ways of War and Peace* (New York: W.W. Norton, 1997).
8. See Erik Gartzke, "The Capitalist Peace," *American Journal of Political Science* 51 (2007), 166–191.

9. See Baron de La Brède et de Montesquieu, *The Spirit of the Laws*, vol. 36 (David W. Carrithers, ed.) (Berkeley, CA: University of California Press, 1971), and Immanuel Kant, *Perpetual Peace* (Lewis W. Beck, ed.) (New York: Macmillan, 1957).

10. See Michael W. Doyle, "Liberalism and Foreign Policy," in Steve Smith, Amelia Hadfield, and Tim Dunne (eds.), *Foreign Policy: Theories, Actors, Cases* (New York: Oxford University Press, 2008).

11. For more on illiberal regimes, see Fareed Zakaria, "The Rise of Illiberal Democracy," *Foreign Affairs* 76 (Number 6, 1997), 22–43.

12. See Robert Axelrod and Robert O. Keohane, "Achieving Cooperation under Anarchy: Strategies and Institutions," in Kenneth Oye (ed.), *Cooperation under Anarchy* (Princeton, NJ: Princeton University Press, 1986).

13. For more on APEC, see its website online at http://www.apec.org/apec/about_apec .html. For more on the EU, see its website online at http://europa.eu/abc/panorama /index_en.htm. For more on the UN, see its website online at http://www.un.org/en /aboutun/index.shtml. For more on the IMF, see its website online at http://www .imf.org/external/about.htm.

14. Jeffrey T. Checkel, "Constructivism and Foreign Policy," in Steve Smith, Amelia Hadfield, and Tim Dunne (eds.), *Foreign Policy: Theories, Actors, Cases* (New York: Oxford University Press, 2008), p. 72.

15. See Alexander Wendt, *Social Theory of International Politics* (New York: Cambridge University Press, 1999), p. 1, and Yale H. Ferguson and Richard W. Mansbach, *The Elusive Quest Continues: Theory and Global Politics* (Upper Saddle River, NJ: Prentice Hall, 2003), p. 205.

16. For more on these perceptions, see Kristin Archick, *European Views and Policies toward the Middle East* (Washington, DC: CRS Report for Congress, Congressional Research Service, March 9, 2005), available online at http://www.globalsecurity.org /military/library/report/crs/44134.pdf. For more on the Bush administration's views on Saddam Hussein, see Bob Woodward, *State of Denial: Bush at War, Part III* (New York: Simon & Schuster, 2006).

17. For more on these Russian perceptions, see Robert H. Donaldson and Joseph L. Nogee, *The Foreign Policy of Russia: Changing Systems, Enduring Interests* (Armonk, NY: M.E. Sharpe, 2005).

18. Hillary Rodham Clinton, "Foreign Policy Address at the Council on Foreign Relations," Washington, DC, July 15, 2009, available online at http://www.state.gov /secretary/rm/2009a/july/126071.htm.

19. U.S. Department of State Bureau of European and Canadian Affairs, "Report to the Congress on the Enlargement of the North Atlantic Treaty Organization: Rationale, Benefits, Costs and Implications," February 24, 1997, available online at http:// www.state.gov/www/regions/eur/9702nato_report.html.

20. Ibid.

21. For more on the general consistency regarding foreign policy goals and institutions across both publics and elites in liberal democracies, see Thomas Risse-Kappen, "Public Opinion, Domestic Structure, and Foreign Policy in Liberal Democracies," *World Politics* 43 (Number 4, 1991), 479–512.

22. Survey Reports, "Public Indifferent about NATO Expansion," Pew Research Center for the People & the Press, January 24, 1997, available online at http://people-press .org/report/114/public-indifferent-about-nato-expansion.

CHAPTER 3

The Context of Policy Making

How do leaders like U.S. president Barack Obama and Russian president Vladimir Putin overcome a history of mutual mistrust between their governments?
Source: Carolyn Kaster/AP Images

LEARNING OBJECTIVES

- Describe the impact of context on foreign policy makers.

- Differentiate among external, internal, and ideational contexts.

- Illustrate the differences between post–Cold War and post-9/11 contexts.

- Assess the current priorities of U.S. foreign policy makers.

Introduction

Policy makers must envy academics who begin an analysis with the phrase "all other things being equal ...." In the foreign policy setting, few things are equal and everything seems to affect everything else—especially policy choices. Constraints push policy makers away from some choices, and opportunities lure policy makers toward others. Consequently, policy makers rarely start with the proverbial "blank sheet of paper" when considering a possible policy initiative. They are affected by what is going on in the external political context, the domestic political context, and the ideational context at the time. In this chapter, we will discuss each of these different contexts and then illustrate how such factors can serve as inputs to the foreign policy–making process.

The External Context

The external context can be found in the international political system that lies beyond U.S. borders. That context or setting shapes foreign policy choices in numerous ways, but clearly international norms and power relationships are two of the most important. Let's talk about them.

International Norms

The international system is like a society, and societies are marked by **norms**—unwritten rules of behavior—and these change over time and impact foreign policy makers. A century ago, the international system was dominated by imperial powers governing vast expanses of the globe through a combination of brute force, economic influence, and often the cooptation of local elites. An important norm of this era was that of gunboat diplomacy, of the strong preying on the weak. **Social Darwinism** seemed to justify this approach to international interactions. More powerful societies dominated less powerful ones, and that seemed to be the natural order of things.

A century later, norms have changed drastically. As the industrial age made technologies of warfare more lethal and destructive, international society moved to limit the damage. The 1899 and 1907 Hague Conferences began a diplomatic process to promote the peaceful settlement of disputes and limitations on the technology of warfare.[1] While such diplomacy did not prevent the outbreak of wars in the 20th century, the growing destructiveness of modern warfare—particularly shown in World War II—caused changes in international perceptions. The horrors of the Holocaust and the advent of nuclear weapons increasingly drove states to reject the acceptability of the strong coercing the weak, at least as far as the blatant use of force was concerned.

The use of force was increasingly seen as a legitimate tool of statecraft only if all other means of influence had failed. Thus norms involving the peaceful resolution of disputes and a commitment to multilateralism marked the post–World War II period. Given their destructiveness, nuclear weapons became a grave concern, and the norm of nuclear nonproliferation developed in the latter half of the 20th century.

At the same time, the norm of safeguarding **human rights** became well established in international politics. **First-generation rights** have been around since the 1700s and involve the rights of each individual, like civil and political rights such as the freedoms of speech, assembly, and religion. **Second-generation rights** are generally associated with the 19th-century rise of socialism and Marxism. Such rights include the material rights that should apply to entire societies, like the right to education, employment, medical care, or sufficient food. **Third-generation rights** date from the end of World War II and apply to groups at risk in society, whether unpopular minorities, women, children, the elderly, and so on.

Most recently, the Westphalian norm of state sovereignty based on the inviolability of borders has been seriously eroded. In 2005, the World Summit at the UN General Assembly endorsed the norm that states had a **Responsibility to Protect (R2P)** their population from war crimes, genocide, and other crimes against humanity. In 2006, delegates passed **UN Security Council Resolution 1674**, which reaffirmed the responsibility to protect people from such gross abuses of human rights.[2] Since then, the R2P norm has evolved in the direction of a more generalized sense that states have a responsibility to protect their people from preventable harm and that, if they cannot do so, the international community has a right, if not a duty, to intervene in the public's behalf.

Some international norms evolve into more formal international law, but whether they are norms or laws, these ideas matter to policy makers. They become parameters within which options are considered, and consequences arise when U.S. foreign policy fails to conform to these parameters. When policy falls short of these norms, policy makers have to spend considerable time defending the legitimacy of their actions. At worst, others may band together to resist U.S. actions viewed as illegitimate in the eyes of the global community.

The power of such norms was demonstrated in the U.S. decision to go to war with Iraq in 2003. When the George W. Bush administration began pressing for an allied invasion to topple the Saddam Hussein regime, major U.S. allies like France and Germany—as well as major powers like Russia and China—insisted on the need for taking the case for war to the United Nations. In their view, if the UN Security Council could be convinced that a case for war existed, then the use of force would be legitimate. The United States tried to make such a case, but members of the Security Council were unconvinced and the Security Council refused to authorize going to war against Iraq; instead it only warned Iraq of more serious penalties to come if it did not allow international weapons inspections to continue by the IAEA.

Without the legitimacy of such a UN authorization, the Bush administration was forced to rely on a "coalition of the willing"—troops from Britain, Australia, Spain, Poland, Denmark, and Italy. Major powers like Germany, France, Russia, and China steadfastly opposed the U.S.-led war, resulting in a major rift between the United States and its European allies. It took both the elections of new leaders in Germany and France and U.S. commitments to begin the process of disentangling itself from Iraq, before the rift within NATO could be mended. Thus for a number of years, U.S.-European relations were largely poisoned by the U.S. failure to live up to international norms. Beyond the roles that norms play in setting the context of foreign policy making, power relationships also shape the foreign policy choices of leaders. They are our focus next.

Power Relationships

The political realities of power—who has it and how much do they have relative to the United States—create both opportunities and constraints to U.S. foreign policy makers and thus provide an array of inputs for the U.S. foreign policy–making process. Consider the current position of the United States in the international system. When the **Cold War** ended in 1989 and the Soviet Union fragmented into 15 component parts in 1991, the United States was left as the lone remaining superpower. Was that an opportunity for foreign policy makers to expand U.S. national influence, or were there still constraints to be faced?

For many, the answer was simple. The United States had won the Cold War, its opponent was vanquished, and now U.S. military power eclipsed that of any other state, and if nuclear arms were considered, of arguably all other states combined. According to realists, the United States was poised to pursue any of a number of potential national interests. Yet according to constructivists, others took this notion farther. The more top members of the George W. Bush foreign policy–making team talked about the possibilities of this new era, the more they convinced themselves that a new reality was at hand—one they had constructed through their social interactions. With such military power they thought, the United States could go out and win any objective, right any wrong, and impose its well-intentioned will on the world. For example, backed by American arms a new democratic Afghanistan could be created, and democracy could be imposed by military force on old nemesis Iraq. Bush administration advocates thought these military moves would remake the Middle East, helping to transform it into a peaceful, democratic region.[3] Supporters and critics alike began talking about a new American empire linked by a global network of military bases.[4]

Still, the exercise of military power does not come without costs. Even the world's largest single economy was stressed by trying to fight two simultaneous wars on the other side of the world. At least in the case of the war in Afghanistan, some allies were there to help. After the Taliban regime in

Kabul was deposed, member states of **NATO** contributed combat or support personnel totaling approximately 50,000 troops to help stabilize the country and consolidate the power of the new regime led by Hamid Karzai.[5] However, the invasion and occupation of Iraq was another story. Few U.S. allies saw any need to overthrow the government of President Saddam Hussein by force, and the UN Security Council refused to authorize military action to oust the regime. So only a few allies agreed to participate in the U.S.-led invasion of Iraq. The choices of other allies not to participate left U.S. military resources stretched so thin across both Iraq and Afghanistan that other regimes—like Iran and North Korea—were emboldened to undertake provocative acts, knowing the unlikelihood of U.S. military responses.

External constraints face the United States in nonmilitary arenas as well. Over time, the U.S. economic position relative to others has fallen. While the U.S. economy is still the largest national economy in the world, others are catching up. As a group, the economies of the **European Union** (**EU**) are now larger than the U.S. economy. China is the second largest national economy in the world and growing quickly, as is the economy of India. Thus in either military or economic terms, the United States is still very powerful, but it is not a **hegemon** capable of imposing its will whenever and wherever it desires. Unless a superpower is willing to ask its population to make significant sacrifices in their lifestyles to subsidize its foreign initiatives, there are limits on what that regime has the resources to do.

This combination of military and economic realities provides some interesting challenges for U.S. policy makers. A good illustration came in 2008 when the United States approved a nuclear cooperation agreement with India, which is discussed in Box 3.1.

BOX 3.1

The U.S.-India Civil Nuclear Cooperation Agreement

In 2008, the United States reversed 30 years of policy by engaging in nuclear trade with a country that had not signed the **Nuclear Nonproliferation Treaty** (**NPT**). Despite the fact that India had not signed the NPT, the agreement allowed U.S. corporations to sell nuclear fuel and nuclear technology to India; in return, India agreed to international inspections of its civilian nuclear power plants. Why would the United States overturn such a long-standing policy? The inputs for this policy shift were both external and internal.

Externally, cozying up to India by providing it nuclear fuel and technology served two purposes: one major and one minor. The major purpose was to seek a counterbalance to growing Chinese military power in Asia. China's military might is growing rapidly, and China has brandished thinly veiled military threats (if veiled at all) toward both Taiwan and Japan—both good friends of the United States. The other major rising military power in Asia is India, which fought a border war with China in 1962. While selling civilian nuclear fuel and technology to India does not directly benefit India's military, it does allow more of India's existing supplies of nuclear fuel and technology to be diverted to military uses, and that should worry the Chinese. Also China will likely worry that such civilian fuel and technology could always be diverted to military uses in an emergency. Finally, any closer U.S. ties with a Chinese rival have to concern the officials in Beijing.

The minor purpose here is that the agreement sent a very harsh signal to Pakistan. Pakistan has lost three major wars to India and has long been a U.S. military ally. After 9/11, U.S. military aid to Pakistan increased, because of Pakistan's importance in the war on terror.

Yet Pakistan's cooperation in the war on terror was mixed. While Pakistani forces launched some military operations against terrorist groups operating inside its borders, most of the military aid sent to Pakistan was used to build up defenses and military capabilities against India. Some in Pakistan's military establishment even supported terrorist groups that launched attacks against India. The U.S. agreement to sell nuclear fuel and technology to India was a rebuke to Pakistan and a signal that U.S. patience with Islamabad was not unlimited, and this rebuke came three years before it was learned that Osama bin Laden not only had lived in Pakistan for years but had done so in a town with a large military presence!

Internally, two major groups in the United States pressed for this agreement. The first was the U.S. nuclear energy industry. With one billion people, India was going to need far more electricity, and it wanted to buy nuclear power stations. These U.S. corporations wanted a piece of that pie, as the cost of each power plant would be measured in the billions of dollars.

Second, the growing size and clout of the Indian-American population came into play domestically. Indian-Americans are a rapidly growing segment of the U.S. citizenry, and there is now an India Caucus in the U.S. House of Representatives. Most important though, lobby groups like the U.S. India Political Action Committee and the U.S. India Business Alliance worked long and hard to secure congressional approval of the nuclear fuel agreement. Thus domestic inputs to foreign policy making cannot be ignored in this case either.

So what do you think? Were external or internal inputs more responsible for the reversal of a 30-year-old policy? Which of our major theories seems to apply most here? Why?

Sources: Jayshree Bajoria and Esther Pan, "The U.S.-India Nuclear Deal," *Backgrounder,* November 5, 2010, Council on Foreign Relations; Jason A. Kirk, "Indian-Americans and the U.S.-India Nuclear Agreement: Consolidation of an Ethnic Lobby?" *Foreign Policy Analysis 4* (2008), 275–300.

Yet for many liberals, there is reason for cautious optimism in the international system. Mechanisms of cooperation exist and are at times used. As noted earlier, NATO took on an important role in providing military personnel and support for the mission to stabilize Afghanistan, and NATO members launched air strikes against Libyan leader Muammar Qaddafi's forces when those forces waged war against their own citizens in 2011. Also with the help of the **International Monetary Fund (IMF)**, leaders of both the Group of 8 (**G-8**) major industrial powers and the Group of 20 (**G-20**) largest economies and emerging markets cooperated in trying to adjust their national economic policies to meet the demands of global recovery from the Great Recession of 2008–2010. In short, the external context provides a variety of inputs to policy makers—some positive and others less so. But policy makers must also deal with the inputs from the domestic arena, and we turn to those next.

The Internal Context

Like the external context, the internal context also presents inputs to foreign policy makers in the form of both opportunities and constraints.[6] The values that make up U.S. political culture push policy makers in certain directions and not others. For example, one constant in U.S. political culture is the widely shared idea of **American exceptionalism**. Most Americans believe that the United States is not just different from other countries or societies, *it is better*. Both U.S. leaders and the public generally believe that the United States is uniquely blessed with a set of liberal values and ideas (e.g., the commitments to individual liberty, representative democracy, and free-market capitalism) that have worked to produce the most powerful, richest, and best society on the planet.[7]

Such an exceptionalist viewpoint can both pull and push policy makers. On the one hand, if you think you are special, leadership on international issues becomes an easier choice. Being special, you have something valuable to share with others. Pushing other states to embrace democracy or capitalism is a long-standing trait of U.S. foreign policy that flows fairly directly from this sense of exceptionalism. On the other hand, when others see you lead on multiple issues over time, they come to expect it—even when you would prefer *not* to lead. Thus when U.S. policy makers choose not to lead on high-profile issues—like intervening to stop genocide in places like Rwanda or Darfur or acting to slow global climate change—international criticism ensues. Other international actors who rarely lead on international issues are spared this expectation and potential criticism. When was the last time you heard the Swedes being criticized?

Another important aspect of the domestic context is the nature of the U.S. foreign policy–making system. Compared to that of other states, it is very open to inputs and fragmented in structure. It is considered open because it can receive policy-making inputs from a wide variety of sources. Inputs to the foreign policy–making process can come from not only legislative and executive branch officials but also domestic opinion makers, public opinion polls, interest groups, think tanks, the media, court rulings, foreign officials, and so on. Yet the system is fragmented in the sense that policy-making roles are shared between executive branch actors and members of Congress—and occasionally federal courts. Each can get a piece of the policy-making action. The result of such an open and fragmented system is that, with so many trying to get their hands on the helm, the ship of state is difficult to control and steer. Sometimes it goes in directions no specific policy makers sought but instead are the result of compromises or accommodations that became necessary to get anything done on the issue at hand. Yet beyond the domestic context shaped by values, culture, and the structures of foreign policy making, there is the ideational context—the current state of major ideas about the ends and means of foreign policy and the priorities that thus exist. We turn to it next.

The Ideational Context

Overlaying this open and fragmented policy-making system are dominant ideas that provide inputs to policy makers. The open and fragmented foreign policy–making system we just discussed is populated in part by officials elected as members of political parties, and the ideas that form the basis of partisanship matter in foreign policy too. While many will assert that politics *should* stop at the water's edge, this has rarely been the case. One can speak of Democratic or Republican foreign policy agendas, and those policy agendas tend to be different in terms of both ends and means.[8] Regarding ends, in recent years Republican policy makers have generally focused more on global issues involving national security matters or free trade. While most Democratic foreign policy makers would argue they are neither hostile nor indifferent to national security matters, they might elevate other global issues to a higher priority than their Republican counterparts—like environmental protection, human rights, or assuring that basic life necessities are met in developing societies. Regarding means, in recent years many Republican policy makers seemed to prefer unilateral approaches that rely primarily on military tools to achieve their goals. Democratic policy makers generally appeared more open to multilateral approaches that involved more international actors and a greater use of diplomatic tools to achieve desired ends. While exceptions to such crude generalizations can always be found (e.g., defense hawks who happen to be Democrats or Republicans committed to refugee relief), these generalizations capture something important about what most members of each political party tend to think is important in foreign policy and how such goals should be addressed.

Another aspect of the ideational context is the set of inputs that come from public opinion.[9] Top U.S. foreign policy makers are either elected by the public or appointed by those who are. Thus public opinion cannot be totally ignored. Two broad orientations toward foreign policy held by the public at times come into play. On the one hand, most Americans believe in **internationalism**. That is, they believe that U.S. national interests are advanced by interacting with other countries and peoples and such regular, ongoing contacts with others may contribute to the greater good of all. Consistently in public opinion polls since the end of the Vietnam War, at least two-thirds of the American public has favored regular engagement with the world beyond U.S. borders. Such internationalists may feel either that it is simply good to know more about other societies and peoples or that there are distinct advantages to be gained—such as military allies or expanded opportunities for U.S. trade.

On the other hand, some Americans are isolationists. **Isolationism** refers to the belief that the dangers of regular and ongoing engagement with the world beyond U.S. borders outweigh the advantages. Isolationists may stress that such engagement draws the United States into other people's wars or contact with other cultures undermines traditional U.S. values, for example. While isolationism was stronger in the 1930s than now, since the end of the Vietnam War between 10 and 20% of Americans typically express isolationist themes in public opinion polls.[10] Recently isolationists have gotten somewhat of a boost by the popularity of U.S. Representative Ron Paul's candidacy for the Republican presidential nomination. By forcefully advocating an isolationist foreign policy agenda, Representative Paul has won a small but vocal band of supporters. However, the intensity shown by his supporters should not obscure the fact that only a small proportion of Americans share these views.

More generally, public opinion about specific issues may push policy makers in certain directions—toward some possible options but not others. Depending on the congruence between what the public and key policy makers seem to want, public opinion can either constrain or empower those policy makers. In some instances, the public may not care about an international issue. In those circumstances, policy makers may be relatively free to do whatever they think is best. In other instances, public opinion may be strong enough to force policy makers to address an issue and to do so in a particular way, such as imposing economic sanctions on South Africa over its **apartheid** policy in the 1980s.

Foreign policy goals are part of this ideational context as well. It would be easy to say that U.S. foreign policy makers confront three overarching foreign policy goals: enhancing U.S. security, power, and interests.[11] But what such overarching goals involve varies in the eye of the beholder. Like policy makers elsewhere, U.S. foreign policy makers share the minimalist goal of protecting the physical safety of their population and possessions from attack. More ambitious goals include actively safeguarding the economic security of their population as well. However, the combined effects of American exceptionalism and a commitment to liberal values often mean that U.S. policy makers publicly embrace maximalist goals such as making the world safe for democracy, expanding the number of democratic states, acting in a global police function to protect the weak from bullies abroad, or, more broadly, just going out to "do good" in the world.

How and when foreign policy makers choose to act on those goals reflects their policy priorities at that moment in time, and those priorities are shaped by the external, internal, and ideational contexts in which policy making occurs. In addition to the points covered earlier, that setting is shaped by what happened in the past, particularly in the recent past. The impact of history is part of the context of ideas that shape U.S. foreign policy, but because history is so important, we will give history its own section to show how the United States came to be in its present situation.

Recent U.S. Foreign Policy History

From roughly the end of World War II until the Berlin Wall was torn down in 1989 and the Soviet Union collapsed in 1991, the Cold War dominated U.S. foreign policy. Rivalry with the Soviet Union—in political, economic, and military terms—produced an era in which small wars between the client states of each superpower could erupt at any time. Yet the overwhelming concern was preventing the two superpowers from going to war directly against each other, as that seemed likely to lead to nuclear war and **mutual assured destruction**.

When economic weaknesses caused the Soviet Union's collapse and the Cold War ended, many assumed a new, more peaceful era had arrived.[12] Events proved otherwise, as nasty but geographically limited military conflicts erupted in the 1990s in places like the Persian Gulf, the former Yugoslavia, and central Africa. Occasionally, U.S. citizens or military personnel became the targets of those with grievances against the United States or its foreign policy. However, such incidents of **terrorism** were either isolated or tended to occur far from U.S. shores.

For example, U.S. support for Israel at the expense of Palestinians and the Saudis' invitation to U.S. troops to be stationed in their country after the Iraqi invasion of neighboring Kuwait in 1990—thus inviting new "crusaders" into the Muslim world's holiest land—were cited by Saudi multimillionaire Osama bin Laden as justification for attacks on the United States or its interests abroad. His group of Takfirist extremists called **al Qaeda** ("the base") was linked to the 1993 bombing of a parking garage beneath New York City's World Trade Center. That attack killed six and injured about 1,000 (but failed to bring down the tower), and bin Laden also later claimed credit for his followers' involvement in the 1993 killing of 18 U.S. military personnel in Somalia—an event immortalized in the film *Blackhawk Down*. Five Americans were killed in a 1995 bombing in Riyadh, Saudi Arabia, that was later attributed to al Qaeda.

In 1996, bin Laden issued a fatwa (or religious directive) calling on all devout Muslims to take up arms against Americans in the Middle East, and an apartment building housing U.S. military personnel in Khobar, Saudi Arabia, was bombed, killing 19 U.S. service members. In 1998, bin Laden issued a second fatwa calling on Muslims to kill Americans and Jews (this time specifically including women and children to be killed) wherever the opportunity presented itself, and truck bombs went off at the U.S. embassies in both Kenya and Tanzania. Over 200 people, mostly Kenyan passersby, were killed, and President Bill Clinton responded by ordering cruise missile attacks on al Qaeda training bases in Afghanistan and a Sudanese pharmaceutical plant that had been linked (apparently erroneously) to chemical weapons and bin Laden. In 2000, two suicide bombers attacked the USS *Cole* as it arrived in the port of Aden, Yemen, killing 17 members of its crew.

So when President George W. Bush took office in January 2001, top security officials of his administration were well aware of Osama bin Laden and al Qaeda. However, there seemed little sense of urgency in confronting this terrorist threat. As a candidate during the presidential campaign, Bush had stressed domestic initiatives like education reform and tax cuts over foreign policy matters, and he said the United States should avoid the "nation-building" initiatives of the Clinton administration that Bush saw as unduly adventuresome.

Events soon changed Bush's presidential agenda. On September 11, 2001, four civilian airliners were hijacked by 19 members of al Qaeda. Two of the aircraft were flown into the twin towers of New York City's World Trade Center. The resulting fires collapsed both buildings, killing more than 2,600 people. Another aircraft flew into the U.S. Department of Defense headquarters building—better known as the Pentagon—across the Potomac River from Washington, DC, in Arlington, Virginia. The death toll from that attack was 125. The fourth airplane crashed in a Pennsylvania field. The passengers on board the aircraft apparently learned of the other incidents and forced the airplane down short of its target—thought to be either the Capitol building or the White House in Washington, DC. The death toll of the individuals on the four combined aircraft was 256, making the total of nearly 3,000 dead in this coordinated attack exceed the death toll of the 1941 Japanese attack on Pearl Harbor.[13]

President Bush's first response to the attacks was to go after bin Laden and those harboring him. In late 2001, the United States went to war against the Taliban regime in Afghanistan that had sheltered bin Laden. Despite an aggressive bombing campaign and a ground assault by indigenous anti-Taliban Afghan forces known as the Northern Alliance, bin Laden escaped capture by entering the mountainous region of Pakistan along the Afghan border where he went into hiding. In 2011, bin Laden was finally tracked down and killed in a U.S. covert operations assault on his compound in Abbottabad, Pakistan.

The U.S.-proclaimed "war on terror" took a different turn in 2003 when the focus turned to Iraq. Saddam Hussein's regime had used chemical weapons in the past against both Iranians in the Iran–Iraq War of 1980–1988 and Iraqi Kurds in the town of Halabja in 1988, and intelligence reports suggested the regime was pursuing biological and nuclear weapons in the 1980s as well. Given these factors, Bush administration officials claimed that the Iraqis might make weapons of mass destruction available to international terrorists, and some officials (prominently led by Vice President Dick Cheney) said they would not be surprised to learn that Iraq had something to do with the 9/11 attacks. When the UN Security Council refused to authorize a collective attack on Iraq, a force comprised primarily of U.S. and British troops (along with others) invaded Iraq, overthrew the Hussein regime, and ultimately created a new Iraqi government led by Prime Minister Nouri al-Maliki.[14]

While the invasion of Iraq was a quick success, the occupation of Iraq proved difficult. Sectarian tensions quickly arose. Many Iraqi Sunnis felt marginalized and threatened by both the new Shi'a-dominated regime and the Shi'a militias the regime said it did not control. Large numbers of Iraqis who had been government employees or members of the military under Saddam's regime lost their jobs when the U.S.-led Coalition Provisional Authority ordered all Ba'ath Party members banned from public service, regardless of their role in the party during Saddam Hussein's rule or the fact that oftentimes membership in the regime's ruling party was a required condition of employment.

Adding to this combustible mix was the fact that the U.S. occupation of Iraq acted like a magnet, drawing **jihadists** from all over the Islamic world to come to Iraq where they had the opportunity to kill Americans. Although Iraq was not a stronghold of al Qaeda prior to 2003, after the intervention foreign jihadists flocked there, and the group known as "al Qaeda in Iraq" was formed.

In 2007, the momentum of the Iraqi occupation began to change. Prompted by the indiscriminate killing of Iraqis by al Qaeda in Iraq, many Sunni insurgents stopped fighting the U.S. occupation troops, began working with U.S. troops to fight the largely foreign al Qaeda forces, and were later put on the U.S. payroll for their efforts. U.S. efforts to identify, track, and assassinate the leaders of al Qaeda in Iraq helped neutralize the group's effectiveness. Also effective was the military surge in 2007, an increase of approximately 30,000 more U.S. troops deployed to Iraq, bringing the total number there to approximately 130,000.[15]

As fighting wound down in Iraq, fighting in Afghanistan escalated, as the Taliban reconstituted itself and took control of large areas of the countryside. U.S. and NATO forces sought to extend the control of the government led by President Karzai beyond the areas adjacent to the capital city of Kabul. At the same time, U.S. strikes on al Qaeda safe houses in Afghanistan and Pakistan increased, by both unmanned drone aircraft and clandestine or covert action teams on the ground. Not surprisingly, U.S. military operations inside Pakistan not authorized by the Pakistani government were highly unpopular with the Pakistani people, as was Pakistan's support for the U.S.-led war on terror.

The Bush administration's war on terror had other unfortunate consequences as well. Thousands of terrorist suspects were rounded up in Afghanistan, Iraq, and other locations and detained indefinitely. Hundreds were housed at the U.S. military base at Guantanamo Bay, Cuba, where they were held without charges or legal representation. Ultimately, the U.S. Supreme Court ruled that such detainees could not be held indefinitely without recourse to the legal system.[16] The fact that the tactics used in the war on terror seemed to put traditional U.S. values at risk created disillusionment both at home and abroad. Such disillusionment increased when it was learned that some detainees had been "waterboarded" during interrogation (a process that simulates drowning and is considered by many to be a form of torture), that detainees at the **Abu Ghraib** Prison had been degraded and humiliated by U.S. military police, and that the National Security Agency had illegally engaged in warrantless electronic eavesdropping on U.S. citizens.[17] Actions such as these made U.S. statements that it was a nation that followed the rule of law seem hypocritical, and the international image of the United States was tarnished.

Beyond the war on terror, a second broad theme of the Bush administration was to avoid constraints on how the United States chose to act in the international arena. Again, this was nothing new. During the Clinton administration, the United States chose not to go along with multilateral approaches to address a number of global problems that had been endorsed by U.S. friends and allies. Among other examples, these multilateral efforts to deal with global problems included the **Kyoto Protocol** to limit global climate change, the creation and operation of the **International Criminal Court (ICC)**, and the **Mine Ban Treaty**.

The Bush administration's opposition to such multilateral approaches to global problems was generally based on a preference for unilateral initiatives that preserved U.S. sovereignty or U.S. freedom of action. Regarding the Kyoto Protocol, President Bush opposed mandatory restrictions on fossil fuel emissions because imposing them would hurt the U.S. economy. Bush not only opposed the creation of the ICC, which might in the future bring U.S. military personnel to trial, he rescinded the U.S. signature on the treaty creating the court and signed the **American Service Members Protection Act** that made it illegal to cooperate with the ICC. That act also threatened non-NATO countries with the loss of U.S. military aid if they did not sign Status of Forces Agreements exempting U.S. forces from being turned over to the ICC. The Bush administration also scuttled action on a potential international convention to regulate the trade in small arms, as administration officials said they feared any effects such a convention might have on the U.S. Constitution's Second Amendment right to keep and bear arms. In addition, President Bush reinstituted the Reagan administration's **Mexico City Policy,** which prohibited federal funds from going to any international entity that might use them to promote the use of abortion, a policy at odds with the United Nations and most U.S. allies.

The most potent illustration of U.S. unilateralism came with the new **U.S. National Security Strategy** announced in 2002. This strategy statement stressed that the nature of the threats facing the country had changed. According to the strategy statement, with weapons of mass destruction becoming increasingly commonplace and with nonstate actors as enemies, some of the old rules of conflict no longer applied. International law's traditional justification of the use of force only in self-defense meant one had to let an aggressor attack first before retaliating. As President Bush noted, letting the opponent strike first might condemn an entire U.S. city to destruction. Similarly, past deterrence strategies worked against state actors whose cities provided immovable retaliatory targets, but nonstate actors (whose members could easily move about) could not be so readily deterred by threats of retaliation. Thus this new **Bush Doctrine** said that the United States would not wait for the first blow; it would strike preemptively against potential aggressors.

To critics, this "strike first" approach meant those who earned the ire of the administration could be labeled as either terrorists or supporters of terrorism and then attacked. In their eyes, the invasion of Iraq in 2003 demonstrated their fears of a hegemonic power that used force as a first resort simply because it could. Thus the propensity of foreign audiences to view the United States as a threat grew as a result.[18]

A third major theme for the Bush administration was another carryover from the Clinton administration. It involved largely ignoring Russia's concerns when pursuing U.S. national interests. During both the Clinton and Bush administrations, U.S. officials seemed to expect the Russians to appreciate U.S. views without any need for the United States to appreciate Russian perspectives in return. This dynamic was well illustrated in debates about NATO expansion. The Russians were alarmed at the inclusion of Hungary, Poland, and the Czech Republic in NATO in 1999, as NATO had now crept into the former Soviet sphere of influence. In 2004, Russians were further alarmed when four more former Soviet sphere states were added (Slovenia, Slovakia, Bulgaria, and Romania) along with three countries that had been part of the Soviet Union itself (Estonia, Latvia, and Lithuania). Now NATO members actually abutted

Russian borders, and Russian president Vladimir Putin warned NATO against stationing any troops in these forward areas. Despite Russia's repeated objections, Albania and Croatia were invited to begin the process of joining NATO in April 2008. At that time, President Bush supported the invitation of Ukraine and Georgia to join as well, but other NATO members did not agree. The August 2008 Russian invasion of Georgia could be seen as Russia's attempt to forcibly prevent Georgia's entry into NATO and as its delayed response to NATO's invasion of Russian ally Serbia in 1999. In 2009, Albania and Croatia formally joined NATO, but Georgia and Ukraine were told they could join only at some future date.

Another illustration of the United States pursuing its interests at the expense of Russian interests involved the creation of a new missile defense system. In 2008, the Bush administration signed agreements that would create a theater missile defense system in Europe by placing a radar installation in the Czech Republic and interceptor missiles in Poland. According to U.S. officials, the intent of the system was to defend Europe and North America against missile launches from Iran or other "rogue" regimes in the Middle East. However, for years top Russian officials had said that the real target of such a defense system was Russia, because Russia had nuclear missiles and Middle East states largely did not. New Russian president Dmitry Medvedev and senior Russian military officials warned that they would be forced to target Russian missiles at such a European antimissile system in the future. In each of these instances, NATO expansion and European missile defense, U.S. leaders paid little or no heed to Russia's perceptions of its national interests, and bad blood ensued.

As a result, in their first meeting both Presidents Obama and Medvedev spoke of the need to "hit the reset button" in the U.S.-Russian relationship. One result of this effort was the **New START** Treaty, which was signed in 2010 and went into force in 2011. This treaty reduced the number of U.S. and Russian deployed nuclear warheads from 2,200 to 1,550 per side and limited each side to no more than 700 deployed heavy bombers and missiles.

As this historical account shows, the current international environment facing U.S. foreign policy makers is a complex one. On the one hand, the United States is unquestionably the only military superpower at this time. Its defense spending alone represented 42.8% of the global total in 2010. By comparison, the next largest countries by expenditure were China (7.3%), the United Kingdom (3.7%), and both France and Russia (3.6%).[19] However, this appearance of a **unipolar system** does not mean the United States is omnipotent; that is far from the case. Conflicts in both Iraq and Afghanistan stressed U.S. military resources to the point that major new military initiatives could not readily be undertaken, and others know this. When the Bush administration pressed Iran over its nuclear program, Iranian Supreme Leader Ali Khamenei pointedly asked what the United States could do about it, given that U.S. forces were overstretched in both Iraq and Afghanistan at the time.

Further, other major regional powers insist on being taken seriously. China has been a rising military power in recent years, and India's 2009 deployment of its first self-built nuclear-powered submarine completes its efforts to join the

United States, Russia, France, the United Kingdom, and China in being able to launch nuclear weapons from land-based missiles, sea-based missiles, or bomber aircraft.[20] Russia is a major military power in the Eurasian region and demands that its interests be considered in Asia, Eastern Europe, the Balkans, and the Caucasus. European leaders have sought to make NATO a military alliance that has the ability to act without requiring U.S. participation, and the EU possesses a larger economy than that of the United States.

Although far behind the others in this listing, Venezuela is an aspiring regional power in Latin America, and former president Hugo Chávez upgraded Venezuela's military assets by increasing the size of the armed forces and purchasing assault rifles, attack helicopters, armored fighting vehicles, four Kilo-class diesel-electric attack submarines, and 24 SU-30 multipurpose fighter aircraft from Russia.[21] In addition to his goal of fending off a presumed U.S. invasion, Chávez sought to replace U.S. influence in the region with a Venezuelan-led economic integration effort known as the **Bolivarian Alternative for the Americas (ALBA)**. The history of poor relations between the United States and the Chávez regime is an interesting one, as indicated by Box 3.2.

BOX 3.2

The United States and Venezuela: Can a History of Mutual Suspicion Be Overcome?

In 1998, the Venezuelan people elected former military officer Hugo Chávez as their new president. His populist campaign stressed that the country's economic elites had squandered Venezuela's oil wealth, promised an end to endemic corruption, and proclaimed a socialist revolution on behalf of the country's poor majority.

U.S.-Venezuelan relations quickly became strained. Each side had grievances against the other. U.S. distrust of Chávez was based upon a number of factors, including things such as Chávez's

- denunciation of capitalism as an exploitative and corrupt economic system and his embrace of socialism,
- embrace of Fidel Castro and the Cuban revolution, and

- efforts to offset U.S. influence in Latin America with a left-of-center coalition of Latin states.

For his part, Chávez's distrust of the United States was based on

- a long history of Latin America being seen as part of the U.S. sphere of influence;
- U.S. support of the previous, and in his view, corrupt Venezuelan government;
- Washington's tactics in the war on terror, which Chávez called "fighting terror with terror"; and
- his perception of U.S. meddling in the social revolution next door in Colombia.

Matters came to a head in 2002 when Chávez was briefly deposed in a coup led by Venezuelan business leaders who opposed his socialist revolution. The Bush administration condemned the coup but still recognized the new government of Pedro Carmona—one of Venezuela's leading business executives. The coup lasted only two days. Facing violent protests in the streets by the Venezuelan masses who elected Chávez, the military switched sides and restored Chávez to power.

Chávez immediately blamed the U.S. government for organizing the coup. News accounts suggested that Carmona and other coup leaders had met repeatedly with top U.S. officials to plan the coup in the months preceding it. According to press accounts, those officials included Assistant Secretary of State for Western Hemisphere Affairs Otto Reich; Special Assistant to the President and Senior Director for Democracy, Human Rights, and International Operations at the National Security Council Elliott Abrams; and UN Ambassador John Negroponte. Regarding Chávez's allegations, the Bush administration's official position was that it had no role in the coup, had known a coup might occur but had no idea when, and had passed that warning along to President Chávez.

Not surprisingly, U.S.-Venezuelan relations did not improve as long as the Bush administration was in office. In a 2006 speech before the UN General Assembly, Chávez referred to Bush as "the devil," castigated the United States for its imperialist behavior, and

characterized Bush's speech to the General Assembly the day before as "talking as if he was the owner of the world." Citing his fears of a U.S. invasion, from 2006 to 2009 Chávez purchased $4.4 billion worth of weapons from Russia and arranged Russian financing for $2.2 billion in additional weaponry. The weapons ranged from assault rifles to supersonic combat jets and submarines.

In 2011, Chávez revealed that he had cancer for which he was treated in Cuba. Following several surgeries, he died in 2013, and his vice president, Nicolas Maduro, assumed the presidency. Maduro was later elected president in his own right, and he pledged to continue Chávez's policies.

So, what do you think? Will President Obama be able to convince Maduro that the United States means Venezuela no harm? Will Chávez's passing help lessen Maduro's suspicions of U.S. intentions? What will it take to overcome this history of mutual suspicion, or will it take generational change?

Sources: Daniel Cancel, "Russia to Finance $2.2 Billion for Venezuela Arms (Update1)," *Bloomberg News*, September 13, 2009; "Chavez: Bush 'Devil'; U.S. 'On the Way Down,'" CNN World, September 20, 2006; "Profile: Hugo Chavez," BBC News, July 1, 2011; "Profile: Pedro Carmona," BBC News, May 27, 2002; Reuters, "Chavez' Cancer Diagnosis Divides Venezuelans," *The Guardian*, July 1, 2011; Ed Vulliamy, "Venezuela Coup Linked to Bush Team," *The Observer*, April 21, 2002.

Economically as well, the United States faces significant rivals and challenges. As noted earlier, the U.S. economy is the largest single economy in the world, but in recent years the story of the international economy has been "the rise of the rest."[22] As noted earlier, the economy of the EU is actually larger than that of the United States, and unless growth rates change, the length of time it takes for the gross domestic product (**GDP**) of China to overtake that of the United States will be measured in decades, not centuries. As Table 3.1 shows, China's economy grew by more than 10% in 2010 whereas the U.S. economy grew at less than 3%. When wealth is measured in terms of GDP per capita, the United States ranks ninth in the world, behind Qatar, Liechtenstein, Luxembourg, Bermuda, Singapore, Norway, Brunei, and Hong Kong. In terms of the human development index—a figure created by the United Nations that combines life expectancy, literacy, education, and standards of living—the United States places fourth, behind Norway, Australia, and the Netherlands.

TABLE 3.1 U.S. Placement in Selected National Rankings, 2011

GDP in Trillions of U.S. Dollars	Annual GDP Growth Rate	GDP Per Capita in Thousands of U.S. Dollars	Human Development Index
1 United States (15.00)	Mongolia (17.5%)	Qatar (98.9)	Norway (0.943)
2 China (7.20)	Turkmenistan (14.7%)	Liechtenstein (89.4)	Australia (0.929)
3 Japan (5.87)	Ghana (14.4%)	Luxembourg (80.6)	The Netherlands (0.910)
4 Germany (3.60)	Qatar (14.1%)	Bermuda (69.9)	United States (0.910)
5 France (2.78)	Solomon Islands (10.7%)	Singapore (59.7)	New Zealand (0.908)
6 Brazil (2.48)	Timor-Leste (10.6%)	Norway (53.4)	Canada (0.908)
7 United Kingdom (2.43)	Panama (10.6%)	Brunei (49.5)	Ireland (0.908)
8 Italy (2.20)	Zimbabwe (9.4%)	Hong Kong (49.4)	Liechtenstein (0.905)
9 India (1.90)	China Lanka (9.2%)	United States (48.3)	Germany (0.905)
10 Russia (1.86)	Iraq (8.9%)	United Arab Emirates (47.7)	Sweden (0.904)
157 Fiji (0.04)	United States (1.8%)	Indonesia (4.7)	Nepal (0.458)

Sources: United Nations at: http://en.wikipedia.org/wiki/List_of_countries_by_GDP_(nominal); CIA World Factbook at: http://en.wikipedia.org/wiki/List_of_countries_by_real_GDP_growth _rate_(latest_year); https://www.cia.gov/library/publications/the-world-factbook/rankorder /2004rank.html and United Nations Development Program at: http://en.wikipedia.org/wiki /List_of_countries_by_Human_Development_Index.

The greatest contemporary economic challenge the United States faces is how to climb out of the Great Recession of 2008–2010. In 2007, a speculative bubble in the U.S. real estate market burst. Financial institutions had to foreclose on unpaid mortgages, but the real estate they took back was then worth less than what they had lent the buyers to purchase it. As a result, financial institutions overexposed to these risks began to fail. Those that did not fail basically stopped lending money out of an overabundance of caution. The result became a larger credit crisis; businesses could not get short- or long-term loans to operate. Given the worldwide interdependence of modern economies and investment, the resulting economic recession quickly went global.

In its last few months in office, the Bush administration persuaded Congress to pass legislation that raised billions of dollars to protect some American corporations. Companies thought to be "too big to be allowed to fail" received federal funds to continue operating. Others were allowed to go bankrupt or be sold to competitors. Shortly after the November 2008 general election, outgoing President Bush hosted a two-day meeting in Washington of the G-20 major industrial and emerging market states. There the leaders agreed to urge more regulation of national credit markets and to stimulate their national economies.[23] These leaders met again in London in April 2009. While the G-20 leaders raised new contributions to the IMF, vowed to more closely regulate tax havens and hedge funds, and called for a new early warning system to monitor the global economy, new President Barack Obama was unable to convince others to initiate more sweeping economic stimulus packages, and both French President Nicolas Sarkozy and German Chancellor Angela Merkel were unable to persuade others of the need for more stringent economic regulation to prevent future abuses.[24]

Finally, there is always the unexpected. In 2011, the Arab Spring erupted, in which the masses turned out in opposition to corrupt or repressive regimes in the Middle East and North Africa. New governments were the result in Tunisia and Libya, and a longtime U.S. ally in Egypt, Hosni Mubarak, was forced from power. However in Egypt, the election of a Muslim Brotherhood–sponsored candidate to the presidency, Mohammad Morsi, did not satisfy many opponents of the regime, who felt one tyrant was being replaced with another, and more violence ensued. In Bahrain, opposition demonstrations were dispersed with tanks, and a civil war erupted in Syria. With the exception of contributing some limited military assistance to NATO in its intervention to protect Libyan citizens, the United States was forced to stand largely by and watch as these events unfolded. Either the political will or the policy options were limited, or simply not enough was known to be able to tell the "good guys" from the "bad guys" in these civil eruptions. In such cases, who do you help, and how?

In summary, the current context in which foreign policy is set provides a mix of both positive and negative inputs to policy making. The United States is a superpower, and others in the international system expect U.S. leadership on important issues. Yet there are limits on its freedom of action; the United

States is not a hegemon, one that readily imposes its will on others. Similarly, American exceptionalism at home pushes the United States to lead on international issues, but the effects of the global recession have made some wary of the costs of such leadership. Partisan gridlock in the nation's capital complicates efforts, as Democrats and Republicans typically disagree on both foreign policy ends and means. Thus policy makers have to contend with a global foreign policy agenda that receives mixed signals both from home and abroad.

Conclusion: Foreign Policy Priorities in the Current Context

Given the policy inputs arising in this current international and domestic context, four major U.S. foreign policy priorities seem to be clear. The first is fixing the economy and its debt problems, through selective support of those corporations whose failure would cause massive job losses or economic dislocations, extra government spending to stimulate the economy, cutting spending where appropriate to please taxpayers, new regulation of domestic and international credit markets, and possibly the raising of government revenues by raising taxes or closing tax loopholes. Fixing the problems in the domestic economy should have beneficial ripple effects throughout the global economy.

The second major priority is keeping the national security focus on those who encourage or conduct terrorism against the United States. For President Obama, that means addressing the conjoined problem called "Af-Pak." Obama's first effort was to send more U.S. and NATO troops into Afghanistan to take back control of the countryside from Taliban militias. Such an approach demanded an effective counterinsurgency strategy of removing the enemy by force, keeping troops in place, and providing sufficient benefits to the local inhabitants so they prefer control by government forces to control by the Taliban. However, that strategy did not produce sufficient results, and in 2011 President Obama signaled a change in policy by promoting the general associated with that strategy, David Petraeus, to become the director of central intelligence. The U.S. goal in Afghanistan shifted from a counterinsurgency approach that supports the Karzai regime to one of (1) hunting down the terrorists there and removing them by force and (2) approaching more moderate Taliban leaders to negotiate some form of peaceful solution to this violence.

However changes in Afghanistan will not matter unless the government of Pakistan can control militant groups located there. Some of these groups have operated with the tacit approval of the Pakistani military and its Inter-Services Intelligence (ISI) branch. Osama bin Laden was able to live for years apparently undetected deep inside Pakistan. That fact has embarrassed the Pakistani military, but not nearly as much as the fact that U.S. military forces were able to enter Pakistan, locate bin Laden in a city known as a military garrison town, kill him, and then escape undetected. The Pakistani military has a lot of explaining to do to the Pakistani people, and gaining Pakistani cooperation in the hunt for terrorists is now limited and difficult to maintain.

The third major foreign policy priority involves gradually pivoting U.S. foreign policy attention from the Middle East to Asia and the Pacific. Given the growth of Chinese economic power and China's increasing defense spending, the United States has become increasingly concerned by the new assertive actions taken by the Chinese of late. These include contesting Japanese ownership of the islands known by the Japanese as the Senkaku Islands and by the Chinese as the Diaoyu Islands. Territorial disputes between both fishing vessels and naval vessels have occurred in the waters of the South China Sea, and in 2011 the United States reached an agreement to position a Marine detachment in Australia so as to be closer should it be needed to protect U.S. interests. In 2013, China announced an expanded air defense zone around the contested territories. The United States responded by flying two B-52 bombers through the airspace without asking Chinese permission. A heightened U.S. presence in the region might help prevent any new provocations from spiraling out of control and sparking regional conflict.

The fourth major foreign policy priority involves "resetting" U.S. relations with many other international actors. As President Obama stressed in various statements, that means showing a bit more humility when dealing with others. In operational terms, this priority means persuading others that the United States seeks to be a team player in addressing problems of global scale and recognizing that Washington's answers to global challenges may not be the only correct answers. Such a multilateral change of focus can be manifested by working through problems with groups like the United Nations, NATO, EU, G-8, and G-20. In bilateral terms, it also means being willing to listen to and give greater consideration to the points of view of others. That means showing more respect not only for established powers like its long-time European allies but also for the points of view of rising powers like Russia, China, India, and Brazil. In the post-9/11 era, only time will tell if U.S. leaders pursue such priorities wisely and well, but inputs from the external, internal, and ideational contexts will continue to prompt policy makers to act.

Glossary Terms

Abu Ghraib   a prison in Iraq where detainees in the U.S. invasion of Iraq were mistreated, degraded, and in some cases sexually humiliated by U.S. military police.

Al Qaeda   "the base" in Arabic. The name for the group of Islamic militants dedicated to opposing the U.S. military presence in the Middle East and U.S. support for Israel. It was created by Saudi Arabian multimillionaire Osama bin Laden from a core group of Islamic freedom fighters who had battled the Soviet presence in Afghanistan in the 1980s.

American exceptionalism   the idea that not only was the United States unique and thus different from other countries but also those differences made it better than other countries.

American Service Members Protection Act   a law that essentially prohibited U.S. cooperation with the International Criminal Court. The law also threatened non-NATO countries with the loss of U.S. military aid if they did not sign Status of Forces

Agreements exempting U.S. forces from being turned over to such a court, and it justified the use of any means necessary to free any U.S. military personnel arrested for trial before the International Criminal Court.

Apartheid   the policy of the Republic of South Africa of according different levels of political and human rights to its citizens based on their skin color. Blacks had the fewest rights, whites had the most rights, and those considered "colored and Asians" fell in between the other two extremes. While the roots of this policy can be found in the 18th century, it was enshrined in law from 1948 until the constitution was changed in 1994.

Bolivarian Alternative for the Americas (ALBA)   an effort at Latin American economic integration based on a socialist model led by Venezuela's President Hugo Chávez. Besides Venezuela, its members include Cuba, Bolivia, Nicaragua, Dominica, and Honduras.

Bush Doctrine   George W. Bush's idea of responding to imminent threats by striking enemies before they can attack the United States. See the **U. S. National Security Strategy**.

Cold War   a period of hostile competition between a Western bloc of anticommunist states led by the United States and an Eastern bloc of communist states led by the Soviet Union, which was to last 42 years (1947–1989). While the two bloc leaders never went to war directly against each other, members of their respective blocs did, and the risks of a global and nuclear World War III could not be discounted.

European Union (EU)   an economic and political partnership of 28 European countries.

First-generation rights   individual human rights such as the freedoms of speech, assembly, and religion.

G-8   the Group of Seven major industrial nations (Canada, France, Germany, Italy, Japan, the United Kingdom, and the United States) who meet annually to coordinate their economic policies plus Russia.

G-20   the Group of 20 major industrial powers and key emerging markets formed in 1999 to coordinate economic policy. The 20 members are Argentina, Australia, Brazil, Canada, China, France, Germany, India, Indonesia, Italy, Japan, Mexico, Russia, Saudi Arabia, South Africa, South Korea, Turkey, the United Kingdom, the United States, and the European Union.

Gross domestic product (GDP)   the total value of goods and services a state actor produces within its borders.

Hegemon   an international actor so powerful it can basically do whatever it wants, even if all other major powers oppose it.

Human rights   rights that societies assume should apply to all people.

International Criminal Court (ICC)   an international court created by the Rome Statute of 1998. Its purpose is to act as a court of last resort for individuals accused of war crimes, crimes against humanity, genocide, and more recently, aggression. It went into effect in 2002.

International Monetary Fund (IMF)   part of the UN family of organizations, this international organization acts as a global bank to protect the value of its members' currencies and took on new roles coordinating the global monetary response to the Great Recession of 2008–2009.

Internationalism   the belief that U.S. national interests are advanced by interacting with other countries and peoples and such regular, ongoing contacts with others may also contribute to the greater good of all.

Isolationism   the belief that the dangers of regular and ongoing engagement with the world beyond U.S. borders outweigh the advantages.

Jihadists   Muslims who seek to conduct a "holy war" (or jihad) against nonbelievers.

Kyoto Protocol   essentially an amendment passed in 1997 to the International Convention on Climate Change. It specified mandatory reductions in fossil fuel emissions by developed countries, but not by developing countries, in the international effort to slow down global warming.

Mexico City Policy   a policy, announced by President Reagan, rejected by President Clinton, reinstituted by President George W. Bush, and now rejected by President Obama, that said no U.S. federal funds could go to any international groups or entities that endorsed abortion as a method of population control.

Mine Ban Treaty   a 1997 treaty, also known as the **Ottawa Convention** that bans the use of antipersonnel landmines and governs their destruction. That same year, the Nobel Peace Prize was awarded to Jody Williams and her organization, the International Campaign to Ban Landmines.

Mutual assured destruction   the idea that a direct military conflict between the United States and Soviet Union during the Cold War would inevitably escalate into a full-blown exchange of nuclear weapons, thereby destroying both societies. Based on this, mutual assured destruction (or **MAD**) became a nuclear strategy; if neither country would survive a nuclear war, then starting such a war would be irrational and thus unlikely.

New START   a 2011 strategic arms reduction treaty between the United States and Russia that limited the deployment by each country to no more than 1,550 nuclear warheads and 700 heavy bombers and missiles.

Norms   unwritten rules; expectations of appropriate behavior in international society.

North Atlantic Treaty Organization (NATO)   formed in 1950, its permanent structure ensured that a multinational military organization was in place to repel any sudden attacks on its members. Its original 12 members were Belgium, Canada, Denmark, France, Iceland, Italy, Luxembourg, the Netherlands, Norway, Portugal, the United Kingdom, and the United States. It later expanded to include Greece and Turkey (1952); West Germany (1955); Spain (1982); the Czech Republic, Hungary, and Poland (1999); Bulgaria, Estonia, Latvia, Lithuania, Romania, Slovakia, and Slovenia (2004); and Albania and Croatia (2009).

Nuclear Nonproliferation Treaty (NPT)   a 1970 treaty that seeks to control the spread of nuclear weapons. Signatories that have nuclear weapons agree not to transfer them to nonnuclear states, and states without nuclear weapons agree not to seek nuclear weapons. The treaty also established a process of international inspections and agreed-upon safeguards for nuclear weapons and technologies.

Responsibility to Protect (R2P)   the idea that states have a responsibility to protect their people from gross abuses of human rights, such as genocide, war crimes, and crimes against humanity, at the very least.

Second-generation rights   the material rights of societies, like the right to food, shelter, education, and medical care.

Shia's or Shi'ites   members of the largest minority sect within Islam, comprising approximately 10 percent of all Muslims worldwide. However, they form the majority of the population in only a few Islamic states, such as Iran, Iraq, Lebanon, and Bahrain. Considered heretics by some Muslims, they are often a persecuted minority in majority Sunni societies.

Social Darwinism   the idea that, like species, societies evolve by the "survival of the fittest," and thus it is the natural order of things for the strong to prey on the weak.

Sunnis   Members of the majority sect within Islam, comprising nearly 90 percent of all Muslims worldwide.

Terrorism   violence directed at noncombatants (either civilians or unarmed military personnel) in an attempt to generate terror among the target society. According to U.S. law—*U.S. Code Title 22, Ch.38, Para. 2656f(d)*—terrorism involves "premeditated, politically motivated violence perpetrated against noncombatant targets by subnational groups or clandestine agents."

Third-generation rights   rights assigned to groups at risk, whether they are unpopular minorities, women, children, or the aged.

Unipolar system   an international system with one major power. This is in contrast to a **bipolar system** that has two major powers or a **multipolar system** that has three or more major powers.

UN Security Council Resolution 1674   the 2006 UN Security Council resolution reaffirming that states have a responsibility to protect their people from gross abuses of human rights, such as genocide, war crimes, and crimes against humanity, and that others have the right to intervene if states do not meet that responsibility.

U.S. National Security Strategy   a 2002 statement that, because of the increasing availability of weapons of mass destruction and the hostility of nonstate actors less susceptible to conventional means of deterrence, the United States would not wait until its enemies struck first. Instead, it would strike preemptively at its opponents to eradicate threats before they could materialize. Also known as the Bush Doctrine.

Endnotes

1. For more on the laws of war, see "The Laws of War," part of the Avalon Project, Yale Law School, available at http://avalon.law.yale.edu/subject_menus/lawwar.asp.
2. See "Key Developments on the Responsibility to Protect at the United Nations 2005–2010," International Coalition for the Responsibility to Protect, available at http://responsibilitytoprotect.org/ICRtoP%20Latest%20Developments%20at %20the%20UN%20Aug%202010(2).pdf.
3. See Thomas E. Ricks, *Fiasco: The American Military Adventure in Iraq* (New York: Penguin Press, 2006) or Bob Woodward, *State of Denial: Bush at War, Part III* (New York: Simon & Schuster, 2006).
4. For an approving viewpoint on American empire, see Robert Kagan, "The Benevolent Empire," *Foreign Policy*, 111 (Summer 1998), 24–35 or Sebastian Mallaby, "The Reluctant Imperialist: Terrorism, Failed States, and the Case for American Empire," *Foreign Affairs*, 81 (March–April 2002), 2–7. For a disapproving viewpoint, see Andrew J. Bacevich, *American Empire: The Realities and Consequences of U.S. Diplomacy* (Cambridge, MA: Harvard University Press, 2004) or Chalmers Johnson, *The Sorrows of Empire: Militarism, Secrecy, and the End of the Republic* (New York: Holt Paperbacks, 2004).
5. See "NATO's Role in Afghanistan," available at http://www.nato.int/cps/en/natolive /topics_8189.htm.
6. For a classic view on the interaction of these contexts and modern interpretations thereof, see Richard C. Snyder, H. W. Bruck, Burton Sapin, Valerie M. Hudson, Derek H. Chollett, and James H. Goldgeier, *Foreign Policy Decision Making (Revisited)* (New York: Palgrave Macmillan, 2002). For a more recent treatment of the importance of political context, see Barbara Farnham, "Impact of the Political Context on Foreign Policy Decision Making," *Political Psychology*, 25 (No. 3, 2004).

7. For more on American exceptionalism, see Seymour Martin Lipset, *American Exceptionalism: A Double-Edged Sword* (New York: W.W. Norton, 1996).

8. Identifying differences in foreign policy ends and means based on one's partisanship goes back a long way. See, for example, George Belknap and Angus Campbell, "Political Party Identification and Attitudes toward Foreign Policy," *Public Opinion Quarterly*, 15(Winter, 1951–1952), 601–623.

9. See, for example, Ole R. Holsti, "Public Opinion and Foreign Policy: Challenges to the Almond-Lippmann Consensus," *International Studies Quarterly*, 36 (1992), 439–466.

10. See the surveys conducted periodically by the Chicago Council on Global Affairs, available online at http://www.thechicagocouncil.org/iMIS/ContentManagement /Search.aspx?SearchTerms=public%20opinion%20polls.

11. For the classic version of these ideas, see Hans J. Morgenthau, *Politics among Nations: The Struggle for Power and Peace* (3rd ed.) (Chicago: University of Chicago Press, 1954). For a more contemporary discussion, see Daniel Deudney and Jeffrey Meiser, "American Exceptionalism," in Michael Cox and Doug Stokes (eds.), *US Foreign Policy* (Oxford: Oxford University Press, 2008).

12. See Francis Fukuyama, *The End of History and the Last Man* (New York: Free Press, 2006).

13. See *The 9/11 Commission Report: Final Report of the National Commission on Terrorist Attacks on the United States*, executive summary online at http://www.c-span .org/pdf/911finalreportexecsum.pdf. The number of dead attributed to this attack can be expected to rise over time, as first responders and others affected there at the time succumb to long-term illnesses caused by their exposure to the toxic chemicals produced by the fires and collapse of buildings.

14. At its height, the "coalition of the willing" in Iraq produced a force of about 300,000 troops. About 250,000 of those were U.S. troops and 40,000 were British. The remaining contributions to the coalition varied from 2,000 Australians to 70 Albanians. So while the coalition was officially composed of 38 states, the Iraqi invasion and occupation was fundamentally a U.S.-British military operation. See Chelsea J. Carter, "Last Two Partner Nations of U.S. Pull Forces Out of Iraq," Associated Press, *Fort Worth Star-Telegram*, August 2, 2009, p. 16A.

15. For more on how and why the Iraqi response to the occupation changed, see Bob Woodward, *The War Within: A Secret White House History, 2006–2008* (New York: Simon & Schuster, 2008).

16. For a good discussion of the rights of detainees, see Linda Cornett and Mark Gibney, "The Rights of Detainees: Determining the Limits of Law," in Ralph G. Carter (ed.), *Contemporary Cases in U.S. Foreign Policy: From Terrorism to Trade* (5th ed.) (Washington, DC: CQ Press, 2014).

17. For more on the warrantless eavesdropping, see Louis Fisher, "NSA Eavesdropping: Unchecked or Limited Presidential Power?" in Ralph G. Carter (ed.), *Contemporary Cases in U.S. Foreign Policy: From Terrorism to Trade* (5th ed.) (Washington, DC: CQ Press, 2014).

18. To track such global public opinion, see the Pew Global Attitudes Project online at http://pewglobal.org.

19. "Background Paper on SIPRI Military Expenditure Data, 2010," Stockholm International Peace Research Institute, April 11, 2011, available online at http://www.sipri .org/research/armaments/milex/factsheet2010.

20. Ashok Sharma, "Nuclear-Powered Sub Build in India Makes Its Debut," Associated Press, found in the *Fort Worth Star-Telegram*, July 27, 2009, p. 7A.

21. See the Global Security website, online at http://www.globalsecurity.org/military
/world/venezuela/army.htm; http://www.globalsecurity.org/military/world/venezuela
/navy.htm; and http://www.globalsecurity.org/military/world/venezuela/airforce.htm.
22. Fareed Zakaria, *The Post-American World* (New York: W.W. Norton, 2008), p. 2.
23. David Ellis, "Leaders Vow to Tackle Economic Crisis," *Special Report Issue #1,
America's Money Crisis*, CNNMoney, November 15, 2008, available online
at http://money.cnn.com/2008/11/15/news/economy/g20_meeting/?postversion
=2008111512.
24. "Obama Hails G-20 Summit as 'Turning Point,'" MSNBC, April 2, 2009, available
online at http://www.msnbc.msn.com/id/30004815/ns/world_news-europe//.

CHAPTER 4

Governmental Policy-Making Actors

Does it look like President Barack Obama and House Speaker John Boehner agree on policy issues?
Source: Jim Watson/AFP/Getty Images/Newscom

LEARNING OBJECTIVES

- Identify the major governmental actors making U.S. foreign policy.

- Explain the roles typically played by executive branch, congressional, and judicial foreign policy actors.

- Analyze the circumstances that favor executive branch, congressional, or judicial foreign policy actors.

- Evaluate the degree to which separate governmental institutions share power in making foreign policy.

Introduction

In Part 1, we looked at the nature of the foreign policy-making process, the theoretical ideas that help us (and foreign policy makers) interpret and understand international phenomena, and the inputs that can come from the external, internal, and ideational contexts in which foreign policy is made. Beginning here in Part 2, we turn our attention to the major actors who participate in making U.S. foreign policy and the processes by which they do so. In other words, we examine how policy inputs are transformed into policy outputs and by whom. In this chapter, we will look at the major governmental actors and their roles in foreign policy making and then in the following chapters look at typical decision-making processes found.

So, who actually makes U.S. foreign policy? Such a simple question defies easy answers. As illustrated in Chapter 1, the "concentric circles" model of policy making puts the president (assisted by advisers) at the center of the process, and with good reason. Presidents are usually the most influential foreign policy makers for many foreign policy issues. However, they are not the only foreign policy makers, and as the "shifting constellations" model of policy making indicated in Chapter 1, they are sometimes not the most important ones. Other governmental actors are significantly involved in the foreign policy-making process as well. We will explore these actors, taking executive branch actors first, congressional actors next, and judicial actors last.

Executive Branch Actors

There are many different officials and agencies in the executive branch that help shape U.S. foreign policy. The president is the single most important, so let's start with the presidency first.

The President

Presidents shape U.S. foreign policy through their words and deeds. As we noted in Chapter 1, their constitutional powers make them the commander in chief of the military, the chief executive, and effectively the U.S chief diplomat. These roles put presidents in a position to control the general direction of U.S. foreign policy through their control of the governmental agenda. Such powers implicitly put presidents in the position to be, as the U.S. Supreme Court noted in 1936, the "sole organ" representing the nation in foreign affairs.[1] Thus, presidents can use their access to the media to assert what the foreign policies of the United States are, ask Congress to authorize and/or fund such policies as required, order executive branch officials and personnel to carry out such policies, and negotiate and sign treaties or other executive agreements affirming such policies as necessary.

When it comes to foreign policy, presidents are clearly *more* than just the "first among equals," but they are not dominant across the board, as their power lies primarily in the power of persuasion.[2] Presidential influence over foreign policy is often like a driver's control of a vehicle traveling on an ice-glazed street. Presidents can point the government in a preferred policy direction, but rarely do they have precise control over what happens next, for at that point other actors (both at home and abroad) often get involved and events take their own course. Still if you want to influence U.S. foreign policy, it's hard to beat being president.

Presidential Advisers

The good news for presidents is that they receive lots of help in shaping U.S. foreign policy. A number of advisers are available to assist presidents. Some occupy formal roles while others are selected on an as-needed or as-desired basis.

Three official forums for such advisers are the National Security Council, the Homeland Security Council, and the National Economic Council. The **National Security Council (NSC)** dates back to the **National Security Act of 1947**. Its purpose is to advise the president on national security matters and coordinate U.S. national security policy across the various governmental actors and agencies involved. Its statutory members are the president, the vice president, and secretaries of state and defense. By statute, the director of central intelligence advises it on intelligence matters, and the chairman of the Joint Chiefs of Staff (JCS) advises it on military matters. Other officials are routinely invited to its meetings, as dictated by the issues involved and the president's preferences.

However, the NSC as a whole typically does not meet that often. Instead, it subdivides its work through a series of interagency committees. The Principals Committee is composed of secretaries of relevant Cabinet departments, the Deputies Committee is composed of deputy secretaries from those departments, and a third grouping is composed of Interagency Working Groups (also known as Interagency Policy Committees), typically organized around recurring issues (e.g., nonproliferation or intelligence) or specific geographic regions. The work of the Principals Committee and the Deputies Committee is guided by the national security adviser and that individual's deputy. The Interagency Working Groups are typically chaired by an assistant secretary from the most relevant Cabinet department concerned, and their members come from the experts drawn from across the administration's various units. All these NSC committees are assisted by members of the NSC staff, who also do their own research and draft position papers on anything falling within the realm of national and international security.

The **Homeland Security Council (HSC)** was created by an executive order in 2001 by President George W. Bush following the 9/11 attacks on New York City and the Pentagon. Like the NSC, its purpose is to coordinate planning and policy for the many different areas that fall under the heading of protecting U.S. citizens at home. While some of these threats have natural sources (e.g., hurricane damage), others may be intentional (e.g., terrorism, threats of weapons of mass destruction, or even biological warfare concerns). The council's structure is similar to that of the NSC. Originally, it had its own staff, and the president's homeland security adviser coordinated its operations. However under President Barack Obama, the staffs of the NSC and the HSC were merged into a new entity, the **National Security Staff (NSS)**.

The **National Economic Council (NEC)** is the NSC's counterpart for advising the president on domestic and international economic issues and coordinating economic policy across the various governmental actors and agencies involved. The NEC was created by an executive order in 1993 by President Bill Clinton, and the assistant to the president for economic policy serves as its director. Those who attend its meetings typically include the vice president and secretaries of agriculture, commerce, energy, health and human services, housing and urban development, labor, state, transportation, and treasury. While international economic policy is always important, the global scope of the Great Recession of 2008–2010 reminded all of how economic matters can quickly become high-visibility foreign policy issues.

Among other presidential advisers, the best known is the **national security adviser** (also known as the assistant to the president for national security affairs). Part of the Executive Office of the President, the national security adviser's importance is based on legal statute and frequent contact with the president. The role originated in the National Security Act of 1947, which reorganized parts of the executive branch to handle the looming challenges of the Cold War. National security advisers have considerable contact with the presidents they serve. They typically brief the president every morning about relevant overnight happenings that could affect U.S. foreign and security interests, and their offices are located in the West Wing of the White House on the same floor as the president's Oval Office and private study. They normally travel with the president as well. In practice, national security advisers have evolved from directors of the NSC staff to influential actors in their own right who help shape the content of foreign policy. A few have been particularly associated with certain initiatives—Henry Kissinger with the opening of relations with the People's Republic of China and negotiating the withdrawal of U.S. forces from Vietnam, Robert McFarlane and John Poindexter with arming the rebel contra forces in Nicaragua, and so on.

Presidents listen to others in the West Wing of the White House as well. Due to proximity and contact, the president's chief of staff is always in a position of potential policy influence. Others who may serve as advisers include those with titles such as counselors to the president, senior advisers to the president, press secretaries, and speechwriters. Presidents also often rely on other, more informal advisers. These advisers may be their spouses, other family members, childhood friends, old college buddies, or other acquaintances whose judgment or expertise they trust. For example, two iconic moments in President John Kennedy's administration were traceable to one person. Kennedy got the ideas for both the Peace Corps and his famous "I Am a Berliner" speech (made following the 1961 Berlin Crisis) from Congressman Henry Reuss, a Democrat and German-American from Milwaukee who had helped Kennedy reach out to German-American voters in the 1960 presidential campaign.[3]

Another increasingly important presidential adviser is the vice president. For years, the vice presidency was not considered an influential position. As Franklin Roosevelt's vice president, John Nance Garner is alleged to have said, the job "was not worth a bucket of warm [spit]."[4] The constitutional mandate for the vice president is to preside over the Senate. However in a chamber with relatively unlimited debate, the importance of that role is so reduced that most of the time it is filled instead by the most junior senator available. Vice presidents tend to be present only when a close vote is anticipated on legislation deemed important by the administration, just in case a tiebreaking vote is needed. Beyond that, the vice president's importance used to be solely to help get the president elected and to fulfill the duties of office should the president die or become incapacitated.

Yet in recent administrations, the role of the vice president has dramatically changed. Under Bill Clinton, Vice President Al Gore was delegated primary responsibility for two important bundles of issues—environmental issues and U.S.-Russian relations. George W. Bush also gave a prominent role to his vice president. Particularly during his first term, George W. Bush listened closely to Vice President Dick Cheney on a wide array of issues involving national security, the administration's "war on terror," policies regarding detainees from that conflict, the invasion of Iraq, and energy policy. Cheney consistently encouraged the president to pursue policies and actions that emphasized a presidency that was greatly empowered at the expense of Congress.[5] Following this trend, presidential candidate Barack Obama picked Joe Biden as his running mate in part due to Biden's long history of foreign policy experience as chair of the Senate Foreign Relations Committee. Once in office, Biden served as a key adviser regarding the war in Afghanistan and the response to the Great Recession and often played the important role of "devil's advocate" in decision-making sessions to ensure that multiple points of view were considered.

Cabinet Officials and Departments

There is always the possibility that officials in the president's cabinet will be asked for their views on foreign policy topics. When those requests come, cabinet officials must decide whether to present the views of the organization they lead or their own personal views. At times these views coincide, but not always. The chances for meaningful foreign policy input will be greatest for the secretaries of state and defense, so let's take a closer look at their roles.

The secretary of state has three different roles: serving as the nation's chief diplomat and spokesperson, as the manager of the State Department, and as the presidential adviser. All these roles take considerable effort. Whether or not the secretary of state also serves as an influential shaper of foreign policy depends on the person filling the role and the president's willingness to listen. For example, Presidents Truman and Eisenhower listened to their secretaries— Dean Acheson and John Foster Dulles, respectively. Both were reputed to have considerable foreign policy influence.[6] Apparently, John Kennedy wanted Dean Rusk to be a forceful voice, but Rusk chose not to be a policy advocate.[7] Colin Powell wanted to play such a role for George W. Bush, but the president did not seem predisposed to listen.[8] More recently, Hillary Rodham Clinton has developed a reputation as a sound manager of the State Department, a very well-traveled diplomat, and a serious voice in the White House regarding diplomatic and national security affairs. At this point, it appears her successor John Kerry will be as active a diplomat as she was, but only time will tell if he has the same degree of influence as Secretary Clinton.

Beginning in the 1960s, secretaries of defense began to loom larger as foreign policy advisers to presidents, sometimes pushing secretaries of state into subordinate positions of influence. Part of it was due to the personalities and styles of some less assertive secretaries of state (e.g., Dean Rusk under Presidents Kennedy and Johnson and Warren Christopher under Bill Clinton), part of it was due to some strong willed secretaries of defense (e.g., Robert McNamara under President Kennedy and Donald Rumsfeld under George W. Bush), and part of it was due to the frequent use of military force as an instrument of foreign policy that would propel the secretary of defense into policy discussions more frequently.[9] More recently, Robert Gates developed quite a reputation as a very influential secretary of defense, serving as a key adviser to both George W. Bush and Barack Obama.

The functions and size of each of these two departments also impact their foreign policy roles. The primary functions of the State Department are to staff a network of embassies and consulates abroad, conduct diplomatic communications and negotiations, and administer programs such as foreign assistance. Since the early 1960s, the State Department's budget has diminished steadily when adjusted for inflation.[10] While the State Department has always served as the channel for official U.S. communications to other international actors, its role in diplomatic negotiations varies. State Department personnel are more likely to be engaged early in the negotiations process and when the issues involved are considered highly technical or complex. Finally, after 1962, the funding for foreign assistance generally trended down in constant dollar terms until the George W. Bush administration, when budgeting for programs in Africa and the reconstruction of Iraq pushed the totals back up.[11]

On the other hand, the Defense Department always looms large in U.S. foreign policy making and policy implementation. Entrusted with the maintenance and operation of the Air Force, Army, Marines, and Navy, the military's budget has steadily increased since 1950 when measured in constant dollars.[12] With 1.4 million uniformed personnel, over 700,000 civilian personnel, an annual budget of over $800 billion, over 400 ships and 11 aircraft carriers, approximately 4,000 combat aircraft, and more "smart weapons" than any other country, the Defense Department gives the United States the ability to project force on a global basis.[13] Based on these considerations, the chairman of the JCS, the other members of the JCS, and the overall combatant commanders of important unified regional military commands can also be significant foreign policy makers. Elected political leaders often defer to uniformed generals and admirals in terms of how the military should be used, and some flag officers shrewdly exploit this influence. For example, JCS Chairman General Colin Powell and Army Chief of Staff General Creighton Abrams recommended policy and procedural changes designed to make it harder for civilian leaders to risk the lives of military personnel in combat unless it was absolutely necessary.[14]

The Defense Department's foreign policy uses are many: to deploy forces for combat, to use the threat of force to signal a potential opponent, to affirm commitments to allies, to suggest U.S. resolve, to act as de facto diplomats, to rebuild war-torn or failed states, and so on. The military also possesses significant intelligence resources (see the next section). The human and financial resources devoted to the Defense Department dwarf those of any other foreign policy-related actor. Consequently, it is not surprising that when U.S. foreign policy makers reach into their statecraft toolbox, they often pull out a military tool. Interestingly, a call for redressing the glaring imbalance of funding between the State and Defense Departments was made by none other than Defense Secretary Robert Gates. In November 2007, he noted that the State Department's budget was only $36 billion, and the total number of U.S. diplomats (6,600) was equivalent to the number of personnel for one U.S. naval aircraft carrier strike group. As a consequence, he urged more spending on the State Department and Central Intelligence Agency, arguing that if more was spent on diplomacy and intelligence, less might be needed for defense.[15]

Beyond the Departments of State and Defense and their leaders, other cabinet departments play foreign policy roles. The secretaries of homeland security, treasury, commerce, energy, and agriculture can all play important foreign policy roles at times. Depending on the issues involved, attorneys general may also get involved in foreign policy discussions. However, the remaining part of the executive branch that typically gets the most attention is the Intelligence Community, so we turn to it next.

The Intelligence Community

When most people think of intelligence or counterintelligence, they typically think first of the **Central Intelligence Agency (CIA)**. However, the CIA only represents one of 17 entities that comprise the **Intelligence Community (IC)**, which is nominally led by the **director of national intelligence (DNI)**. The post of DNI was created in 2004, after post-9/11 investigations found that different parts of the IC had different pieces of information suggesting that some sort of terrorist incident might be about to happen. However, such information was not shared, and no one was in a position to put all the pieces of information together.[16] The ability of the DNI to effectively pull the various parts of the IC together seems unlikely. The largest parts of the intelligence budget are found in the Defense Department and thus out of the DNI's control, and bureaucratic loyalties and careerism generally inhibit the sharing of information. While there are numerous components of the IC, two of the most prominent ones are the CIA and the National Security Agency.

The CIA is the nation's primary civilian intelligence agency. Like intelligence agencies the world over, the CIA engages in intelligence gathering (the collecting of information thought to be useful in policy making), analysis of what that intelligence means, and counterintelligence (preventing others from obtaining information the United States would prefer not to share publicly). Where the CIA differs from other intelligence agencies is the degree to which it conducts covert or paramilitary operations—direct actions abroad designed to bring about a desired result without that action being traced back to the U.S. government. According to published reports, the IC's total budget was $75.4 billion in 2012, and the CIA's budget was the largest single component at 19.5% or $14.7 billion.[17] Again, the numbers are classified, but reports suggest that approximately 20,000 employees may work at the CIA headquarters in Langley, Virginia, but no data are available for the number of CIA personnel who work in other locations or abroad or how many private contractors are employed by the CIA.[18]

Far larger in human terms is the **National Security Agency (NSA)**. The job of the NSA is conducting information assurance by preventing vital information from falling into the hands of other powers (often through the use of cryptography), collecting signals intelligence (by eavesdropping on the communications of others), and conducting the research necessary for both information assurance and signals intelligence.[19] According to a 1990s estimate, the NSA employed nearly 40,000 people and had a budget of nearly $4 billion per year.[20] By the turn of the 21st century, NSA staff levels dropped to approximately 32,000—a number that does not include the 25,000 people employed by the Central Security Service to staff listening posts for NSA—and the budget dropped to something in excess of $3 billion per year.[21] After the terrorist attacks on 9/11, spending on electronic surveillance surged, and in 2012, the NSA's budget was the second largest in the IC at $10.8 billion. By 2000, the NSA was reported to be the source for almost 80% of the intelligence information relayed to the rest of the U.S. government, and that number may be higher now.[22]

TABLE 4.1 The 17 Members of the Intelligence Community

Member Agencies of the Intelligence Community
Air Force Intelligence
Army Intelligence
Central Intelligence Agency
Coast Guard Intelligence
Defense Intelligence Agency
Department of Energy
Department of Homeland Security
Department of State
Department of Treasury
Drug Enforcement Administration
Federal Bureau of Investigation
Marine Corps Intelligence
National Geospatial-Intelligence Agency
National Reconnaissance Office
National Security Agency
Navy Intelligence
Office of the Director of National Intelligence

Source: "A Complex Organization United under a Single Goal: National Security," Intelligence Community Website, available online at: http://www.intelligence.gov.

The largest components of the IC in terms of budgets and personnel are the individual military branch intelligence agencies and the combined **Defense Intelligence Agency (DIA)**. Numerous other government entities have IC components, as shown in Table 4.1.

All told, the IC represents much of the federal government's eyes and ears. Beyond their own monitoring of open news sources, foreign policy makers rely on the IC to tell them what is happening in the world, how that information may affect U.S. national interests, and what may be done to further U.S. national interests as a result. At times, members of the IC are relied upon to undertake direct actions to further U.S. national interests as well.

Yet, the makers of U.S. foreign policy are not confined solely to the executive branch. They can be found in Congress as well, and we turn our attention to that institution next.

Congressional Actors

Congress as a whole, a variety of its components, and its individual members play a number of significant foreign policy roles. We address each of these next.

Congress as a Whole

As indicated in Chapter 1, Congress actually has a wider array of foreign policy–making powers than does the president.[23] These include declaring war, approving treaties and appointments, regulating foreign trade, and so on. However, Congress's most significant powers are the ability to pass legislation authorizing some action or policy statement and the ability to provide the funds the federal government needs to work. Thus except for the granting of diplomatic recognition to other regimes, Congress can basically set almost any aspect of U.S. foreign policy by what it chooses to authorize, fund, or require the administration to do. In short, *Congress has tremendous foreign policy powers if and when its members choose to use them.*

The degree to which Congress uses these powers varies by the situation involved. For example, Congress takes its funding powers seriously, so Congress is quite willing to tell the administration what it can or cannot do based on what Congress is willing to fund. Immigration policy is another arena in which Congress has historically not shown any hesitancy to act. Nor does Congress hesitate to send signals to an administration. For example, when the Clinton administration was considering the 1997 Kyoto Protocol on Global Climate Change (which would require Senate approval to be binding on the United States), the Senate voted 95–0 for a nonbinding "sense of the Senate" resolution that essentially said: "Don't send us that treaty."

One situation where Congress has an uneven record involves use of force decisions. On the one hand, Congress has not declared war on anyone since World War II, and since then there have been numerous presidential use of force decisions. So, Congress is often depicted as not wanting the responsibility for use of force decisions, reluctant to challenge presidential uses of force unless things go very badly, and reluctant to be put in a position that could be described as not supporting the troops.

However, there is another way to look at this. Presidential uses of force require money, and Congress has cut off funding for a use of force before. The Vietnam War is a good example. Also, the **War Powers Resolution** of 1973 requires presidents to inform Congress when troops are sent into areas of current or imminent hostilities, and it gives Congress the opportunity to authorize or not authorize such uses of force. According to some in Congress, this situation arose in 2011, as discussed in more detail in Box 4.1. After reading this box, you should be better able to make up your mind as to the legality of that use of force.

So, what is the impact of these considerations? According to a comprehensive study of presidential uses of force, presidents who face at least one chamber of Congress controlled by the opposition party are less likely to use force and wait longer before choosing to use force. Moreover, presidents are wary of Congress's ability to swing public opinion against a use of force or to suggest to foreign audiences that the president lacks important political support back home for a use of force.[24] In short, congressional influence over use of force decisions can be quite direct or subtle and indirect. Yet, Congress does not only

BOX 4.1

Presidential War Powers: The Case of Assisting the Libyan Rebels

The Arab Spring of 2011 began with Tunisians overthrowing the regime of President Zine el Abidine Ben Ali in January. In February, Egyptian protesters forced President Hosni Mubarak out of office. While other Arab societies faced protests and riots, Libya was quickly engulfed in a civil war. In this case, U.S. response to the uprising included the use of force.

On March 17, the UN Security Council authorized military action by UN members to protect Libyan civilians from their own military. On March 18, National Security Adviser Tom Donilon began his morning by meeting via a secure conference call with Defense Secretary Robert Gates, Chairman of the Joint Chiefs of Staff Admiral Mike Mullen, and Secretary of State Hillary Clinton to begin the planning of U.S. military responses. Donilon then held a similar planning session via a secure video conference with his counterparts in the United Kingdom and France. Donilon next briefed President Obama, who in turn met in the Oval Office with Vice President Biden and his assistant Tony Blinken, Secretaries Gates and Clinton, Admiral Mullen, Donilon and his deputy Denis McDonough, Deputy Secretary of State Jim Steinberg, and Under Secretary of State for Political Affairs Bill Burns.

At 12:30 p.m. on March 18, President Obama met for an hour with a bipartisan group of congressional leaders in the White House Situation Room to brief them on U.S. military plans. U.S. air strikes against Libyan targets began on March 19. Within 48 hours of those air strikes, President Obama provided a letter to congressional leaders explaining the military action and saying that it was restricted to air operations to protect Libyan civilians and civilian-held areas. However, the president did not ask for a congressional authorization for a use of force.

Within days, members of Congress began to question whether such a use of force was legal without a congressional authorization, and others began questioning its costs and funding. On March 30, Secretary Clinton and Admiral Mullen held closed-door briefings for members of Congress, and the next day senior administration officials briefed the House and Senate Armed Services Committees and the House Foreign Affairs Committee in open hearings. Representative Dennis Kucinich (D-OH) introduced a bill to cut off funding for the Libyan intervention, and a vote on a Kucinich-sponsored resolution to invoke the War Powers Resolution to force an end to the U.S. military operation was called off on June 1 by Republican leaders in the House. House Speaker John Boehner told reporters that he did not think President Obama had "technically" violated the War Powers Resolution. On June 15, Kucinich and a bipartisan group of nine other House members filed a lawsuit in federal district court challenging the intervention's constitutionality.

While administration officials briefed congressional leaders within the required 48 hours as specified by the War Powers Resolution, Congress did not take a vote to authorize this use of force. President Obama said

the fact that the United States was
not engaged in full-blown hostilities
with Libya made a congressional
authorization unnecessary, but that
did not quiet congressional critics who
include both antiwar Democrats and Tea
Party Republicans. On June 21, House
Speaker Boehner noted:

> The fact is the president has not made
> his case to the members of Congress.
> He's not made his case to the American
> people. We've been in this conflict for
> 90 days and the president hasn't talked to
> the American people for four or five weeks
> about why we're there, what our national
> interest is and why we should continue.

What do you think? Did the president
overstep his bounds in this case by not

seeking a congressional authorization of
force? Was Congress negligent in not
taking an authorization vote? Was the
War Powers Resolution followed here, or
was this an unconstitutional use of force
by the president?

Sources: Donna Cassata, "Boehner Says
Obama Lacks House Support for Libya,"
Associated Press, June 21, 2011; "Congress
Presses Gates, Mullen on Libya," C-SPAN,
April 1, 2011; Reuters, "Dennis Kucinich
Libya Withdrawal Resolution Vote
Scrapped by House," June 1, 2011; Shawna
Shepherd, "Obama Authorizing Force in Libya:
A Timeline,"The 1600 Report, CNN, March 21,
2011; Felicia Sonmez, "Kucinich, Other House
Members File Lawsuit Against Obama on
Libya Military Mission," PostPolitics, *Washington
Post,* June 15, 2011.

influence foreign policy when acting collectively; other parts of Congress can
play independent roles as well. We turn to these next.

Congressional Components

Congress contains various structural components, and some of them have clear
foreign policy roles. Congress is organized to process legislation and engage in
policy oversight via its structure of committees and their various subcommittees. Both the House of Representatives and the Senate have standing committees dealing with armed services, foreign relations/foreign affairs, and homeland
security. Both have special or select committees dealing with intelligence matters. Many other standing committees have jurisdictions that touch on foreign
policy concerns as well. For example, the energy committees deal with national
energy policy; the commerce committees regulate foreign trade; the finance
committees deal with the taxation of foreign trade; the judiciary committees
deal with a variety of issues such as imprisonment of detainees, the protection
of intellectual property (e.g., patents, copyrights, and trademarks), immigration,
and international criminal matters; and the natural resources committees deal
with maritime and fishery resources as well as some petroleum-related matters.

Significant policy actions take place in these committees. Once legislation is
introduced, the closest scrutiny comes in these committees. The actual wording

and substance of bills are most likely determined by these committees. Legislation approved by these committees very often gets approved by the larger chambers in both the House and the Senate. Legislation not approved by these committees typically dies and would have to be reintroduced to be reconsidered. These committees also influence policy by holding hearings, conducting investigations of foreign policy-related matters, and overseeing the activities of the administration.

Members of Congress also form caucuses to coordinate action on issues about which they care.[25] There are about 25 caucuses in the Senate but over 200 in the House of Representatives.[26] For example, there are caucuses focused on specific foreign countries (e.g., Armenia, Brazil, Croatia, Greece, the Netherlands, North Korea, or Sudan), regions (e.g., Central America), global issues (e.g., climate change, human rights, HIV/AIDS, narcotics control, or workers' rights), and national security (e.g., energy security, port security, the uniformed military services, the Out of Iraq caucus).[27] While caucuses have no official role in policy making, informally they can be very important. They provide a forum for concerned members to coordinate their policy-making efforts, garner public attention for the issues that motivate them, and define the problem agenda in a favorable way.

Finally, other component parts of Congress that can play foreign policy roles are nonpartisan research organizations such as the **Congressional Research Service (CRS)** and the **Government Accountability Office (GAO)**. Members of Congress can request CRS reports on policy issues, and those reports can help set the agenda and context of foreign policy making. For example, in a period of rapidly rising global food costs, a CRS report can show Congress what the administration is proposing in the way of food aid in the short-term future and how such aid should be used.[28] The GAO performs similar research and analysis on financial questions. For example, the GAO can evaluate ways to enhance the delivery of civilian foreign assistance to Pakistan and make specific recommendations to Congress regarding how to proceed.[29]

However, perhaps the most overlooked and underestimated way Congress can influence foreign policy is through the individual actions of its members. We now turn to that topic.

Individual Members of Congress

In the final analysis, Congress is composed of 535 individuals, some of whom care about foreign policy issues and will act in the name of Congress.[30] Members of Congress (MCs) can employ means that are direct (seeking to address a particular issue) or indirect (seeking to shape the broader context or policy-making setting) and legislative (specific to a piece of legislation) or nonlegislative (not tied to a specific piece of legislation). Thus, MCs can choose direct-legislative means, indirect-legislative means, direct-nonlegislative means, and indirect-nonlegislative

TABLE 4.2 Congressional Avenues of Influence		
	Direct	**Indirect**
Legislative	Legislation Appropriations Treaties (Senate)	Nonbinding legislation Procedural legislation Appointments (Senate)
Nonlegislative	Letters, phone calls Consultations, advising Hearings Oversight activities Litigation	Agenda setting Framing debate Foreign contacts

Source: Based on James M. Scott, "In the Loop: Congressional Influence in American Foreign Policy," Journal of Political and Military Sociology 25 (1997), 47–76.

means. These dichotomies produce four avenues by which they can shape foreign policy, and examples of them can be found in Table 4.2.[31]

Some MCs choose to act on their own foreign policy agendas without waiting for the administration to do so; these are considered **congressional foreign policy entrepreneurs**. Historically, they have come more often from the Senate than the House (although this difference has narrowed to the point that foreign policy entrepreneurship is now almost as likely in the House as in the Senate), tend to be from the majority party controlling their chamber, and tend not to be members of the president's political party. They gravitate toward all four of the avenues of influence mentioned earlier. For example, they can introduce legislation to keep otherwise out-of-work Russian nuclear weapons' engineers employed in peaceful tasks or reject the Comprehensive Test Ban Treaty (direct-legislative avenues), introduce procedural legislation to oversee the IC more carefully or prohibit political contributions by foreign agents (indirect-legislative), provide the administration the idea for how to bail out the Mexican peso during a currency crisis or encourage U.S. citizens to stop funding the activities of the Irish Republican Army (direct-nonlegislative), or promote peace negotiations in Central America or hold hearings questioning the wisdom of U.S. participation in the Vietnam War (indirect-nonlegislative).[32]

The policy impacts of these entrepreneurs are significant. They stopped U.S. involvement in foreign conflicts (e.g., the Vietnam War and Somalia interventions) and made it harder for presidents to commit troops abroad thereafter.[33] They shifted U.S. policy regarding particular regimes, making relations with some more positive (Spain in the 1950s, Mexico and Russia in the 1990s) and some more negative (South Africa in the 1980s, Cuba and Iran in the 1990s). They encouraged closer U.S. relationships with international organizations (in the 1940s and 1950s) and discouraged closer ties with international organizations that might infringe on U.S. sovereignty (in the 1990s). They pushed administrations to work to topple some foreign governments (e.g., Iraq and Iran) and prevented administrations from toppling others (e.g., Nicaragua). They pressed for greater U.S. participation in efforts to solve some global problems

(e.g., AIDS in Africa or the trade in conflict diamonds) and for less U.S. participation in solving others (e.g., global climate change).

Some of their policy impacts were significant but ultimately counterproduc-
tive. The efforts of Representative Charlie Wilson (D-TX) and others to arm the
Afghan mujahedin in the 1980s led to expulsion of the Soviet Red Army from
Afghanistan and hastened the end of the Cold War. However, that effort also
helped give birth to Osama bin Laden's al Qaeda and provide it with arms to
later attack U.S. military and civilian personnel.[34]

In many ways, the presence of congressional foreign policy entrepreneurs is a
stealth phenomenon, because such policy entrepreneurs are usually more interested
in getting the desired change in policy than in getting individual credit for doing so.
As a result, presidents often take credit for ideas that come from these MCs, and in
other instances administration officials anticipate the reactions of these MCs and
build many of their policy preferences into administration proposals.

While most MCs do not choose to become heavily involved in foreign policy
innovation, a number of MCs have always done so. The numbers of congressional foreign policy entrepreneurs have been significant and growing in the post–
World War II era.[35] Major public policy changes rarely occur in the United States
without individual MCs taking public stances on them, and almost a quarter of
all such public stances taken by MCs since 1789 have involved foreign policy.[36]

In many ways, most U.S. foreign policy is directly made by presidents, other
executive branch officials, and MCs. However in rare instances, courts get involved as well. We turn to their roles next.

Judicial Actors

The federal judiciary rarely gets involved in foreign policy making, because
judges tend to see most foreign policy matters as "political questions"—issues
most appropriately resolved by elected officials rather than courts of law. However as the final arbiters of what the federal government can legally do (and
sometimes how it can be done), there are circumstances where judicial input is
required. The federal courts cannot act unless someone files a lawsuit, and those
suits can involve corporations, individuals, or other government officials.

Several highly significant legal rulings have come from cases involving corporations. The 1936 *Curtiss-Wright* case involved a U.S. aircraft manufacturer
that wanted to sell bomber aircraft to Bolivia despite a presidential order banning such exports. The U.S. Supreme Court ruled that since Congress had previously authorized the president to embargo the sale of arms in South America,
the president had the power to do so and that, moreover, the president should
serve as the country's primary spokesperson in foreign policy.[37] However, such
presidential power was not unlimited. During the Korean War, President Truman
seized control of a steel factory idled due to a strike. In the *Youngstown Sheet
& Tube* case, the U.S. Supreme Court ruled that the administration did not have
the power to take such an action, specifically since strike-related remedies open
to the administration were included in the recently passed Taft-Hartley Act of
1947.[38] Overall, as long as Congress carefully spells out what administrations

are authorized to do in prior legislation, administrations are bound by those specific congressional authorizations. If, on the other hand, those congressional authorizations are vaguely worded or don't exist, courts generally allow presidents considerable leeway in foreign policy actions.[39]

In some instances, other government officials will file suits over U.S. foreign policy matters. For instance, Senator Barry Goldwater (R-AZ) objected to the fact that President Jimmy Carter extended official diplomatic relations to the People's Republic of China, thereby decertifying the Republic of China (now better known as Taiwan) as *the* China in U.S. eyes. Goldwater argued that the U.S. Senate had previously approved a mutual security treaty with Taiwan, the president's action put that treaty into doubt, and the president could not break that treaty without the senatorial input. The Supreme Court ruled against the senator, saying that the Constitution was clear; the Constitution gave the president the sole power to determine official diplomatic relations. Other treaties did not rise above this constitutional prerogative.[40] More recently, in 2011, a bipartisan group of 10 U.S. Representatives, led by Dennis Kucinich (D-OH), filed a federal lawsuit challenging the Obama administration's right to use force in Libya. At the time of this writing, that case had not gone forward (and subsequent events largely rendered it moot). The lawsuit called upon the courts to prevent presidents from going to war, participating in NATO military missions, or participating in UN-authorized military missions without the express approval of Congress.[41] Sometimes, lawsuits come from private citizens, such as Larry Klayman's lawsuit challenging the legality of the NSA's metadata program that collected dialing records of all phone calls in the United States. The 2013 federal district court ruling held the metadata program to be unconstitutional. Time will tell whether the decision in *Klayman et al. v. Obama et al.* will be upheld on appeal.

In recent years, difficult legal issues have arisen regarding the status of detainees captured in the "war on terror." These are discussed in more detail in Box 4.2. These issues are troubling ones, because reasonable people differ greatly in finding a line that separates the benefits of following the rule of law from the benefits of protecting U.S. lives from terrorist attack. After reading this box, you'll be more able to add your view to the mix.

BOX 4.2

The Courts and Detainee Rights: Determining the Limits of the Constitution

When the post-9/11 "war on terror" began in earnest, the result was the capture of thousands of people in Afghanistan who were initially labeled as "enemy combatants." The question quickly arose as to what to do with them. While many were imprisoned in Afghanistan and later Iraq, some were transported to the U.S. naval base at Guantanamo, Cuba. White House and Justice Department lawyers wrote memoranda for President George

W. Bush, arguing that such detainees were neither criminals (and thus not deserving of due process rights under the U.S. Constitution) nor prisoners of war since they did not represent nation-states or wear military uniforms (and thus not deserving rights under the Geneva Conventions).

Therefore, these individuals existed in a kind of legal limbo. The administration claimed that the president's authority as commander in chief *in time of war* allowed him to keep the detainees locked up indefinitely as many were considered too dangerous to release, as they had taken up arms against the United States or were motivated to do so now after their imprisonment. Further, these detainees might know things that would help prevent future terrorist attacks. So, administration lawyers wrote memoranda justifying the use of aggressive interrogation techniques—which others would later call "torture"—in an attempt to gain useful intelligence information from them.

Critics of the administration's actions (including State Department lawyers) were aghast; to them, it was illegal and un-American to simply lock people up and throw away the key, thereby denying prisoners any chance to protest their innocence or challenge their detention. Others also could not abide the idea of aggressive interrogation techniques that included at times the simulated drowning of prisoners (i.e., "waterboarding"). Even more troubling, a few of those incarcerated were U.S. citizens, and the Bush administration's position was that they had forfeited their constitutional rights by fighting for the enemy. Not surprisingly, a number of lawsuits were filed challenging the government's actions. Ultimately, in a series of decisions, the U.S. Supreme Court said that (1) the Constitution's due process rights existed to restrict governments from abusing their powers anywhere, not to give full or partial rights to citizens and no rights to noncitizens being held in foreign locations; (2) detainees had to be provided some access to due process of law through appropriately constituted tribunals; and (3) Congress should authorize such tribunals. Congress subsequently passed legislation authorizing military tribunals for this purpose, but only a limited number of such cases against detainees were expected, as many of the detainees have since been repatriated to other countries.

Unquestionably, determining right and wrong here is difficult after the events of 9/11. How would a realist explain the Bush administration's actions? How would a liberal interpret these events? Would constructivists see these events differently? Does idealism figure into any of these explanations? In your view, what's right and what's wrong here?

Source: Based on Linda Cornett and Mark Gibney, "The Rights of Detainees: Determining the Limits of Law," in Ralph G. Carter (ed.), Contemporary Cases in U.S. Foreign Policy: From Terrorism to Trade, 5th ed. (Washington, DC: CQ Press, 2014).

Conclusion: A Plethora of Governmental Actors

As should now be clear, many different governmental officials and organizations participate in the making of U.S. foreign policy. The individuals involved provide crucial information on issues, concerns, opportunities, and challenges; they help identify and analyze options and possibilities for action; they make the key decisions needed for the government to act; and they implement the decisions made.

In fact, there are so many potential governmental actors involved that tracing who the actual decision makers are can be difficult at times. Further, other societal and external actors get involved as well. We turn to them in Chapter 5.

Glossary Terms

Central Intelligence Agency (CIA)   created by the **National Security Act of 1947**, this civilian agency engages in intelligence gathering and analysis, counterintelligence, and covert operations.

Congressional foreign policy entrepreneurs   members of Congress who choose to act on their own foreign policy agendas without waiting for the administration to do so.

Congressional Research Service (CRS)   a nonpartisan staff agency that assists Congress in its policy-making roles by providing information and analysis.

Defense Intelligence Agency (DIA)   a multiservice agency responsible for intelligence functions in the Defense Department.

Director of national intelligence (DNI)   a position created in 2004 to coordinate the information gathered by the other 16 members of the Intelligence Community.

Governmental Accountability Office (GAO)   a nonpartisan staff agency that assists Congress in its policy-making roles by providing financial information and analysis.

Homeland Security Council (HSC)   the group charged with advising the president on homeland security matters and coordinating such policies across the various governmental actors involved.

Intelligence Community (IC)   17 different entities that participate in the collection and analysis of intelligence information, counterintelligence operations, and at times covert operations.

National Economic Council (NEC)   the group charged with advising the president on domestic and international economic policy and coordinating such policies across the various governmental actors involved.

National Security Act of 1947   the legislation that created the Department of Defense (uniting the Air Force, Army, Marines, and Navy), the Central Intelligence Agency, the National Security Council, and the position of **national security adviser**.

National security adviser   the president's assistant for national security affairs who normally briefs the president daily on national security-related events. Created by the **National Security Act of 1947**.

National Security Agency (NSA)   the NSA provides information assurance by preventing vital information from falling into the hands of other powers (often through the use of cryptography), collects signals intelligence (by eavesdropping on the communications of others), and conducts the research necessary for both information assurance and signals intelligence. It provides nearly 80% of the intelligence information used by the federal government.

National Security Council (NSC)   the group charged with advising the president on national security policy issues and coordinating such policies across the various governmental actors involved.

National Security Staff (NSS)   the combined members of what previously had been the National Security Council Staff and the Homeland Security Council Staff.

War Powers Resolution   a 1973 law requiring presidents to inform Congress of use of force decisions and giving Congress the opportunity to authorize—or not authorize—that use of force.

Endnotes

1. See *United States v. Curtiss-Wright Export Corp.*, 299 U.S. 304 (1936).
2. For more on the power to persuade, see Richard A. Neustadt, *Presidential Power: The Politics of Leadership* (Cambridge, MA: Harvard University Press, 1960).
3. For more on Henry Reuss as a foreign policy maker, see Ralph G. Carter and James M. Scott, *Choosing to Lead: Understanding Congressional Foreign Policy Entrepreneurs* (Durham, NC: Duke University Press, 2009).
4. For more on this, see Patrick Cox, "John Nance Garner on the Vice Presidency—In Search of the Proverbial Bucket," The Dolph Briscoe Center for American History, University of Texas at Austin, available online at: http://www.cah.utexas.edu/news /press_release.php?press=press_bucket.
5. For more on the role of Dick Cheney, see Bob Woodward, *State of Denial* (New York: Simon and Schuster, 2006), and *The War Within: A Secret White House History 2006–2008* (New York: Simon and Schuster, 2008); John W. Dean, *Worse Than Watergate: The Secret Presidency of George W. Bush* (New York: Grand Central Publishing, 2005); and Ivo H. Daalder and James M. Lindsay, "America Unbound: The Bush Revolution in Foreign Policy," *Brookings Review* 21 (Fall 2003), 2–6.
6. For more on Dulles, see Townsend Hoopes, *The Devil and John Foster Dulles* (Boston: Little, Brown, 1973). For more on Acheson, see Robert L. Beisner, *Dean Acheson: A Life in the Cold War* (New York: Oxford University Press, 2009).
7. See David Halberstam, *The Best and the Brightest* (New York: Random House, 1989).
8. See Woodward, *State of Denial*.
9. See Halberstam, *The Best and the Brightest*, and Woodward, *State of Denial*, respectively.
10. See "Outlays for Discretionary Programs in Constant (FY 2000) Dollars: 1962–2014," available online at http://www.gpo.gov/fdsys/granule/BUDGET-2010-TAB /BUDGET-2010-TAB-8-8/content-detail.html.
11. See Curt Tarnoff and Larry Nowells, "Foreign Aid: An Introductory Overview of U.S. Programs and Policy," Congressional Research Service Report for Congress, April 15, 2004, available online at http://fpc.state.gov/documents /organization/31987.pdf.
12. See "Military Defense in the United States: 1950–2018," available online at http:// www.usgovernmentspending.com/downchart_gs.php?year=1950_2019&view =1&expand=&units=k&fy=fy10&chart=30-total&bar=1&stack=1&size=m&title =Defense&state=US&color=c&local=Defense.
13. For uniformed military personnel numbers, see the Office of the Secretary of Defense website, available online at http://siadapp.dmdc.osd.mil/personnel /MILITARY/history/hst0903.pdf. For civilian personnel numbers, see the Office of the

Secretary of Defense website, available online at http://siadapp.dmdc.osd.mil/personnel /CIVILIAN/fy2009/may2009/may2009.pdf. For the current budget figures, see "Declining Defense: Obama's Budget Does Cut One Federal Department," *Wall Street Journal*, March 2, 2009, p. A14, available online at http://online.wsj.com /article/SB123595811964905929.html.

14. For more on this notion, see Andrew J. Bacevich, *The New American Militarism: How Americans Are Seduced by War* (New York: Oxford University Press, 2006).

15. Julian E. Barnes, "Defense Chief Urges Bigger Budget for State Department: Beyond Guns and Steel, the U.S. Should Build up Diplomacy and 'Civilian Instruments of National Security,' Gates Says," *Los Angeles Times*, November 27, 2007, available online at http://articles.latimes.com/2007/nov/27/nation/na-gates27.

16. See the DNI website, available online at http://www.dni.gov/history.htm.

17. "Intelligence Budget Data," Intelligence Resource Program, Federation of American Scientists, available online at http://www.fas.org/irp/budget/index.html; and "The Black Budget," *Washington Post*, available online at http://www.washingtonpost .com/wp-srv/special/national/black-budget/.

18. See the libraryindex.com website, available online at http://www.libraryindex.com /pages/1930/Civilian-National-Security-Infrastructure-CENTRAL-INTELLI- GENCE-AGENCY-CIA.html.

19. See the NSA/CSS (Central Security Service) website, available online at http://www .nsa.gov/.

20. See "Intelligence Agency Budgets: Commission Recommends No Release but Releases Them Anyway," Federation of American Scientists Intelligence Resource Program, available online at http://www.fas.org/irp/commission/budget.htm.

21. James Bamford, *Body of Secrets: Anatomy of the Ultra-Secret National Security Agency from the Cold War through the Dawn of a New Century* (New York: Doubleday, 2001).

22. James Bamford, *The Shadow Factory: The Ultra-Secret NSA from 9/11 to the Eavesdropping on America* (New York: Anchor Books, 2009); and "The Black Budget," *Washington Post*, available online at http://www.washingtonpost.com/wp-srv /special/national/black-budget/.

23. Harold Koh, *The National Security Constitution: Power Sharing after the Iran-Contra Affair* (New Haven, CT: Yale University Press, 1990).

24. William G. Howell and Jon C. Pevehouse, *While Dangers Gather: Congressional Checks on Presidential War Powers* (Princeton, NJ: Princeton University Press, 2007).

25. For more on congressional caucuses, see Susan Webb Hammond, *Congressional Caucuses in National Policymaking* (Baltimore: Johns Hopkins University Press, 2001).

26. Maggie Master, "Got an Issue? Congress Has Your Caucus," *The Hill*, November 28, 2007, available online at http://thehill.com/capital-living/23977-got-an-issue -congress-has-your-caucus.

27. For examples of congressional caucuses, see Master, "Got an Issue?" and the website of Representative Michael Capuano (D-MA), available online at http://www.house .gov/capuano/issues/committees.shtml.

28. Melissa D. Ho and Charles E. Hanrahan, "U.S. Global Food Security Funding, FY2010–FY2012," CRS Report for Congress, April 28, 2011, available online at http://www.fas.org/sgp/crs/row/R41812.pdf.

29. "Department of State's Report to Congress and U.S. Oversight of Civilian Assistance to Pakistan Can Be Further Enhanced," GAO Report, GAO-11-310R, February 17, 2011, available online at http://www.gao.gov/products/GAO-11-310R.

30. For more on this point, see Frans Bax, "The Legislative-Executive Relationship in Foreign Policy: New Partnership or New Competition?" *Orbis* 20 (1977), 881–904.
31. For more on these avenues of influence, see Carter and Scott, *Choosing to Lead*, Chapter 1.
32. For more on these congressional foreign policy entrepreneurs, see Carter and Scott, *Choosing to Lead*.
33. For more on congressional war powers, see Howell and Pevehouse, *While Dangers Gather*.
34. For more on this example, see George Crile, *Charlie Wilson's War: The Extraordinary Story of the Largest Covert Operation in History* (New York: Atlantic Monthly Press, 2003), or watch the movie by the same title.
35. Again, see Carter and Scott, *Choosing to Lead*.
36. See David R. Mayhew, *America's Congress: Actions in the Public Sphere, James Madison through Newt Gingrich* (New Haven, CT: Yale University Press, 2000).
37. See *U.S. v. Curtiss-Wright Export Corp.*, 299 U.S. 304 (1936).
38. See *Youngstown Sheet & Tube v. Sawyer*, 343 U.S. 579 (1952).
39. See Gordon Silverstein, *Imbalance of Powers: Constitutional Interpretation and the Making of American Foreign Policy* (New York: Oxford University Press, 1997).
40. See *Goldwater v. Carter*, 444 U.S. 996 (1979).
41. Stephen Koff, "Dennis Kucinich Files Lawsuit against President Obama, Says Libya War Violates the Law," *Cleveland Plain Dealer*, June 15, 2011, available online at http://www.cleveland.com/open/index.ssf/2011/06/dennis_kucinich_files_lawsuit .html.

CHAPTER 5

Individual and Small Group Decision Making

The group involved in making the decision to go after Osama bin Laden in Pakistan later monitored the May 1, 2011, operation in the White House Situation Room. They included, sitting from left, Vice President Joe Biden, President Barack Obama, Brigadier General Brad Webb of Joint Special Operations Command, Deputy National Security Adviser Denis McDonough, Secretary of State Hillary Clinton, and Secretary of Defense Robert Gates. Standing from left are Chairman of the Joint Chiefs of Staff Admiral Mike Mullen, National Security Adviser Tom Donilon, Chief of Staff Bill Daley, Vice Presidential National Security Adviser Tony Blinken, Counterterrorism Director Audrey Tomason, Presidential Assistant for Homeland Security and Counterterrorism John Brennan, and Director of National Intelligence James Clapper. Just out of the picture is the CIA counterterrorism officer who successfully argued that bin Laden was probably at the compound in Abbottabad, Pakistan.
Source: White House Photo/Alamy

77

LEARNING OBJECTIVES

- Explain the difference between individual and small group decision making.

- Illustrate the types of situations that favor individual versus small group decision making.

- Define a rational actor approach to decision making.

- Evaluate the roles and relevance of cognitive shortcuts and decision heuristics.

Introduction

The image is iconic: a lonely individual sitting at a big desk, perhaps staring out a window while pondering a momentous decision that could impact millions of lives around the globe. Manifested by Harry Truman's proud claim that "the buck stops here" and George W. Bush's self-proclaimed title of "Chief Decider," the notion of presidents making the decisions that shape U.S. foreign policy is commonplace in U.S. political culture. But how accurate is it? Is this how U.S. foreign policy is typically made?

The answer is, "No." As the chapter-opening photo suggests, while presidents may be the ultimate foreign policy decision maker in many cases, *rarely do they act alone or make decisions without the face-to-face input of others.* Richard Nixon was one of the few exceptions to this rule. He was reputed to take input in the form of one-page memoranda into his private office, close the door, and later emerge with a decision of what U.S. foreign policy should be. Such solitary decision making is far from the norm.

When foreign policy decisions are made, a number of formal or informal presidential advisers tend to also be in the room. So, rather than the president acting as the "lone ranger" making U.S. foreign policy, more often foreign policy decision making is the product of small group decision processes. Thus, in this chapter, we will discuss the processes of small group decision making and the roles played by the president and others in the administration.

Small Group Decision Making

Presidents and Their Staffs

Presidents have considerable staff assistance when making foreign policy decisions. As noted in Chapter 4, presidents may call on the vice president, the national security adviser, Intelligence Community officials, Cabinet secretaries, and a host of other personal and National Security Staff aides and administration officials for information and policy input.

The goal of the president and his decision-making team is simple: make a good decision. While luck always helps, a good decision is usually predicated on having good information as well as a good grasp of the relevant options. Even with all the help available to the president, getting both good information and adequate knowledge of the available options when needed can be challenging at times.

As president in the 1950s, former General Dwight Eisenhower relied on his military background and used his Cabinet officials as he had previously used his military staff officers. He pressed them for whatever relevant expertise they could bring to bear on the problem at hand, and Cabinet meetings became real foreign policy decision-making settings. President Eisenhower was followed by the much younger John Kennedy, whose relative inexperience might have initially led him to be too impressed with "experts," as was demonstrated in 1961.

Upon entering office, Kennedy inherited a CIA covert operation to invade Cuba, an initiative long past its final planning stages and about to go operational. Before making the "go or no-go" decision to topple Cuban president Fidel Castro, Kennedy listened to the rosy predictions of success from top CIA officials. Essentially, their message to the new president was, "We've done this before" (in places such as Iran and Guatemala) and "we know what we're doing." However, the other participants in the decision-making group failed to question the tenuous assumptions on which the operation was based, stifled any doubts of their own, and were apparently very concerned with "fitting in" and maintaining the goodwill of the others. Thus, difficult questions were not asked, possible flaws in the plan were not discussed, and the result of the Bay of Pigs invasion was a fiasco in which seemingly everything that could go wrong did. Such decision-making behavior in a concurrence-seeking group is now called **groupthink**, and while it does not guarantee a bad decision, it makes one far more likely.[1]

To be fair, it is not unusual for people who meet regularly to try to minimize or put aside their differences in an attempt to get along. While the downside to such behavior may be negligible in many settings, when making decisions that potentially affect the lives of over 300 million people, the costs of such decision-making mistakes may be catastrophic. Thus, it is hard not to conclude that the decision-making group's emphasis should have been on getting the decision right, not just getting along with the others in the room or avoiding looking foolish. Full and free discussion of the situation, of all the assumptions involved, and of the pros and cons of the relevant options should have been encouraged.

One way to promote such a dynamic discussion would be to use a **rational actor model (RAM)** of decision making. Following the RAM would require the president to ask the staff to identify all the options available in the situation, list each option's strengths and weaknesses, and then discuss all the options, seeking to find the one that was optimal—the overall best option, the one promising the best possible outcome in light of the incurred costs, or the overall least bad option if all options are bad.

What's the downside of such an approach? It requires considerable amounts of time to identify all options and determine their strengths and weaknesses. Presidents may feel they have neither the time nor the inclination to invest so much effort into the particular decision at hand. With more decisions yet to make, more official duties yet to perform, and more position papers yet to read in preparation for the days ahead, they often turn to any available shortcuts to make the decision faster and easier.

One way to do this is to use a **multiple advocacy** approach in which members of the decision-making group are tasked with the responsibility to become advocates for each different option and find the flaws in the options under consideration. If done well, all sides to controversial issues should be fairly presented to the president or other top foreign policy decision makers before a decision is made, thus increasing the chances of making a good decision.[2] While such an approach may produce discord among the participants, particularly for decisions made under stressful conditions, the president can try to promote an environment in which the decision makers can "disagree without becoming disagreeable."[3] However, this approach may still require a lot of time. A more practical alternative may be to ask an influential adviser to play the role of "devil's advocate." Vice President Biden has often been asked to play this role by President Obama, where his job in decision-making groups is to ask tough questions, challenge assumptions, and otherwise "think outside the box."

One of the concerns here, of course, is that the president has a lot more influence than the others in the room. Therefore, if presidents don't want others to simply agree with their boss, presidents would be well-advised to keep their policy preferences under wraps—at least at first. That way, others are encouraged to say freely what they think, so as to get the best ideas out for consideration. Even then, presidents should be mindful of the personalities and responsibilities of those in the room, knowing that some forceful personalities might need to be kept in check and some more reticent advisers might need to be prompted more, particularly if they possess good judgment or the expertise needed in the situation.

On the other hand, presidents and other top administration foreign policy makers are like the rest of us. They often don't want to work any harder than necessary to make a good decision. To make things easier, they will often look for some ways to simplify decision making. We turn to such tactics next.

Cognitive Shortcuts

There are many ways foreign policy makers may use to make decisions easier and faster by simplifying their thinking. Some officials come into office with a relatively fixed image of how the political world works, which they rely on to point them in the right direction. Such an **operational code** provides a blueprint to the decision maker by specifying what is important, what motivates others, and what tends to work best in solving foreign policy problems.[4] President Jimmy Carter relied on his operational code to tell him that what was most important in international politics was how governments treated their citizens, and thus, he made a focus on human rights central to U.S. foreign policy under his administration. He was followed in office by President Ronald Reagan who saw the world through Cold War lenses, who felt the Soviet Union was the source of all evil in the world, and who believed the spread of communism should be contested at every opportunity. Not surprisingly, the foreign policy directions of these two administrations were quite different. For his part, President Obama seems to have an operational code of his own, as shown in Box 5.1.

■■■■■   BOX 5.1   ■■■■■

Obama's Operational Code: Is It Christian Realism?

What makes Barack Obama tick? Does he have an operational code—a blueprint that tells him what tends to motivate others, what ends should be pursued, and by what means? Had Obama been a politician of longer experience, he would probably have had a track record of public commentaries on most foreign policy issues. Yet as a relative newcomer to the national political scene, he did not have much of a track record, and he was careful not to tie himself to very specific policy stances during the campaign.

Obama provided a clue in 2007 when he told the *New York Times* columnist David Brooks that Reinhold Niebuhr was one of his favorite philosophers. When asked what he took away from Niebuhr, a Christian theologian who wrote extensively about public affairs from the 1930s through 1960s, Obama said, "I take away the compelling idea that there's serious evil in the world, and hardship and pain. And we should be humble and modest in our belief we can eliminate those things. But we shouldn't use that as an excuse for cynicism and inaction."

In elaborating what came to be called "Christian realism," Niebuhr stressed a number of key ideas:

- Capable of love, individuals may behave ethically, but societies rarely do.
- Evil exists in the world. While it cannot be eliminated, it must be confronted, contained, and diminished.

- Power corrupts as does self-righteousness, and the watchful eye of democracy is needed to prevent such corruption.

President Obama stressed such themes in his December 2009 acceptance speech for the Nobel Peace Prize when he said, "We must begin by acknowledging the hard truth: we will not eradicate violent conflicts in our lifetimes. There will be times when nations—acting individually or in concert—will find the use of force not only necessary but morally justified." In his view, some wars were just, as he noted that "A nonviolent movement could not have halted Hitler's armies. Negotiations cannot convince al Qaeda's leaders to lay down their arms." To a European audience often skeptical of U.S. policies or motives, he added, "Whatever mistakes we have made, the plain fact is this. The United States of America has helped underwrite global security for more than six decades with the blood of our citizens and the strength of our arms."

Regarding means, Obama stressed that we should not abandon our moral values when fighting evil, for to do so was to become evil ourselves. Regarding ends, Obama pressed the idea that we should improve things where we can, and that partial victories are better than no victories at all. He put that idea into practice a week after the Nobel Prize speech when he worked with China,

India, Brazil, and South Africa to get a political agreement at the Copenhagen Climate Change Conference that made at least some progress on limiting the growth of future fossil fuel emissions by major polluters, but far less progress than had been initially hoped.

Thus, the operational code that Barack Obama follows may well be:

- We have to face the world as it is. Evil exists and must be confronted whenever possible.
- Our goal must be to do as much good as we can.
- Perfect solutions are rare; we should accept whatever progress we can achieve (i.e., a half a loaf is better than none at all).
- We should use the foreign policy tools best suited to progress— soft power in some cases (moral suasion, economic incentives or disincentives, diplomacy) and hard power in others (the threat or use of force).

Do you think this analysis captures the way he sees the world? If so, what meaningful difference does that make in terms of policy outputs? Does this operational code seem similar to or different from that of other presidents as far as you know? Does it seem similar or different than the general beliefs of the U.S. public? Will it lead to the kind of decisions you can support? What objections might liberals or idealists raise to this approach?

Sources: David Brooks, "Obama, Gospel and Verse." *New York Times*, April 26, 2007; David Brooks, "Obama's Christian Realism." *New York Times*, December 15, 2009, p. A37; Jennifer Loven and Ben Feller, "Climate Deal Shows Obama Pragmatism." Associated Press, as reported in the *Fort Worth Star-Telegram*, December 19, 2009, p. 14A; Pew Research Center Publications, "Obama's Favorite Theologian? A Short Course on Reinhold Niebuhr." *Pew Forum on Religion & Public Life*, June 26, 2009; David Sanger, "A Nobel Laureate's Pragmatic Approach to 'the World as It Is.'" *New York Times*, December 12, 2009, p. A9; Jeff Zeleny, "Accepting Peace Prize, Obama Offers 'Hard Truth.'" *New York Times*, December 11, 2009, p. A17.

Some presidents rely more on instinctive approaches to decision making. President George W. Bush repeatedly said that he relied on his "gut" (i.e., his intuition) in making decisions or reacting to others, and he did not question those decisions thereafter.[5] On the other hand, his father President George H.W. Bush appears to have been more instinctively guided by **prospect theory**. This theory holds that when things are going well, decision makers tend to act prudently and become more risk-averse, so as not to upset a status quo that is favorable. When things are not going well, decision makers become prone to risky strategies as they seek to change that unacceptable status quo. Thus, the first President Bush failed to reach out with much aid to Russia after the Soviet Union collapsed—when you are the only superpower left, why aid a potential enemy who might arise again?—but chose to go to war with Iraq in 1990 rather than accept its occupation of neighboring oil-rich Kuwait, even though the Iraqi Army was the fourth largest in the world at the time.

Another instinctive way for presidents to make decisions easier is to compare them with prior situations. Sometimes, they use metaphors. So, when George H.W. Bush called Saddam Hussein a "Hitler" following the Iraqi invasion of Kuwait, that metaphor tilted a U.S. response away from any conciliatory behavior toward Iraq and instead toward a more robust U.S. response to the invasion. How can you compromise with or accommodate a Hitler? Other times, presidents say they apply the lessons of history. President Harry Truman explained his quick reaction to North Korea's 1950 invasion of South Korea by saying that the "lessons of Munich" showed that appeasing aggressors did not work. After all, Adolf Hitler had demanded and gained the German-speaking part of Czechoslovakia at a meeting in Munich in 1938, but instead of being satisfied, Hitler went on to order the invasion of Poland the next year. Later, whenever President Bill Clinton contemplated the use of force to stop the genocide in Rwanda or the ethnic cleansing in the former Yugoslavia, he and his advisers kept remembering the images of dead U.S. servicemen being dragged through the streets of Mogadishu, Somalia, in 1993. That image prevented any serious discussion of putting "boots on the ground" to protect civilians from genocidal violence.

Decision Heuristics

Beyond psychological shortcuts, decision makers often rely on what they might call "common sense" or "rules of thumb" to make decision making easier and faster. Psychologists call such guidelines **decision heuristics.**[6] One such heuristic is **incrementalism**—making only minor changes from what has been done before or from one's current policy position. Such approaches avoid the investment of time and effort that finding an optimal solution requires.[7] So, when the Vietnam War was not going well and the military asked for more troops, President Lyndon Johnson ordered more troops to be deployed. With each small escalation went the hope that perhaps this new troop level would produce a victory, thereby avoiding any painstaking reevaluation of the U.S. role in that war.

Implicit in most incremental approaches is the notion of **satisficing;** the idea that the goal is not to discover the optimal or best solution but rather one that is "good enough" to be satisfactory or sufficient.[8] Any solution that can be portrayed as satisfactory or sufficient to meet the policy need is particularly attractive to an administration when it is under public pressure to "do something" regarding an issue. If such a satisficing solution can be marketed as a "success" by the administration, so much the better. For example, when the Obama administration chose to let Congress largely write the details of an economic stimulus package in 2009, it got a satisficing response. While the results may not have been ideal to many, they did largely quell the public's demands to "do something" about the Great Recession and the administration could claim that a worse depression had been avoided.

Another decision heuristic requires a bit more thought on the part of the administration actors. A **poliheuristic** approach also envisions decision making as a two-step process. The first step is to eliminate as many options as possible (using whatever reasoning that makes sense in the situation). The second step is to devote whatever time is left to carefully evaluate the few remaining options with the goal of maximizing benefits and minimizing risks.[9] The 1962 Cuban Missile Crisis decision—to deploy a naval blockade to force the Soviets to remove their missiles from Cuba—illustrates this approach. Options such as appealing to the United Nations (UN), directly approaching Cuban president Fidel Castro, and invading Cuba were quickly discarded, leaving the majority of the analysis devoted to only two options—a naval blockade or an airstrike. These two options were considered carefully before the airstrike option was discarded (as it could not guarantee that all missiles would be rendered inoperative), and then the blockade option was chosen.[10]

More recently, the Obama administration appears to have used such an approach in making the decision to deploy a troop surge in Afghanistan in December 2009, as shown in Box 5.2. While a poliheuristic approach to decision making is potentially a faster process than the RAM, it is still not a quick way to make a decision, as this box illustrates. The meaningful question is whether the result of such a process was a good decision.

▬▬▬▬ BOX 5.2 ▬▬▬▬

Deciding on the Afghan "Surge": Poliheuristic Decision Making or Indecisiveness?

On December 1, 2009, President Barack Obama announced a long-anticipated policy shift in a speech at the U.S. Military Academy at West Point, New York. He said he would increase the number of troops in Afghanistan by approximately 30,000 within the next six months. Along with 10,000 more troops he hoped would be contributed by NATO allies, the goals of these additional forces would be to beat back the Taliban insurgency against the Afghan government, attack al Qaeda elements in Afghanistan and weaken their ability to attack the United States and its interests, and strengthen Afghan forces so they could provide for their own national security, thus allowing U.S. and NATO forces to leave sooner as opposed to later. The goal, he said, was to begin the process of military withdrawal in July 2011.

This decision—to increase the number of troops in Afghanistan to beat back the enemy so that U.S. troops could begin the process of leaving Afghanistan sooner—was more than two months in the making. The question of what strategy to follow in Afghanistan— where U.S. forces had been fighting for over seven years without much to show for their effort—had been hanging over the new administration since it arrived in Washington. Moreover, news reports indicated Taliban forces were getting stronger; something different needed to be done.

On August 30, 2009, the U.S. commander in Afghanistan—General

Stanley McChrystal—submitted a classified report asking for more troops. The options he outlined were an 80,000 troop increase to undertake a countrywide counterinsurgency campaign against the Taliban and al Qaeda forces, which had the greatest hope for a military success; a 40,000 troop increase to take on the Taliban and al Qaeda in eastern and southern Afghanistan where they were strongest, which might preclude a military failure; or a 10,000–15,000 troop increase to focus on training Afghan forces whose performance could not be predicted.

When considering these options, the president made the ultimate decision, but he was aided by a small group of officials dubbed the "AfPak" national security team. Group members included Vice President Joe Biden, Presidential Chief of Staff Rahm Emanuel, National Security Adviser General James Jones, Deputy National Security Adviser Thomas Donilon, Secretary of State Hillary Clinton, UN Ambassador Susan Rice, Special Envoy to Pakistan and Afghanistan Richard Holbrooke, Secretary of Defense Robert Gates, Chairman of the Joint Chiefs of Staff Admiral Mike Mullen, Chief of U.S. Central Command General David Petraeus, Director of National Intelligence Dennis Blair, and Director of Central Intelligence Leon Panetta. This core group of 13 people—with additional input at times from Senior Adviser to the President David Axelrod, Ambassador to Afghanistan Lieutenant General Karl Eikenberry, and General McChrystal—met on 10 occasions from September 13 to November 29 for a total of 25 hours.

Obama had previously read a book on the Vietnam War called *Lessons in Disaster* by Gordon Goldstein. The lesson the president took away from the book was that the U.S. intervention in Vietnam had failed because both Presidents Kennedy and Johnson had not questioned the underlying assumptions on which U.S. military intervention was based. Obama was determined not to make the same mistake, so he asked the AfPak group fundamental questions such as:

- What are the relationships between the Afghan Taliban, the Pakistani Taliban, and al Qaeda?
- Can al Qaeda be defeated without defeating the Afghan Taliban?
- Can the Afghan Taliban be defeated without the defeat of the Pakistani Taliban next door?
- Did the Afghan regime led by Hamid Karzai have sufficient strength and legitimacy to participate in a counterinsurgency war, or would such a U.S. effort be wasted?
- If the Taliban took control of Afghanistan, would Pakistan be next?

The president initially eliminated the 80,000 troop increase option as too much to consider. From that point on, he listened and encouraged the others to debate the various pros and cons of the remaining options. Proponents of a 40,000 troop increase included Generals Petraeus and McChrystal and Secretary Clinton. Director Panetta pressed for more covert operatives and Predator unmanned drone aircraft to be assigned to Pakistan. Vice President Biden pushed for a more limited military operation directed solely at al Qaeda operatives. Ambassador Rice, Ambassador Holbrooke, Chief of Staff Emanuel, Ambassador Eikenberry, and Adviser Axelrod expressed doubts about any military surge due to the human and financial costs involved or the reliability of the Afghan government.

The president's goal was to give the Karzai regime a chance to prevail against the Taliban and al Qaeda but without locking U.S. forces into an indefinite commitment. Secretary Gates came up with the 30,000 troop option, arguing that NATO could be pressed to put up the remaining 10,000. Admiral Mullen came up with the idea of beginning a withdrawal by July 2011.

Unfortunately, someone leaked General McChrystal's classified report to the media in mid-September. Thus, as the weeks went by, the public question became: When will someone make a decision? The president and his supporters stressed that the decision was too important to be rushed without sufficient consideration of all the relevant facts and factors. Critics led by former vice president Dick Cheney argued that the delay in announcing a decision amounted to indecisiveness, a dangerous trait in a commander in chief.

When the decision was finally announced on December 1, some thought it was a judicious decision that balanced the various concerns that motivated the president. Others were less sure of the decision's wisdom. Some Americans wanted to initiate a U.S. troop withdrawal from Afghanistan, not a surge. Others wanted a targeted operation against al Qaeda, not a surge. Some thought 30,000 more troops were clearly insufficient for the task and, thus, a waste of effort, resources, and lives. Others thought the idea of publicizing a withdrawal date in advance gave the enemy a huge tactical advantage; from the enemy's point of view, they just had to wait for 18 months and the Americans would begin to leave.

Was this a sound poliheuristic process leading to a wise decision, or was it an indecisive response—designed primarily to try to please as many different audiences as possible—and thus, likely to fail? Did it produce a good decision?

Source: Based on Peter Baker, "Inside the Situation Room: How a War Plan Evolved," *New York Times,* December 12, 2009, pp. 1, 24–25.

Perhaps the approach involving the least effort is **cybernetic decision making**—literally decisions with a minimum of thinking or analysis. Here, the decision makers ask questions such as, "Can we do anything? If so, try it." A good example of cybernetic decision processes came when Britain, France, and Israel invaded Egypt in the 1956 Suez Crisis. To force the British out of Egypt, President Eisenhower asked his Cabinet, "What can we do?" When told that the United States had sufficient British currency reserves in its treasury to bankrupt Britain, if all that currency was dumped on global money markets at the same time, Eisenhower threatened the British with just such an action. The British promptly withdrew their troops from Egypt. Who would have guessed that Treasury holdings would be the key to ending the invasion?

However, since most decisions are made by small groups, there is one other factor to consider. As situations vary, so do the inputs facing policy makers and the amount of stresses they experience in seeking policy answers. The nature of the situation thus needs to be considered as well.

Types of Situations

Not all foreign policy decisions are the same. Administrative foreign policy decisions that involve easy choices or routine matters tend to be made elsewhere in the administration (see Chapter 6 on bureaucratic decision making). As President Obama observed on several occasions, the only decisions that get all the way to his desk are the tough ones. Yet, not all tough decisions are the same. The small group dynamics covered up to this point typically applies to noncrisis decision making. As a limited subset of all foreign policy decisions, crises have their own characteristics.

A **crisis** is a situation that represents a significant threat to core values or high priority goals, requires a quick response, and comes as a surprise to decision makers.[11] Despite the fact that most decision makers are quick to label things as crises, most situations tend to meet only one or two of these criteria. Only a small fraction of the many situations facing foreign policy makers truly fit all three of these criteria, and the combination of these criteria produce some commonalities in decision making.

First, the high level of threat quickly kicks the decision all the way up to the top of the administration, so the highest level official available will be involved—and that is almost always the president. Second, the short time frame for a response limits the number of others whose input can be sought, so the decision group is typically even smaller than usual. The group may literally be the president with only a few advisers, as fewer experts happen to be close by and there may not seem to be enough time to round all of them up for inclusion in the decision group. Third, with the element of genuine surprise, the result may be a decision that, to a greater degree than normal, reflects the personal traits and idiosyncrasies of the president. The result may be a quick response that is more extreme than what presidents might otherwise choose to do if they had more time to think things through and consult with more experts.

For example, President Richard Nixon built his early political career on a tough stance against the Soviet Union and the communist threat to the United States, but his almost visceral opposition to whatever the Soviets did seemed to moderate when he became the president. However, the hopes for improving U.S.-Soviet relations in the détente period were seriously jolted in October 1973 when the Soviets suddenly threatened to intervene militarily in the ongoing October War in the Middle East.

In that war, Israeli forces violated a U.S.-Soviet–sponsored UN cease-fire by surrounding the Egyptian Third Army in the Sinai desert, thereby cutting the army off from food, water, and medical supplies. To deal with this genuine emergency, the Soviets proposed a joint U.S.-Soviet military rescue of the Egyptian forces. When President Nixon rejected that idea, the Soviets declared they would intervene unilaterally to save the Egyptians and began loading troopships in the Black Sea for the short cruise to Egypt. Nixon told the Soviets to stop their actions and then ordered *all U.S. military forces around the world to be put on heightened alert status.*

By taking the provocative step of ordering a global military alert instead of a regional military reaction, Nixon risked a wider confrontation with the Soviets, thereby going further than other presidents may have gone in similar circumstances. In a decision apparently made with only one other adviser— Henry Kissinger—involved, the U.S. global response may have been a knee-jerk reaction based on Nixon's long-standing opposition to Soviet military expansionism and distrust of Soviet leaders.[12] Luckily, the Soviets backed down and the Israelis allowed supplies to be brought to the Egyptian forces, thereby defusing the crisis. Yet the point remains: With only a few voices being heard, crisis decision making tends to be quite different than the noncrisis decision making, as illustrated in Box 5.1.

Presidents are virtually guaranteed to be involved in crisis decision making. However, the opposite of crises are those occasions for decision when presidents may not be involved at all. Various reasons can explain such presidential decisions to step out of the decision-making process. Sometimes, presidents feel that their presence in the group may stifle a robust discussion of all alternative options or any change from their previously announced public schedule would have negative consequences in the situation. A good example of these concerns came in the 1962 Cuban Missile Crisis. The missiles the Soviets were deploying in Cuba would have threatened an arc of the United States—stretching roughly from Washington, DC, to Houston, Texas—meaning a possible nuclear attack with only a few minutes warning.

After feeling misled by the "experts" in the 1961 Bay of Pigs debacle, President Kennedy sought to ensure the consideration of a wide array of views. He did so by creating a group of advisers dubbed the Executive Committee of the National Security Council—or "ExComm" for short—which would meet without him present to determine the appropriate response. The ExComm included members from the State, Defense, and Treasury Departments and the director of central intelligence. It also included members personally close to the president: his brother—the attorney general, the national security adviser, and a presidential counsel. The president was kept abreast of the group's deliberations while he maintained his normal schedule of activities so the Soviets would not realize his administration had discovered the missile threat. After nearly two weeks of tense deliberations, the group recommended the blockade of Cuba, which was the course of action the president apparently preferred but did not want to order without the input of the others.[13]

Sometimes, presidents have other reasons to want to be out of the decision-making loop. In some cases, deniability may be desired. For example, in the late 1980s, President Reagan felt the leftist Sandinista leadership in Nicaragua represented a communist threat to the United States. What if Soviet aircraft were based in Nicaragua? Would they be within range of Texas and Louisiana oil fields? Correspondingly, Reagan provided U.S. military assistance to the Nicaraguan counterrevolutionaries—the contras—who were fighting the Sandinista regime. When Congress passed the Boland amendments making such military aid illegal, a National Security Council staff aide—U.S. Marine Colonel Oliver North—came up with a plan to sell arms secretly to Iran and divert the proceeds to the Nicaraguan contras. His boss, National Security Adviser Admiral John Poindexter, approved the plan, and it was put into action with the help or at least knowledge of the CIA. When this illegal operation became public knowledge, Admiral Poindexter resigned, Colonel North was fired, both were indicted and convicted of federal crimes, and their convictions were later overturned on appeal.[14] More to the point, President Reagan was able to claim no direct knowledge of the matter.[15]

Other times, presidents want to be out of the loop because they want to preserve their time for other policy matters that are simply more important to them. President Bill Clinton entered office with a distinctly domestic policy emphasis and a foreign policy agenda largely limited to promoting free trade. Perhaps due to this greater domestic focus, the more benign image of the new Russian regime under Boris Yeltsin, the relatively reduced global role of the Russian Federation weakened by the breakup of the Soviet Union, and other such factors, Clinton quickly delegated most issues involving U.S.-Russian relations to Vice President Al Gore. In 1993, this delegation was formalized in the creation of the U.S.-Russian Joint Commission on Economic and Technological Cooperation, cochaired by Vice President Gore and Russian prime minister Viktor Chernomyrdin (hence, the Gore–Chernomyrdin Commission).

The commission's initial goals were to coordinate U.S.-Russian cooperation regarding space and energy issues. Its roles soon expanded into a wide array of economic cooperation initiatives, the conversion of defense infrastructure to civilian use, and cooperation in scientific, health, and environmental areas. Thus, key foreign policy decisions affecting U.S. policy toward Russia were being made by Gore and the other U.S. representatives on the commission: the secretaries of agriculture, commerce, defense, energy, and health and human services; the administrators of the Environmental Protection Agency and National Aeronautics and Space Administration; and the director of the President's Office of Science and Technology Policy. These officials were aided by officials from the National Security Council staff, the vice president's national security adviser, and State Department experts on Russia and the other former Soviet republics.[16] Led by Gore, this group of administration officials made most U.S. policy toward Russia, with the president's role confined largely to announcing the policy decisions and representing the United States at U.S.-Russian summit conferences.

Conclusion

To repeat, the image of the president as the sole maker of U.S. foreign policy is largely misplaced. Presidents occasionally make foreign policy decisions by themselves, and they certainly represent the face of the United States to external audiences. However, the foreign policy decisions deemed by presidents to be most significant are almost always the product of small group decision making, in which the president works with a handful of people who are experts on the subjects at hand or whose judgment and advice are trusted by the president. For the many more foreign policy decisions that are more routine in nature or do not rise to the level of importance to compel interest from the White House, the most important decision makers are often bureaucratic officials, and it is to them we turn in Chapter 6.

Glossary Terms

Crisis   a foreign policy situation that represents a threat to core values or high priority goals, requires a quick response, and comes as a surprise to decision makers.

Cybernetic decision making   mindlessly trying available options until an option produces a satisficing response or all available options have failed.

Decision heuristics   rules of thumb to make decision making easier and faster.

Groupthink   the phenomenon that occurs in a concurrence-seeking group when the desire by members to get along outweighs their willingness to challenge the dominant viewpoints of the group, resulting in assumptions not being examined, doubts not being expressed, and poor decisions often being made.

Incrementalism   making only minor changes from current policy or from what has been done before in similar circumstances.

Multiple advocacy   an approach to decision making in which an official (e.g., the national security adviser) is responsible for ensuring that all major options and considerations are examined and fairly presented to the president prior to a decision being made. The aim is to have vigorous advocates presenting their cases to the president to ensure that all relevant facts are considered before making a decision.

Operational code   a relatively fixed blueprint or set of beliefs decision makers use to specify what is important, what motivates others, and what tends to work best in solving foreign policy problems.

Poliheuristic decision making   a two-step decision-making process in which as many options as possible are quickly eliminated in the first step, and then in the second step whatever time is needed is devoted to carefully evaluating the few remaining options with the goal of maximizing benefits and minimizing risks.

Prospect theory   the idea that when things are going well, decision makers tend to act prudently and become more risk-averse, so as not to upset a status quo that is favorable. When things are not going well, decision makers become prone to risky strategies as they seek to change that unacceptable status quo.

Rational actor model (RAM)   a decision-making process that attempts to identify all possible options available, considers systematically each option's strengths and weaknesses, and then selects the optimal option. The optimal option is the one which promises the best overall result, the best result in light of the incurred costs, or the result which is least bad if all options are bad.

Endnotes

1. For more on the groupthink phenomenon and the Bay of Pigs example, see Irving L. Janis, *Groupthink: Psychological Studies of Policy Decisions and Fiascos* (2nd ed.) (Boston: Houghton Mifflin, 1983).

2. For more on the multiple advocacy approach, see Alexander L. George, "The Case for Multiple Advocacy in Making Foreign Policy," *American Political Science Review* 66 (1972), 751–785; or *Presidential Decisionmaking in Foreign Policy: The Effective Use of Information and Advice* (Boulder, CO: Westview Press, 1980).

3. This phrase is attributable to former U.S. House Speaker Jim Wright (D-TX) who uses it often in conversation.

4. The concept of an operational code was initially developed by Nathan Leites in *The Operational Code of the Politiburo* (New York: McGraw-Hill, 1951) and reinvigorated by Alexander L. George in "The 'Operational Code:' A Neglected Approach to the Study of Political Leaders and Decision-Making," *International Studies Quarterly* 13 (1969), 190–222. For a more contemporary treatment of this approach, see Mark Schafer and Stephen G. Walker (eds.), *Beliefs and Leadership in World Politics: Methods and Applications of Operational Code Analysis* (New York: Palgrave Macmillan, 2006).

5. For more on this decision-making style, see Bob Woodward, *State of Denial: Bush at War Part III* (New York: Simon and Schuster, 2006); or Ron Suskind, *The One Percent Doctrine: Deep Inside America's Pursuit of Its Enemies Since 9/11* (New York: Simon and Schuster, 2006).

6. For more on such decision-making heuristics, see Herbert A. Simon, "Theories of Decision-Making in Economics and Behavioral Science," *American Economic Review* 49 (1959), 253–283; or Daniel Kahneman, Amos Tversky, and Paul Slovic (eds.), *Judgment under Uncertainty: Heuristics & Biases* (Cambridge, UK: Cambridge University Press, 1982).

7. See Charles E. Lindblom, "The Science of 'Muddling Through,' " *Public Administration Review* 19 (1959), 79–88.

8. Simon, "Theories of Decision-Making."

9. Alex Mintz, "How Do Leaders Make Decisions? A Poliheuristic Perspective," *Journal of Conflict Resolution* 48 (2004), 3–13.

10. See Graham T. Allison and Philip Zelikow, *Essence of Decision: Explaining the Cuban Missile Crisis* (New York: Longman Publishers, 1999).

11. Charles F. Hermann, "Some Issues in the Study of International Crisis," in Charles F. Hermann (ed.), *International Crises: Insights from Behavioral Research* (New York: Free Press, 1972).

12. For more on this crisis from the inside, see Henry Kissinger, *The Anatomy of Two Major Foreign Policy Crises: Based on the Record of Henry Kissinger's Hitherto Secret Telephone Conversations* (New York: Simon and Schuster, 2003).

13. For more on this, see Allison and Zelikow, *Essence of Decision.*

14. They had been granted immunity and forced to testify before Congress about the Iran-Contra Affair. The court ruled that their convictions would not have occurred without the information revealed in their testimony before Congress.

15. For more, see Bob Woodward, *Veil: The Secret Wars of the CIA, 1981–1987* (New York: Simon and Schuster, 1987).

16. "The Gore-Chernomyrdin Commission," Federation of American Scientists, available online at http://www.fas.org/news/russia/2000/russia/part05.htm.

CHAPTER 6

Bureaucratic Politics and Policy Making

Former Secretary of State Hillary Clinton and former Secretary of Defense Robert Gates were among the most influential officials to hold those posts in recent years; their influence was based in part on their personalities and on the bureaucratic organizations they led.
Source: Chris Usher/CBS/Landov

Introduction

For many issues, foreign policy making involves doing today what has been done before in similar circumstances. Policy making by inertia, as this has been called, is fairly commonplace and tends to feature the bureaucratic organizations identified in Chapter 4.[1] A focus on the bureaucracy raises intriguing questions about these actors as foreign policy makers. Thus, we will examine what motivates them, the phases of the policy-making process where their impact is most felt, the types of issues that lend themselves to bureaucratic policy making, the processes by which bureaucratic actors make their foreign policy decisions, and the advantages and disadvantages bureaucrats bring to the policy-making arena. We turn to their motivations first.

Bureaucratic Motivations

Nearly half of the 2.11 million civilian employees of the U.S. government work in the foreign policy/homeland security/national security arena, and the uniformed military adds nearly 1.5 million more.[2] An array of professional motivations exists for these individuals.

One way of understanding the motivations of bureaucratic actors comes from the idea of a **principal–agent model**. In this view, bureaucratic personnel are the agents who are assigned tasks by their principals—the president and members of Congress.[3] By being responsive to elected officials, these bureaucratic actors are responding indirectly to the needs of the broader voting public.

Two potential difficulties arise from the principal–agent perspective. First, these bureaucratic agents typically know far more about their professional subject matter than do either the principals to whom they report or the people who elected those officials. Obviously, this knowledge gap can cause tensions at times, particularly when what's popular with the public or elected officials does not coincide with what bureaucratic experts think is good for the country or for their agency or department. This happens more often than one might think. What is the bureaucratic official to do in such circumstances? Second, elected officials come and go (particularly in the White House), but the vast bulk of the federal bureaucrats stay for a very long time—oftentimes, for their entire careers. In such situations, bureaucrats may be motivated by more parochial goals that make sense to them, such as:

- equating what is in their bureaucratic organization's interest with what is in the national interest,
- putting their narrow, organizational success and survival ahead of broader national interests, or
- putting their personal career goals ahead of national interests.

Literally, what a president may think is best for the country may not be what the organization most directly affected thinks is best for the country—or for it.[4] As one can imagine, policy-making problems quickly arise when national and organizational goals come into conflict. We'll illustrate this later when we talk about the 1962 Cuban Missile Crisis.

Bureaucratic motivations become important whenever bureaucratic actors play significant roles in making U.S. foreign policy; such participation may be found in various phases of the foreign policy–making process. We turn to those phases next.

Policy-Making Phases

Elected foreign policy makers such as the president and members of Congress are heavily reliant on bureaucratic actors. The first phase of the policy-making process involves information collection, analysis, and the identification of policy-making options. With the exception of what they already know or glean from the news media, elected officials typically depend heavily on bureaucratic actors for such information and analysis. For example, presidents rarely make final decisions on diplomatic issues without consulting with relevant State Department personnel first. Members of Congress routinely consult with Defense Department officials and top military officers before making national security policy changes. Such bureaucratic actors have the specific expertise these elected policy makers need to make good decisions, so they are important in the policy-making phases that precede decision making.

Bureaucratic actors often help shape U.S. foreign and national security policy decisions in more direct ways during this input phase of the policy-making process. When they tell elected leaders what is possible in a situation, they may at times structure the options, so their preferred option seems to be the only prudent choice.

For example, in 1949, the Soviet Union detonated its first atomic bomb and the Chinese Communist Party took control of mainland China. Thus, the inputs from the international context seemed sharply more negative than they had been just a few months earlier. Paul Nitze, who led the State Department's Policy Planning Staff at the time, was convinced that the United States was not spending enough on defense to contain the threat posed by what he saw as a global communist menace. So, he convinced the National Security Council (NSC) to authorize a broader examination of U.S. strategic policy. That NSC study was largely written by Nitze's staff, *because they volunteered to do the work.*[5] The resulting document, **NSC-68**, outlined the communist threat and identified four options: doing nothing, engaging the Soviets with diplomatic approaches, launching a preemptive war against the Soviets, or undertaking a massive rearmament campaign to build up U.S. military capabilities. The document recommended massive rearmament as the optimal choice.

Following the invasion of South Korea by North Korean Communist forces in 1950, options such as doing nothing and engaging the Soviets diplomatically seemed to fall far short of what was then needed. President Truman and other top officials embraced massive rearmament as the only prudent option, and U.S. defense spending virtually tripled.[6] Nitze got the decision he wanted, at least in part because of the way the options were structured.

Sometimes, bureaucratic actors dominate the decision-making phase of the policy process. State Department travel warnings are one example of bureaucratic actors making decisions that directly affect U.S. relations with other countries. In January 2014, 37 countries were included on the State Department's "Current Travel Warnings" list. While the potential impact of fewer Americans traveling to Somalia, Iran, or Madagascar might be negligible, travel warnings to other destinations can have more far-reaching consequences. Haiti's presence on the list affected its economic recovery following the 2010 earthquake by slowing the flow of the few tourist dollars that normally come into the Haitian economy through the stops made by cruise ships. Even more impacted was Mexico. Not only did putting Mexico on the warning list insult Mexican officials, but doing so risked very harmful impacts on the Mexican tourist industry—a major source of revenue for Mexico.[7]

A more controversial example of bureaucratic decision making came in the mid-1980s. While Iran and Iraq fought a war, Iran secretly sought to purchase arms from the United States. Despite the presence of economic sanctions against Iran, President Ronald Reagan was persuaded by the then National Security Adviser Robert McFarlane to proceed with the arms sale to Iran secretly, because such a sale might improve U.S. relations with both Iran and Lebanon and might contribute to the release of seven Americans being held in Lebanon. Once the "arms-for-hostages" deal became known, the public outcry led to an internal investigation during which Attorney General Edwin Meese discovered that $18 million of the $30 million Iran paid for the weapons was missing. As we noted previously, NSC staff member Marine Lieutenant Colonel Oliver North had diverted the missing money to supply the contras, the counterrevolutionaries who were fighting the leftist Sandinista regime in Nicaragua. North had done so with the approval of newly appointed National Security Adviser Admiral John Poindexter but apparently without the knowledge of the president or higher elected officials. The resulting Iran–Contra scandal damaged the credibility of the Reagan presidency and tainted the image of the United States in Latin America, but it was the product of decisions by bureaucratic actors who thought they were acting in line with the president's interpretation of the U.S. national interest.[8]

Far more often, bureaucratic actors are heavily involved in the last phase of the policy-making process: implementation of the decision. Following the September 11 attacks, much of the world was sympathetic to the United States and supported the U.S. military effort to go after al Qaeda units in Afghanistan and the Taliban forces protecting them. However, that global support eroded quickly when military and intelligence personnel went too far in interrogating detainees captured on the battlefields of Afghanistan and later Iraq. Leaked photographs revealing the torture and humiliation of detainees at Iraq's Abu Ghraib prison scandalized the international community, the United States lost the moral high ground, and many Muslims around the world began interpreting U.S. policy as a war on Islam.

In another example, U.S.-Chinese relations were severely damaged in 1999 when the Chinese embassy in Belgrade was bombed as part of NATO's bombing campaign against Yugoslavia in the war over Kosovo. The Clinton administration maintained that the bombing of the embassy compound, in which several Chinese government personnel were killed and others were wounded, was a tragic mistake based on the use of an out-of-date map by the mission's planners. The official explanation was that the embassy compound had previously been a headquarters and communications facility for the Yugoslavian army (and thus, a legitimate military target) and that the CIA-supplied map had not been updated to show that the Chinese had purchased the site for their embassy.

However, a subsequent investigation by the British news media reported that the CIA knew at the time it was the Chinese embassy and that the building was targeted intentionally, because the Chinese were electronically tracking U.S. and NATO cruise missile attacks and allowing the Yugoslavian army to use the embassy's radio transmitter to communicate with Yugoslavian army and air defense units in the field.[9] Two interpretations of this event thus seem possible. First, the bombing mission may have been an implementation mistake, which was the product of human or organizational error. Second, the CIA and military planners were acting to protect U.S. and NATO aircraft and crews and did so either on their own without the knowledge of President Clinton or in such a way that Clinton could later claim that the bombing was an accident. Whichever interpretation is chosen, the result of this implemented action was the deaths of several Chinese government employees, days of anti-U.S. rioting in China, and considerable harm to U.S.-Chinese relations.

If implementation of governmental decisions can be problematic when the implementers are government employees, what happens when they are not? Increasingly and for a variety of reasons, governmental bureaucracies turn to private contractors to handle certain aspects of U.S. foreign policy. These choices to "outsource" policy implementation carry risks as well, as illustrated in Box 6.1.

Just as some phases of the policy-making process are more open to significant bureaucratic input and roles (notably the input and implementation phases), some types of issues also lend themselves to bureaucratic input. We turn to a discussion of these issue types next.

Issues and Organizational Roles

Certain types of issues lend themselves to increased bureaucratic involvement while others do not. Bureaucracies typically handle routine or recurring issues reasonably well, usually creating **standard operating procedures (SOPs)** for that purpose. SOPs are a pattern of steps learned (and maybe even perfected) over time that allow the organization to produce a coordinated response to a situation, thereby freeing the individuals in the organization from having to come up

BOX 6.1

Bureaucratic Outsourcing: Private Contractors and U.S. Foreign Policy

The use of private contractors to perform functions otherwise handled by governmental employees is nothing new. For example, in the 1970s, the CIA reportedly contracted with French and South African mercenaries to fight pro-Soviet rebel groups in the Angolan civil war. In this case, the CIA needed to be able to disavow any connection to these forces should they be captured. Beyond the benefits of such official separation, government agencies often hire private contractors as a way to cut their costs. Since contractors are paid by the project, the government is not required to keep those employees on the payroll on a permanent basis; when the contract ends, so does the government's payments. The result is money saved.

Contractors fill many needed roles. For example, no one is surprised when the Defense Department goes outside the uniformed services to hire cooks, housekeeping staff, laundry personnel, maintenance workers, and so on for operations in places such as Iraq or Afghanistan. Such hiring practices mean permanent government employees are freer to do the jobs they were primarily trained to perform. However, as government budgets tighten and government personnel get stretched too thin, other hires can be more problematic.

The "poster child" for bad behavior by a private security contractor is Academi (formerly known as Xe Services and before that known as Blackwater USA). As early as 2004, the CIA hired Blackwater USA to find and assassinate al Qaeda operatives in Afghanistan. Then, Blackwater personnel were hired to provide security to U.S. diplomatic personnel in Iraq. In 2007, Blackwater personnel providing security for U.S. diplomats in Baghdad mistakenly killed 17 Iraqi civilians. Five lower-level Blackwater employees were indicted on manslaughter charges for the killings, but the charges were later dropped. In late 2008, two former Blackwater employees filed a lawsuit charging Blackwater with systematically defrauding the U.S. government by overbilling—as well as by charging the government to pay for the services of strippers and prostitutes. Following the filing of that lawsuit, government inspectors said the State Department overpaid Blackwater for security services in Iraq by $55 million. In 2009, news reports claimed that Blackwater was working with the Defense Department's Joint Special Operations Command in Pakistan to identify and target senior leaders of al Qaeda and Taliban for assassination. However, it is not clear whether senior Obama administration officials were aware of the operation. Following a raid on its corporate headquarters, in 2010 five former top Blackwater executives (including the former president of Blackwater Worldwide) were indicted on federal weapons charges and making false statements to investigators.

Yet, Blackwater/Xe Services/Academi is not the only private contractor to cause problems for its governmental employer. One incident occurred at the U.S. Embassy in Kabul, Afghanistan, among members of the Armor Group (a subsidiary of Wackenhut, which in turn is owned by the British firm G4S) who participated in lewd and drunken hazing rituals. In 2009, it was reported that the Defense Department contracted with an Afghan firm, Watan Risk Management, to provide security to truck convoys carrying supplies to U.S. troops in Kandahar, Afghanistan. Watan is owned by the Popal brothers, who are cousins to Afghanistan President Hamid Karzai. One of the brothers, Ahmad Rateb Popal, is a former mujahedin member, a translator for the former Taliban regime, and an indicted heroin smuggler. According to a senior Afghan government official, at least 10% of the funds the U.S. military pays for logistical support goes directly to the Afghan insurgents U.S. forces are fighting. More recently, a Defense Department official was reported to have created his own network of multiple private contractors to identify, locate, and assassinate militants in both Afghanistan and Pakistan. According to Defense Department representatives, that operation was shut down and the official is under investigation for possible criminal wrongdoing.

Obviously, the Defense Department is aware of these problems. According to its Inspector General's report, the lessons not learned from the use of private contractors on contingency operations in Iraq could imperil DoD operations in Afghanistan. These problems include poor contract job descriptions, lack of accountability by contractors, lack of oversight of contractors, overpricing and fraud in billing, other financial mismanagement, contractors performing functions that are inherently governmental, and even terrorism-related acts by contract personnel. To some extent, the question thus becomes, Who is actually conducting U.S. foreign policy? Who should be doing so? Would the implementation of U.S. foreign policy be improved if government employees resumed many of these roles, or would the financial costs seem too high in an environment where cutting government spending is in vogue?

Sources: Mark Mazzetti, "2 Ex-Workers Accuse Blackwater Security Company of Defrauding the U.S. for Years." *New York Times*, February 11, 2010, p. A22; Office of Inspector General, "Contingency Contracting: A Framework for Reform" (U.S. Department of Defense, Report No. D-2010-059, May 14, 2010); James Risen and Mark Mazzetti, "Federal Prosecutors Indict 5 Ex-Officials of Blackwater." *New York Times*, April 17, 2010, p. 8. Aram Roston, "How the US Funds the Taliban," *The Nation*, November 11, 2009, available online at: http://www.thenation.com/article/how-us-funds-taliban. Jeremy Scahill, "Blackwater: CIA Assassins?" *The Nation*, August 31, 2009, available online at: http://www.thenation.com/article/blackwater-cia-assassins. Jeremy Scahill, "BP and US Government 'Command Center' Guarded by Company from Afghan Embassy Hazing Scandal," *The Nation*, May 28, 2010, available online at: http://www.thenation.com/blog/bp-and-us-government-command-center-guarded-company-afghan-embassy-hazing-scandal. Jeremy Scahill, "DoD Investigating Nine Cases of 'Terrorist-Related Acts' by US Military and Contractors," *The Nation*, May 27, 2010, available online at: http://www.thenation.com/blog/dod-investigating-nine-cases-terrorism-related-acts-us-military-and-contractors. Jeremy Scahill, "The Secret US War in Pakistan," *The Nation*, December 7, 2009, available online at: http://www.thenation.com/article/secret-us-war-pakistan. Tim Shorrock, *Spies for Hire: The Secret World of Intelligence Outsourcing* (New York, NY: Simon and Schuster, 2008).

with new responses each time a similar occasion for decision or action arises. In other words, the wheel does not have to be continually reinvented. For example, when the U.S. Agency for International Development (USAID) funds a public health program involving prescription drugs abroad, it can rely on SOPs that have been developed for drug management in laboratories and for different types of diseases and recipients.[10] SOPs exist for other recurring behaviors, such as how to administer the transfer of military weaponry to allied states or how to handle routine diplomatic negotiations.

On the other hand, issues that are nonroutine or that require creative solutions each time they arise do not lend themselves to bureaucratic SOPs. Given that bureaucratic organizations exist primarily to handle repeated tasks well, it is hard to order bureaucrats to be innovative. When faced with such challenges, bureaucratic actors may have to create ad hoc task forces to deal with them or send them up the chain of command for resolution by higher officials.

The latter is certainly the case with crisis situations. In crises, bureaucracies may be highly involved in gathering relevant information or identifying options for decision makers, and they are often involved in implementing those decisions. However, they rarely play a significant role in the actual decision-making process in a true crisis (i.e., a surprise situation that threatens core values and demands a response). As noted in Chapter 5, crisis decision making heavily favors the president and a small number of other executive branch actors. But when they do get heavily involved in making policy, how do bureaucratic actors typically perform? Let's address that next.

Bureaucratic Policy Making

When bureaucracies engage in the decision phase of policy making, they may have neither the time nor more likely the inclination to follow the idealized decision-making steps of the rational actor model—identifying all possible options, evaluating them, and choosing the optimal one. Just as important, bureaucratic officials operate in a specific organizational context that conditions both how they approach policy making and the policies that they choose. The operative phrase usually is, "Where you stand on an issue depends upon where you sit." In other words, bureaucratic officials tend to view occasions for decision based on the face of the issue they see, and the face of the issue seen is a function of how that issue typically affects their bureaucratic organization. Depending on that face of the issue seen, the officials will take whatever stands they feel appropriate. Then, the question of who prevails in the decision-making game may not be who has the best response to the situation but may depend upon who has more influence, has more formal or informal power, has the ear of more powerful officials, is stubborn longer, and so on.

A variety of examples of bureaucratic organizations in action can be found in the 1962 Cuban Missile Crisis.[11] In September 1962, there were reports coming into the CIA that the Soviet Union *might* be placing missiles in Cuba. On September 19, Intelligence Community officials (represented at that time by the U.S. Intelligence Board) made the determination that enough indicators were present to justify a reconnaissance overflight, specifically to look for evidence of missiles in Cuba.

From that point, it took 14 days to get authorization from another bureaucratic entity—the Committee on Overhead Reconnaissance—to send a high-flying U-2 spy plane over Cuba to take the pictures. This delay was the result of several factors. First, the State Department was worried about the diplomatic costs if a U-2 aircraft was shot down over Cuban airspace. Not only had a U-2 been shot down over the Soviet Union in 1960, but on September 9 one being operated by the Taiwanese regime had been shot down over the People's Republic of China, so the risks of losing a very expensive aircraft and its pilot were quite real. Moreover, each prior incident had resulted in considerable negative diplomatic fallout.

Second, there was the obvious question of where exactly in Cuba to look. Cuba is an island, but that doesn't mean it is small. CIA officials had to sift through all the available bits of information to determine the most likely locations for such missiles, and they also had to guess where they would put missiles if they were the Soviets. That took time too.

Third, how to conduct the flight was another decision. Flying directly over the areas in question might result in the best pictures but also might put the pilot at the greatest risk of being shot down. Instead, it was decided to fly along the periphery of the areas in question so the pilot would be in a position to evade any surface-to-air missiles that might be launched against him by leaving Cuban airspace as quickly as possible.

Once the authorization was made, another 10 days were consumed in determining who would conduct the flight. Both the CIA and the Air Force operated U-2 aircraft. Both wanted the mission, and each thought they were better suited than the other to conduct it. The Defense Department pressed the case for the Air Force, noting that if the plane was shot down, it would be better if the pilot was in a military uniform. The penalty for a uniformed military officer might be prisoner-of-war status, whereas a civilian-attired pilot might be considered a spy and be executed. The CIA countered with the argument that this was an intelligence mission and that was its primary jurisdiction. The CIA claimed more experience and possibly better equipment for such a mission, whereas the Air Force claimed that its pilots were unsurpassed. Ultimately, a compromise was reached after 10 days. The Air Force provided the pilot and the CIA provided the aircraft.

Once the presence of the missiles in Cuba had been confirmed by U-2 photographs, how to respond to them depended on who was asked at the meeting. Not surprisingly, in the decision-making phase of the process, the State Department pressed for a diplomatic response. Whether it was a diplomatic appeal to the Soviets, the new Castro regime in Cuba, or the United Nations, this option would give State the mission, and all bureaucratic organizations want appropriate missions to justify their continued existence, budgets, and importance. Further, the State Department argued that, should diplomacy fail, more forceful options could still be used later.

Defense Department representatives responded that, in the time needed for a diplomatic approach to be tried, the missiles might become operational. If they became operational, the entire southeastern United States would be at risk of a nuclear attack with only a couple of minutes of warning. Led by the Air Force, Defense Department representatives argued instead for an air strike to take out the missiles. After all, removing the threat was the real goal. Bombing could do that.

However, others at the meeting raised objections to air strikes. First, could air strikes guarantee success? In an air strike, all the missiles had to be destroyed. If just one missile with a nuclear warhead survived the attack, it might be launched against the United States. When pressed, Air Force representatives acknowledged that an air strike had only a 90% chance of getting all the missiles. Their 90% figure was based on their estimates, given that Intelligence Community reports said the missiles were mobile. If they were mobile, they might have moved in the interval between the last overflight photo and the actual bombing mission. With antiaircraft batteries and surface-to-air missiles firing at them, the bomber pilots might not be able to linger in the area looking for missing missiles to bomb. Only later did Air Force representatives learn that the missiles were mobile in the same way as a small house was mobile; they could be moved, but it was a slow and difficult process.

When asked what an air strike might involve, Air Force officials said it might take 500 bombing sorties against Cuba to get the missiles. What political officials had assumed would be a "surgical" strike with limited damage now looked like "saturation" bombing instead. Might such air strikes run the risk of starting World War III? A heavy bombing attack would surely kill Soviet and Cuban military personnel and possibly any Cuban civilians living near the bombing area. How might the Soviets or Cubans respond? Would the Soviets attack U.S. missile installations near the Soviet border in Turkey? Would they retaliate against West Berlin, a noncommunist enclave deep inside communist East Germany? Where and how would the Soviets respond to such an attack?

Shared values also came into play. After being the victims of a Japanese surprise attack on the U.S. naval fleet at Pearl Harbor in 1941, did U.S. officials want to do that to someone else? Was the moral high ground being abandoned with such an approach? At least the president's brother, Attorney General Robert Kennedy, thought so.

Based on a variety of factors, a mid-range approach was chosen. Rather than the diplomatic option that seemed too timid or the air strike option that might start a world war, decision makers chose to impose a naval blockade against Cuba. That option would convey a strong message (after all, a military blockade was traditionally considered an act of war), but it would not necessarily initiate a shooting conflict. The next decision would then be back in the hands of Soviet leaders. While a naval blockade did nothing to remove the threat of missiles already in Cuba, it would stop additional Soviet cargo ships from delivering more military supplies to Cuba, and it would buy time for the Soviets to reconsider their decision to base offensive missiles in Cuba.

A bureaucratic factor that helped this option was that a naval blockade against Cuba was well within U.S. organizational capabilities. The United States had a large navy, whereas the Soviet Union did not. Moreover, the operation would occur practically in the U.S. backyard; the U.S. East and Gulf Coasts had multiple naval and air bases nearby from which a blockade could be launched, and Soviet personnel in Cuba were far from home.

Once the blockade option was announced, bureaucratic actors were called upon to implement it. As per its SOPs, the Navy positioned its ships 500 miles off the Cuban coast. That distance was not by chance. At 500 miles from Cuba, the ships were considered safe from attack by Cuban aircraft, which did not have the combat range to attack the ships and return to land without running out of fuel and ditching in the ocean.

When the president decided to give his Soviet counterparts more time to decide whether to try to run the blockade with their cargo ships, the secretary of defense ordered the Navy to pull the blockade line back closer to Cuba. When the crisis was over, officials learned that naval commanders had ignored that order, because it put their ships and crews in danger. Here was a case of insubordination, where military officers were sure that they knew better how to run this operation than did the commander in chief. The Navy also took another action that was in its bureaucratic interest. It used this opportunity to show off the antisubmarine warfare capabilities for which it had been requesting additional funding. Without authorization from higher officials, the Navy engaged Soviet submarines and forced some to surface, thereby risking a more deadly confrontation and possibly the start of World War III.

The Cuban Missile Crisis thus shows the many ways in which bureaucratic actors become important in all phases of the foreign policy–making process. Policy makers typically rely on bureaucratic organizations for what they know or bureaucratic expertise for what it means. They often ask bureaucratic actors for advice in determining options to consider and sometimes to get involved in the decision-making phase, and then they almost always have to rely on bureaucratic actors to implement the decisions made. So, bureaucratic actors can be important players in making U.S. foreign policy. Is that a good or a bad thing?

Bureaucratic Advantages and Disadvantages

Bureaucratic involvement in foreign policy making and implementation carries with it both advantages and disadvantages. Advantages include expertise, competence, and consistency over time.

Expertise is a fairly obvious advantage. Bureaucracies developed in the first place to have the same people handle a similar set of issues repetitively, thereby using SOPs to make governmental responses to similar issues a matter of routine. In this way, different officials did not have to waste their time constantly reinventing the wheel. By being immersed daily in a restricted range of issues, bureaucratic actors come to know those issues well, expertise is developed, and more rational policy making should be the result.[12] Thus, for example, if presidents want to evaluate the nuclear programs of states such as Iran or North Korea, there are multiple sources of expertise to tap within the administration. Experts on various aspects of nuclear weapons—including their research and development, production, testing, and maintenance—can be found within the various members of the Intelligence Community, the National Security Staff, and the Departments of Defense (Air Force; Navy; Joint Chiefs of Staff; International Security Affairs; Science and Technology), Energy (the National Nuclear Security Administration), State (Bureau of International Security and

Nonproliferation; Bureau of Verification, Compliance, and Implementation; Bureau of Intelligence and Research), and Commerce (the National Technical Information Service). For virtually any foreign policy issue, there are bureaucratic officials with expertise in that subject matter.

The other side of expertise is competence. By building their expertise, bureaucratic officials come to know what works and what does not. By doing something repeatedly, officials can get better at the task—whether that involves tracking international financing for suspected terrorist organizations, analyzing how other regime leaders tend to act, conducting military operations, or distributing foreign aid in developing countries. Take diplomatic negotiations for example. Diplomats who are calm, patient, and unrelenting in their efforts to get what they desire may often simply wear down their counterparts who may lack such patience or need to move on to other issues. According to a story told about Warren Christopher, the secretary of state for Bill Clinton, he was highly respected by other foreign service officers at the State Department because of something that had happened early in his career. Apparently, Christopher was an accomplished negotiator who at one point wore down a counterpart in a negotiating session by sitting at the table—without getting up for any reason—for hours and hours, thereby refusing to stop negotiating until he got what he desired.

Consistency over time is another advantage provided by bureaucracies. Humans like order, and other regimes appreciate knowing what to expect from the United States in certain circumstances. By relying on competent experts for policy guidance, policy making, or policy implementation, administrations gain the benefit of consistency over time. While national policies may need to change occasionally, others in the international system respect or appreciate those changes if they result from changed circumstances and not just the personal whims of policy makers. Thus, the vast majority of foreign policy actions by an administration for any particular issue tend to be constant, and at least in part, that is a result of bureaucratic participation.

Nonetheless, bureaucracies come with some clear disadvantages as well. As noted earlier, there is a tendency for bureaucratic officials to see issues from the perspective of their specific organization (**parochialism**) and their personal role in it (**careerism**). Thus, what is good for the organization or the officials personally may come to be more important than what is good for the United States. An example of parochialism comes from the experience of the Air Force and Army. For years, the culture of the Air Force stressed the importance of strategic bombardment, the idea of carrying the fight to the heartland of the enemy.[13] Thus, the Army was never able to get the Air Force to devote sufficient resources (at least from the Army's perspective) to the low altitude, close-air support mission that troops on the ground required, because that mission was not in line with Air Force culture. Finally, the Army chose to develop its own close-air support capability, and it now possesses a large air support capability with hundreds of attack helicopters as well as other aircraft for its use. A careerist example occurs when those viewing a 25–30-year career in a particular department or agency say, "presidents come and go every four or eight years, but my department will always be here." Such thinking can easily color their judgment.

As suggested earlier, different parts of the bureaucracy often do not cooperate well with each other. Parochialism suggests they typically compete to get the most desirable missions, the largest budgets, the ear of the president, and so on. Such rivalries can spawn bureaucratic empire-building, with bureaucratic organizations seeking to become bigger (in personnel or budgets) at the expense of their rival organizations.

A classic instance of this was seen in the investigations that followed the September 11 terrorist attacks on the United States. In the years leading up to the attacks, various officials knew Osama bin Laden and his al Qaeda group were threats to the United States. In the months leading up to the attacks, various parts of the Intelligence Community, the Defense Department, the Immigration and Naturalization Service, and the Federal Bureau of Investigation knew the names of some al Qaeda members, that some of them were in the United States, that aircraft could potentially be used as terrorist weapons, that some Saudis were taking flying lessons in the United States but were unconcerned about learning to take off or land, and that something "big" was about to happen.[14] Yet, these individual bits of information were not shared with others in a way that these dots could be connected and the threat of using commercial aircraft as weapons against buildings could be foreseen. In a bureaucratic environment where "information is power," sharing information is *not* the norm.

Another disadvantage of bureaucracies is rigidity in both their thinking and their actions. As noted earlier in this chapter, organizations designed to do certain things repetitively and well are not structurally suited to creativity or innovation. A good example of this came at the end of the Cold War. For two generations, intelligence officers had been tasked with helping to prepare the United States to deal with its superpower rival—the Soviet Union. When one's rival has thousands of nuclear weapons and its leader publicly has said "we will bury you," it is only prudent to assume worst-case scenarios when planning. Thus, the strengths of the Soviet Union were stressed while its weaknesses, to the extent they were known, tended to be underestimated. Signs that the Soviet Union was weakening by the mid-1980s, particularly in its economic performance, were either totally missed or misinterpreted. Analysts were so focused on the smaller details of the Soviet military threat that they missed the bigger picture of a superpower in serious decline. As a result, most members of the Intelligence Community were just as surprised as anyone else when the Soviet Union abruptly fell apart in 1991.[15] In short, bureaucratic structures reflect organizational assumptions, those assumptions are not checked at the door by those who work there, and such shared assumptions or attitudes can limit creativity.

Both rigid thinking and a failure to cooperate across agencies marked the post-2003 reconstruction efforts in Iraq. These pathologies of bureaucratic behavior are described in more detail in Box 6.2.

Finally, speed is not typically a hallmark of bureaucratic organizations. The more complex the organization and more layers of administration reflected in its organizational chart, the slower it tends to operate. Most information flows from the bottom of an organization up, and important decisions or actions flow from the top down as they require high-level authorization.

Take this hypothetical example. Several relatively new foreign service officers posted at the U.S. Embassy in Paris get what they think is a great idea for improving U.S.-French relations. They write a memo and send it to their supervisor. The supervisor tweaks it a bit, approves the memo, and sends it up the embassy's food chain. At some point, the embassy's chargé d'affaires (its top foreign service officer) has to approve it, and then it goes to the ambassador. If the ambassador approves it, the memo then goes to the French desk at the State Department back in Washington, DC. If the desk officer approves it, it goes up the organizational chart at State headquarters until someone with an appropriate level of authority can formally approve it. That might be the assistant

▰▰▰▰▰ BOX 6.2 ▰▰▰▰▰

Policy Planning and Implementation: The Tale of Postwar Iraq

The 2003 U.S. invasion of Iraq easily toppled the regime of Saddam Hussein, but the postwar occupation and reconstruction of Iraq was another story. Faulty assumptions, wishful thinking, and poor policy implementation and coordination plagued the effort from the start.

By November 2001, the planning for an invasion of Iraq had begun, but little effort was invested in planning what would happen after the Hussein regime was ousted. By late 2002, numerous public and private warnings had been issued to Secretary of Defense Donald Rumsfeld, Deputy Secretary of Defense Paul Wolfowitz, Under Secretary of Defense for Policy Douglas Feith and other top Defense Department officials by concerned State Department officials, current and former senior uniformed military officers, and dozens of Mideast experts at conferences at both the National Defense University and the Army War College. Despite these many warnings, officials from the Office of the Secretary of Defense continued to believe that U.S. forces would be greeted as liberators, not occupiers; the Iraqis could and would provide for their own security; and Iraqi

oil revenues would pay for any costs of reconstruction.

Unfortunately, the critics had a better sense of what would happen when a 30-year-old police state suddenly collapsed than did senior Defense Department officials. Domestic security broke down almost immediately. Retired Army General Jay Garner, who had successfully led Operation Provide Comfort for Kurdish refugees in Iraq after the 1991 war, was brought in to administer the transition back to Iraqi self-rule. After only three months on the job, he was unexpectedly replaced by former Ambassador Paul Bremer, who immediately rejected Garner's plan to use former Iraqi military personnel for police and security services. For most of his year-plus service in Baghdad, Bremer engaged in a running bureaucratic battle with Rumsfeld. Rumsfeld insisted Bremer report to him, but Bremer insisted he had been appointed by the president and was answerable only to him.

In this environment of bureaucratic wrangling, the postwar occupation and reconstruction of Iraq began. Iraq's infrastructure needs turned out to be far greater than senior government officials realized, multiple bureaucratic actors were involved, and there was still no clarity as to who was in charge of Iraqi reconstruction. The results were predictably poor. By 2008, over $100 billion had been spent, but that only restored some of the infrastructure and social services that had been destroyed or disrupted in ousting Hussein. Overall however, little was done to improve the quality of life for most Iraqis, and these poor results made it difficult for the U.S. government to earn the trust of the Iraqi people. That lack of trust in U.S. promises then helped fuel the Iraqi resistance to the U.S. occupation.

Yet, this may not be anything new. The official governmental report on the reconstruction effort concluded that "Every President since Harry Truman has faced at least one contingency operation requiring the deployment of civilian and military resources abroad. Even so, the government as a whole has never developed a legislatively-sanctioned doctrine or framework for planning, preparing, and executing contingency operations in which diplomacy, development, and military action all figure" (Bowen 2009, 585). Not surprisingly, some effort is now being devoted to combining and coordinating such diplomatic, development, and military operations in chaotic settings. The most prominent example of this effort is the new AFRICOM military command, whose mission for Africa calls for it to put fostering local development efforts at the same priority as achieving military security.

So, was the poor U.S. effort to help rebuild Iraq the result of a series of human errors by well-meaning officials who were out of touch with the realities of Iraq or an organizational failure that could have been avoided? Who should take the blame for this policy debacle: various bureaucratic organizations starting with the Department of Defense, key individuals such as Bremer or Rumsfeld, or their ultimate boss President George W. Bush?

Sources: Stuart W. Bowen, Jr., *Hard Lessons: The Iraqi Reconstruction Experience* (Washington, DC: U.S. Government Printing Office, February 2, 2009); James Glanz and T. Christian Miller, "Official History Spotlights Iraq Rebuilding Blunders." *New York Times,* December 14, 2008, p. 1; Thomas E. Ricks, *Fiasco: The American Military Adventure in Iraq* (New York, NY: Penguin Press, 2006); Bob Woodward, *State of Denial: Bush at War, Part III* (New York, NY: Simon and Schuster, 2006).

secretary for European and Eurasian affairs, the undersecretary for political affairs, the deputy secretary of state, or finally even the secretary of state. Assuming the memo gets final approval and goes back to those junior foreign service officers who first drafted it, considerable time has probably elapsed, and the approved memo may only bear a slight resemblance to the one originally drafted.

This hypothetical example is drawn from real life. Consider the organizational chart of the State Department at the beginning of the Obama administration in Figure 6.1. Multiple layers are found, and each of the offices indicated are really smaller organizations in their own right, with multiple people of multiple ranks working there and reporting to their superiors who then have to deal with their superiors, and so on. The Department of Defense is similarly complex, with each component containing many subcomponent organizations, as shown in its organization chart in Figure 6.2.

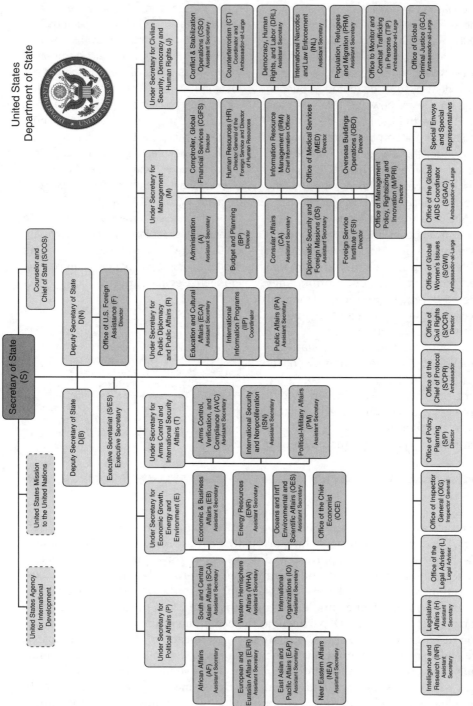

FIGURE 6.1 The organizational chart of the Department of State reveals that it is a complex organization composed of multiple, smaller organizations, each with their own responsibilities.

Source: http://www.state.gov/documents/organization/187423.pdf

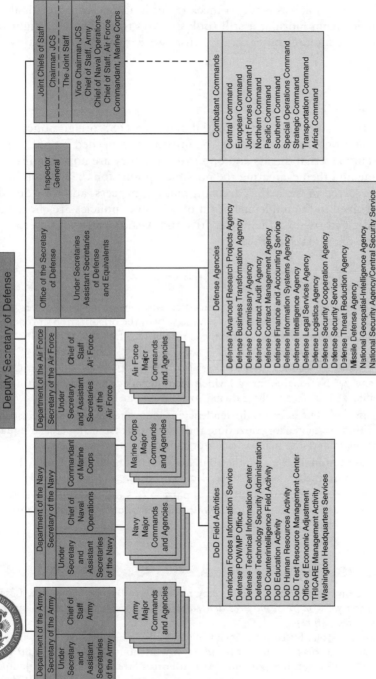

FIGURE 6.2 The organizational chart of the Department of Defense shows a far larger, and arguably more complex, organization compared to the Department of State.

Source: http://www.netage.com/economics/gov/USDefense-chart-top.htm

The pace of bureaucratic behavior slows even more when multiple organizations are involved. Consider again the Cuban Missile Crisis example. Once a determination was made to check to see if nuclear-capable missiles were only 95 miles from Florida, it still took *24 days* to get the U-2 flight implemented because multiple bureaucratic actors were involved—and that was considered a *crisis*.

Conclusion

Bureaucratic organizations are essential actors in U.S. foreign policy making. They are instrumental in collecting the information needed by policy makers to understand external threats and opportunities, they are normally involved in formulating and then evaluating the possible options for U.S. actions, at times they are involved in the actual decision-making process, and they are almost always involved in the implementation of whatever policies are chosen. Thus, bureaucratic actors—and their strengths and weaknesses—are interwoven in the foreign policy–making process.

Glossary Terms

Careerism   in a bureaucracy, being so concerned with one's individual career prospects (merit raises, promotions, etc.) that it gets in the way of the organization's broader goals; in essence, substituting what is good for the career official for what is good for the organization—or perhaps the country.

NSC-68   a National Security Council paper formally entitled "United States Objectives and Programs for National Security," which recommended the massive rearmament of the U.S. military in the face of the growing Soviet threat in 1950.

Parochialism   in a bureaucracy, the tendency to limit one's viewpoint to just the perspective of that particular organization and, in worst-case instances, to equate the broader national interest to that particular organization's narrower interests.

Principal–agent model   the idea that bureaucrats are the agents who carry out the wishes of their principals, who tend to be elected officials.

Standard operating procedures (SOPs)   a pattern of steps developed over time and followed by bureaucratic actors that have produced coordinated organizational responses to situations.

Endnotes

1. For more on this idea of inertial policy making, see Barbara Hinckley, *Less Than Meets the Eye: Congress, the President, and Foreign Policy* (Chicago: University of Chicago Press, 1994).
2. "Table 17.1—Total Executive Branch Civilian Full-Time Equivalent (FTE) Employees: 1981–2013," available online at http://www.whitehouse.gov/sites/default/files/omb/budget/fy2013/assets/hist.pdf; and "Armed Forces Strength Figures for January 31, 2013," available online at http://siadapp.dmdc.osd.mil/personnel/MILITARY/ms0.pdf.

3. See, for example, Terry M. Moe, "The New Economics of Organization," *American Journal of Political Science* 20 (1984), 734–749; and B. Dan Wood and Richard W. Waterman, "The Dynamics of Political Control of the Bureaucracy," *American Political Science Review* 85 (1991), 801–828.
4. See Christopher M. Jones, "The Foreign Policy Bureaucracy in a New Era," in James M. Scott (ed.), *After the End: Making U.S. Foreign Policy in the Post-Cold War World* (Durham, NC: Duke University Press, 1998).
5. See Graham T. Allison, *Essence of Decision: Explaining the Cuban Missile Crisis* (Boston: HarperCollins, 1971), p. 161.
6. See "NSC-68, 1950," U.S. Department of State, Timeline of U.S. Diplomatic History, 1945–1952, available online at http://www.state.gov/r/pa/ho/time/cwr/82209.htm.
7. See U.S. Department of State, "Current Travel Warnings," available online at http://travel.state.gov/content/passports/english/alertswarnings.html.
8. For a concise history of this affair, see Julie Wolf, "The Iran-Contra Affair," PBS *People and Events, The American Experience*, available online at http://www.pbs.org/wgbh/amex/reagan/peopleevents/pande08.html.
9. John Sweeney, Jens Holsoe, and Ed Vulliamy, "Nato Bombed Chinese Deliberately: Nato Hit Embassy on Purpose," *The Observer*, October 17, 1999, available online at http://www.guardian.co.uk/world/1999/oct/17/balkans.
10. "Pharmaceutical Management—Assuring the Quality and Safety of Medicines," *USAID Impact*, available online at: http://blog.usaid.gov/2011/01/pharmaceutical-management-%E2%80%93-assuring-the-quality-and-safety-of-medicines/.
11. For more on this example, see Allison, *Essence of Decision*.
12. For more on this subject, see Max Weber, *Economy and Society*, eds. Guenther Roth and Claus Wittich (Berkeley: University of California Press, 1968).
13. See Lynne E. Vermillion, "Understanding the Air Force Culture," Air War College, Air University, Maxwell Air Force Base, Report AU/AWC/RWP/258/96-04, April 1, 1996, available online at http://www.dtic.mil/cgi-bin/GetTRDoc?AD=ADA393915&Location=U2&doc=GetTRDoc.pdf.
14. See Thomas H. Kean and Lee H. Hamilton, *The 9/11 Report: The National Commission on Terrorist Attacks Upon the United States* (New York: St. Martin's Paperbacks, 2004).
15. See John Diamond, *The CIA and the Culture of Failure: U.S. Intelligence from the End of the Cold War to the Invasion of Iraq* (Stanford, CA: Stanford University Press, 2008).

CHAPTER 7

Congressional Foreign Policy Making

Here's a picture former House Speaker Nancy Pelosi (D-CA) might want to forget—meeting with Syrian President Bashar al-Assad in Damascus.

Source: LOUAI BESHARA/AFP/Getty Images/Newscom

Introduction

News reports often begin with "Today the administration announced ..." as if the president and administration officials are the only foreign policy makers who matter. They matter tremendously, yet, as noted in Chapter 4, the Constitution provides Congress more foreign policy roles and powers than it does for the presidency. Day in, day out, Congress is the second-most significant foreign policy maker in the United States, only trailing the presidency. Moreover, at certain times or for some selected issues, Congress makes U.S. foreign policy, not the president. The congressional role in foreign policy making should therefore not be underestimated. In this chapter, we will examine the congressional actors most likely to become highly involved in making foreign policy, the inputs that motivate Congress and its members, the avenues or processes through which Congress influences (if not makes) foreign policy, and the overall congressional record in terms of foreign policy outputs.

Who in Congress Makes Foreign Policy?

All of the 435 members in the House of Representatives and the 100 members in the Senate present and voting make foreign policy, at least when dealing with issues that result in floor votes in their respective chambers. However, not all issues are handled in such ways, and the number of members of Congress (MCs) highly active on foreign policy issues is usually considerably smaller. Still, this smaller subset often acts in the name of the larger Congress. Those who tend to act in the name of Congress are typically elected party leaders, members of congressional caucuses, members of relevant committees and their subcommittees, and congressional foreign policy entrepreneurs. We will discuss each of these in turn.

Elected Party Leaders

Some of these MCs active in foreign policy making are the elected party leaders in each chamber—the House and Senate majority and minority leaders and the Speaker of the House. The House speaker decides who can speak on the House floor during debate on an issue and who cannot. These elected leaders also canvas their party members so the leaders know how others are likely to vote on an issue. This allows leaders to schedule floor votes appropriately—either when support is greatest for bills they support or when opposition is greatest for bills they oppose. While the leaders of the president's party in each chamber can generally be expected to support the president's foreign policy agenda, the leaders of the nonpresidential party will often find partisan reasons to disagree with the administration's position on foreign policy issues. When the nonpresidential party is the majority party in a chamber of Congress and thus controls it, that party leader—the Speaker of the House or the Senate majority leader—often emerges as a focal point of opposition to the president's foreign policy agenda.

Many examples come to mind: House Speakers Jim Wright (D-TX) pressing the Reagan administration to assist the peace process in Central America in the 1980s, Newt Gingrich (R-GA) pressing the Clinton administration for National Missile Defense (NMD) and covert operations to undermine the Iranian regime, and Nancy Pelosi (D-CA) pushing for global climate change legislation against the wishes of the George W. Bush administration. In the Senate, majority leader Bob Dole (R-KS) was a constant critic of the Clinton administration regarding what he saw as too little U.S. support for Bosnians facing the threat of ethnic cleansing from the Serbs in the 1990s, and his successor Trent Lott (R-MS) challenged the Clinton administration over additional funding for the International Monetary Fund during the Asian Financial Crisis of 1997–1998. Recently in 2013, President Obama had to beseech Senate majority leader Harry Reid (D-NV) not to bring an Iran sanctions bill to the Senate floor that might derail progress in the ongoing diplomatic negotiations with Iran. Thus, elected party leaders can become foreign policy makers as they swing considerable weight with their own party members in Congress.

Congressional Caucuses

Members of congressional caucuses can also become significant players in foreign policy making at times. These informal groups are composed of members who care about an issue, a set of related issues, U.S. policy toward another country or part of the world, and so on. Some of the caucuses deal with foreign policy issues on the basis of their constituents' economic interests (e.g., the Congressional Pro-Trade Caucus or Congressional Steel Caucus). Others focus more on the link between constituents' identity interests and another country or region (e.g., the Congressional Asian Pacific-American Caucus, the Congressional Czech Caucus, or the Congressional Caucus on Turkey and Turkish Americans). Others focus on specific policy issues (e.g., the Congressional Coalition on Adoption or the Out of Iraq Caucus).

A good example of how a caucus can mobilize MCs on an issue came in the late 1980s and early 1990s. The Marine Corps needed a new vehicle to replace a fleet of aging CH-46 helicopters, but the United States was in a recession and the George H.W. Bush administration was trying to hold down spending. Bell and Boeing proposed their jointly built V-22 aircraft to meet the needs of the

Marines Corps—a tilt-rotor, vertical takeoff and landing aircraft that could fly faster and further and carry more troops or cargo than the helicopters it would replace. The Marine Corps wanted the aircraft badly, but the George H.W. Bush administration wanted to save money by buying more helicopters instead. Led by Representatives Curt Weldon (R-PA) whose district included a Boeing plant and Pete Geren (D-TX) whose district included a Bell plant, the Congressional Tilt-Rotor Caucus was formed. It pooled the efforts of those MCs who believed in this new technology, whose districts benefited from the contracts and subcontracts the V-22 would bring, or who were pro-Marine Corps in their orientation. These MCs played a major role in protecting the V-22 from the administration's budget cutters—led by President Bush and his Secretary of Defense Dick Cheney—who wanted to terminate the program. Based on the success of the Tilt-Rotor Caucus, the Marine Corps got its new aircraft.

Committees and Subcommittees

Structurally speaking, the place where most MCs involve actively on foreign policy issues is the congressional committees and subcommittees that deal with foreign policy, but those committees and subcommittees include far more than the obvious ones like armed services or foreign relations. House and Senate committees dealing with foreign policy include agriculture (promoting exports of agricultural products), appropriations (funding foreign policy), armed services (authorizing national security spending), banking and financial services (pushing international financial policy), commerce (regulating foreign trade), energy (decreasing reliance on foreign oil suppliers and providing for the safety of nuclear weapons), environment (promoting global climate change and pro-environmental policy), foreign relations (overseeing foreign policy and authorizing foreign aid spending), homeland security (protecting Americans at home from foreign threats), intelligence (learning what others may be planning or doing), and science and technology (promoting global competitiveness).

Most committee members typically develop expertise on the subject matter of their committees or subcommittees. Those who serve for long periods on their respective committees and subcommittees often come to know as much or more about their subject than do the administration's own experts, and if they do not, they will be able to identify others who do. Consequently, such committee members often put their mark on U.S. foreign policy by relying on such expertise and political power. One example came in the 1960s when senators like Edward Kennedy (D-MA), Stuart Symington (D-MO), John Sherman Cooper (R-KY), and Philip Hart (D-MI) got tired of the Johnson administration's experts telling them that they did not sufficiently understand the technical details of nuclear weapons issues to justify their opposition to a proposed anti-ballistic missile (ABM) defense system. Undeterred, the senators identified their own group of rocket scientists whose expertise could not be discounted and who also questioned the expense and performance of an ABM system. By continuing to attack the ABM proposals of Johnson's successor, Richard Nixon, these senators ultimately led Nixon to seek a negotiated limit with the Soviets on ABM systems. In another example, a few years earlier Senator William Fulbright (D-AR) used his chairmanship of the Senate Foreign Relations Committee to hold televised hearings questioning the wisdom on American involvement in the Vietnam War, in which non-administration experts were invited to testify who could credibly challenge the assumptions of Defense Department officials testifying on behalf of continued U.S. participation in the war.

A well-known example of such committee power being lodged in just a couple of people can be seen in the movie *Charlie Wilson's War*. Charles Wilson (D-TX) was a representative who served on the House Appropriations Committee and, even more importantly, on its Defense and Foreign Operations Subcommittees. When he chose to help the Afghan mujahedin acquire the weaponry they needed to defeat the Soviet invaders of their country, he was in the right place to do it. All he had to do was to convince Clarence "Doc" Long (D-MD), the chairman of the Foreign Operations Subcommittee, that the Central Intelligence Agency (CIA) needed to get more arms to the mujahedin, and then Long could get the other subcommittee members to go along. Then the entire Appropriations Committee would go along with what the subcommittee had recommended. He was successful in that effort. Wilson was able to send millions of dollars worth of weapons to the mujahedin, including portable Stinger antiaircraft missiles that could shoot down the Soviet helicopter gunships which the Afghans particularly feared. The good news is that his efforts turned the tide in Afghanistan in the 1980s and helped to hasten the end of the Soviet Union. The bad news was that he was unable thereafter to get members of other Appropriations subcommittees to provide the funding to build the schools in Afghanistan that might have prevented the rise of the Taliban there.[1]

Congressional Foreign Policy Entrepreneurs

As the earlier anecdote shows, some MCs care more about foreign policy than others. Those who are willing to invest their time and energy to act on their own foreign policy agendas rather than to await administration action on those issues can be considered **congressional foreign policy entrepreneurs**.[2] These policy innovators are a source of significant congressional initiative regarding foreign affairs. They can be found most often on the foreign policy–related committees of Congress, because their foreign affairs interests typically lead them to seek out membership on those committees. However, those who cannot attain such relevant committee memberships can still be entrepreneurs; they just have to use other forums for their activity. A forum available to all MCs is their respective chamber floor, where they can introduce legislation, introduce amendments carrying their substantive message, make speeches, and build coalitions in support of their policy views. All such entrepreneurs also have access to the media, and they can use the news media to press their policy concerns. Those entrepreneurs who are elected party leaders have another bit of leverage they can bring to bear for the issues they champion; they can press their party cohorts in ways other MCs cannot.

The examples of Bob Dole, Newt Gingrich, Trent Lott, Nancy Pelosi, William Fulbright, Jim Wright, and Charlie Wilson all illustrate congressional foreign policy entrepreneurs at work. Such entrepreneurs can be found across the entire post–World War II era. Early in the post–World War II era, they were more likely to come from the Senate than from the House, but over time that difference has eroded to the point that they are practically as likely to come from the House now as the Senate. Moreover, their numbers are growing. With each passing year, more MCs are engaging in foreign policy entrepreneurship, and as Table 7.1 shows, their policy impact can be substantial.

So what motivates all these MCs to try to shape foreign policy? In other words, what are the inputs to the congressional foreign policy process? We turn to that next.

TABLE 7.1   The Impact of Congressional Foreign Policy Entrepreneurs

Specific U.S. Initiatives with Congressional Roots

The creation of the UN and what later became the European Union

Spain's inclusion in the Western alliance and NATO

Immigration restrictions during the Cold War

Cold War homeland security changes not unlike the more recent USA PATRIOT Act

Insistence that the space race with the Soviets be a civilian-run operation through the creation of NASA

The idea for the Peace Corps

Relaxing the economic embargo on Cuba

Returning control of the Panama Canal to Panama

Improving relations with both the Soviet Union and the People's Republic of China

Endorsing reform in UN operations, leading to a reduction in U.S. dues to the UN

Limiting ABM systems

Pressing for an end to the Vietnam War and limiting U.S. participation in other Southeast Asian conflicts

Improving U.S.–Mexican relations

Ending private support for the Irish Republican Army

Limiting or in some cases banning U.S. military aid to repressive military regimes

Promoting a regional peace plan for Central America

Encouraging more relief for international refugees

Sponsoring the V-22 tilt-rotor aircraft

Aiding the Afghan mujahedin

Cutting funds for the intervention in Somalia

Pushing for the creation of an International Criminal Court but repudiating it later when its actions would not be subject to UN Security Council authorization

Saving Mexico's economy by finding a formula to bail out the peso

TABLE 7.1   (Continued)

Ensuring the return of looted Jewish artworks by the Swiss government

Promoting World Bank funding of HIV/AIDS programs

Calling attention to Russian–Iranian missile technology trade

Promoting the protection of Bosnian Muslims

Pressing for the recognition of the People's Republic of Vietnam

Making humanitarian relief supplies exempt from economic embargoes

Abolishing the Arms Control and Disarmament Agency and the U.S. Information Agency as separate entities and rolling their functions into the State Department

Pushing for Iranian sanctions over its nuclear and missile programs

Proposing the enlargement of NATO

Promoting reforms in how the International Monetary Fund operates

Finding the diplomatic formula to end the Kosovo War

Promoting National Missile Defense

Limiting funding for international agencies that allow the use of abortions

Banning the trade in "conflict diamonds"

Source: Based on Ralph G. Carter and James M. Scott, Choosing to Lead: Understanding Congressional Foreign Policy Entrepreneurs (Durham, NC: Duke University Press, 2009), p. 233.

What Motivates MCs?

One might think that the inputs to foreign policy making are fairly obvious. MCs respond to external events that represent either opportunities for advancing U.S. interests or threats to U.S. national interests. However, those events are presumably the same for all MCs, but not all MCs choose to get involved in foreign policy making. So what motivates this smaller group to get involved? The answers can be as diverse as MCs themselves, but some patterns are evident for these inputs to policy. Core values, the desire to make good policy, the desire for influence in the chamber, partisanship, and the desire for reelection can motivate MCs in foreign policy making.

Core Values

A primary motivator for MCs to become engaged in foreign policy making is often their core values. As former House Speaker Jim Wright (D-TX) once noted, MCs were motivated because "they have convictions."[3] Such convictions might be based on their political ideology. For example, more conservative MCs might press for foreign policy initiatives that emphasize free-market principles in international politics, "peace through strength" approaches to national security, or protection of U.S. national sovereignty whenever it seemed threatened.

More liberal MCs might press for more cooperative efforts to solving common problems, working with and through international organizations to meet global needs, or spending somewhat less on the defense budget and somewhat more on foreign assistance.

Another aspect of core values involves the role of personal experiences. We are all shaped by our pasts, and MCs are no different. As Speaker Wright said in an interview, his generation was shaped by participation in World War II. He noted that many MCs who served in combat abroad (as he did) came home with no illusions about how events far from the United States could have profound repercussions back home.[4] Similar life-shaping experiences were shared by Korean War veterans like Representatives John Conyers (D-CA) or Charles Rangel (D-NY),[5] and the same can be said for Vietnam veterans like Senators Chuck Hagel (R-NE), John Kerry (D-MA), or John McCain (R-AZ). We have already begun to see Iraq and Afghanistan war veterans elected to Congress and will likely add their names to this list of MCs shaping foreign policy in the future.

Beyond wartime military service, other personal experiences shape an interest in, or approach to, foreign policy. For Senator Christopher Dodd (D-CT), serving as a Peace Corps volunteer in the Dominican Republic sensitized him to the needs of Latin Americans. In addition to his Vietnam War service, for Hagel it was his prior career in international telecommunication sales.[6] For the then Senator Barack Obama (D-IL), it was his career as a community organizer. In addition to his combat service in World War II, for Representative Henry Reuss (D-WI), it was his role as an administrator in occupied Germany after the war. Experiences such as these shape people in ways that become part of their core values.

Family experiences play a similar role in shaping core values. MCs whose families come from immigrant backgrounds often retain an interest in the old country. That was as true for Irish-Americans like former House Speaker Thomas P. "Tip" O'Neill (D-MA) and former Senator Edward "Ted" Kennedy (D-MA) as it was for Cuban-Americans like Representatives Ileana Ros-Lehtinen or Lincoln Diaz-Balart (both R-FL) or Senator Robert Menendez (D-NJ). Former Representative and later Senator Jacob Javits (R-NY) often noted that his family's history of immigrant status made him more sympathetic to the needs of immigrants and refugees everywhere.[7]

The Desire to Make Good Policy

Another motivating factor for MCs is their personal desire to make good policy.[8] You might assume that this motivates all MCs, but, to be candid, some are more motivated by ensuring their chances for reelection than by engaging in good public policy making. (And isn't that sad to say?) Those who choose to take on foreign policy issues often want to be part of the solution to the country's problems, not part of the problems themselves. To know what policies will be good in a particular situation, MCs will rely on their own values, ideas, and predispositions, on the advice of their own or committee staff members, on the cues given to them by other MCs known to be expert in that subject area, and on what they learn through the media.[9]

Several of these cue-givers deserve special mention. The views of their own office or committee staff members who have earned a reputation for expertise on that subject will generally be taken seriously by MCs, as will some of the "talking head" experts found on television programming. Particularly important cue-givers are those other members of the House or Senate who have developed a reputation for their relevant expertise. In foreign policy matters, Senator Richard Lugar (R-IN) earned such a reputation. Many members from both major parties in both congressional chambers would wait until Lugar announced his position on an issue and then took their cue from his announcement. That way they had the benefit of his expertise and were spared the effort to become more expert themselves.

Desire for Influence in the Chamber

Desire for influence in Congress is another motivating factor for MCs. Every MC who desires to be reelected probably cares about domestic policy, as the public pays close attention to it. Thus, there are potentially 435 domestic policy "experts" in the House and 100 in the Senate. However, fewer members of the public pay close attention to foreign policy, and thus fewer MCs generally invest their scarce time resources in developing foreign policy expertise. As shown by the example of Senator Lugar, developing a reputation of expertise gains respect from one's peers in Congress and with it comes broader influence in Congress.

Yet Senator Lugar is far from the only example of such respect given to MCs due to their command of policy details. Former Senate Foreign Relations Committee Chairman John Kerry (D-MA) was widely respected for his general foreign policy expertise (and served several times as a diplomatic messenger for the Obama administration to Afghan President Hamid Karzai; such knowledge and roles helped him get appointed as secretary of state succeeding Hillary Clinton), Senator John McCain (R-AZ) was often looked to for advice on military matters, former Chairwoman Ileana Ros-Lehtinen (R-FL) of the House Foreign Affairs Committee is an expert on Cuba-related issues, and her colleague on the committee Christopher Smith (R-NJ) is well known for his knowledge of international adoption and abortion-related issues.

Partisanship

Another important motivator of MCs is the push and pull of partisanship. Congress is a highly partisan body because the control of its chambers and its formal distribution of power are based on party membership. The party with the most members in each chamber—the majority party—controls that chamber, which means it has more of its members on every committee and subcommittee, its members serve as the chairs of all committees and subcommittees, and its elected party leaders control the chamber's agenda and schedule. So members of the majority party in both the House and the Senate are structurally well positioned to advance their own policy agendas. Potentially, they have the votes to accomplish any goal they set within their chamber. As long as they can convince their fellow partisans to go along (which is not always as easy as it may sound), they can pass legislation and otherwise act in the name of the chamber.

Partisanship matters in another practical way as well. There is the president's party label to consider. While MCs desire to get things done, there is an additional partisan motivation to help presidents who are members of their party. If the president and the MC are from the same party, then by acting together they can help each other look good to the American public. To some degree, they share electoral fortunes. A popular president may help get other members of his party elected to Congress.

Conversely, being a member of the nonpresidential party matters as well. While one might hope that some objective measure of the national interest trumps all other considerations when MCs are deciding how to act on a foreign policy matter, history shows that the bipartisan era—when MCs put aside their partisanship and worked closely with the president to present a united front to the rest of the world—largely ended in the 1950s. Since then, MCs from the nonpresidential party tend to be quicker to oppose a presidential initiative in foreign policy than is the case with MCs from the president's own party. Even when opposition party MCs share a president's foreign policy goal, they may prefer other means by which to achieve it than what the president recommends. For most issues in Congress, the best predictor of how MCs will vote is whether they share the president's party label.

In recent years, partisanship has become so pronounced in Washington, DC, that to cooperate with members of the other party is often seen as a sign of disloyalty by some elected officials. While this development has proven toxic at times to effective government, often leading to legislative gridlock when Congress and the presidency are controlled by different parties, it need not necessarily be a bad thing. By carefully scrutinizing a president's foreign policy requests and initiatives, the opposition party may be in a position to uncover any weaknesses or flaws in those proposals. If weaknesses are identified and are corrected, sounder U.S. foreign policies may be the result.

The Desire for Reelection

Finally, many would argue that the most important motivator of almost all MCs is getting reelected, and attending to the needs of one's constituents is a very good way to help one's reelection. While some MCs claim that foreign policy has no natural constituency (as in "Pakistan is not in my district"), at times clear constituency concerns are evident.

Take foreign aid, for example. Most U.S. foreign aid is conditional in nature. If the United States provides foreign aid to Pakistan in the form of loans for agricultural investment and Pakistan chooses to purchase farm equipment and fertilizer with those funds, the farm equipment and fertilizer will be purchased from U.S. companies. Such a condition is routinely inserted into foreign aid bills. Thus, for MCs with manufacturers of farm equipment and fertilizer in their districts, supporting that foreign aid bill means good business for some constituents back home. Similarly, U.S. food aid means more sales for U.S. farmers, medical aid means more sales for the pharmaceutical and medical equipment industries, military assistance means more sales for arms manufacturers, and so on. MCs are well aware of such businesses in their districts or states.

In addition to the many economic groups that might benefit from a U.S. foreign policy decision, some constituents may have a personal interest in U.S. foreign policy toward a particular country, region, or issue. As noted earlier, Americans with immigrant roots might have a continuing interest in the old country, so Irish-Americans may care more about U.S. policy impacting Ireland or Northern Ireland than do others. Thus, it was not surprising that the lead roles in getting the Irish-American community to stop contributing money to the Irish Republican Army so it could carry on its war with British police and troops in Northern Ireland were played by two Irish-American MCs—House Speaker Tip O'Neill (D-MA) and Senator Ted Kennedy (D-MA). Similar policy connections can be found for Italian-Americans, Greek-Americans, Armenian-Americans, Mexican-Americans, and so on, regarding policies impacting their earlier countries of origin. They may care more in general, or they may still have relatives in those countries. More broadly, Latin Americans may have a greater interest in the entire Latin American region, and those originally from Cuba, Haiti, the Dominican Republic, and elsewhere might care more about U.S. policy toward the Caribbean region. Finally, there are some citizens who simply care about a particular issue and press their MC to act in the direction of their preferences. That issue might be AIDS/HIV relief in Africa, the proliferation of nuclear weapons globally, the environment, protecting the rights of women and children, ensuring religious freedom abroad, or global monetary policy.

These constituency influences on MCs can work in several ways. The norm of representation suggests that MCs should care to act on the interests of the public back home. Those local concerns are often articulated and conveyed to MCs by representatives of that concerned group of citizens—via personal contacts; phone, fax, e-mail, Facebook, and Twitter communications; letters; and more indirect methods like advertisements in or letters to the editor of the local paper. Sometimes political advertising is used. Some years ago, there was a very prominent billboard on the side of the highway leading out of the Des Moines, Iowa airport. It simply read "Get the United States Out of the UN!" Obviously, someone cared enough to pay for such a sign placed where elected officials who fly in and out of that airport could not fail to see it. If MCs know that a group of constituents cares about a particular issue, they may anticipate the positions likely to be taken on those issues by folks back home and move in that preferred direction without waiting for such a request. In that way, they have anticipated the reaction of constituents even before the constituents have acted. Even if MCs do not always share their constituents' views, they do care about reelection. That provides another motivation to be responsive to the desires of organized groups back home.

How do these inputs turn into policy outputs on Capitol Hill? There are multiple processes used by MCs in this regard, and we turn to them next.

Processes of Congressional Influence

How does Congress actually make foreign policy? The most obvious way is to set foreign policy through legislation, but that is only one way Congress has at its disposal. There are four broad processes or avenues MCs use to make or influence foreign policy.[10] Congressional action can be direct or indirect. Direct actions are specific to a particular issue; indirect actions are less specific but seek to impact the broader policy context involved. Actions can also be legislative or nonlegislative. Legislative actions seek to pass a particular piece of legislation—a bill or an amendment—whereas in the short run, nonlegislative actions do not. Combining these dichotomies produces four different avenues of congressional activity: direct/legislative processes, direct/nonlegislative processes, indirect/legislative processes, and indirect/nonlegislative processes. Direct/legislative processes involve passing bills that could include authorizations to act, appropriations of money, and Senate approval of treaties. Direct/nonlegislative processes involve holding hearings, engaging in oversight activities, communicating with other policy makers in the executive branch, or even filing suits in court. Indirect/legislative processes involve approving personnel appointments in the Senate, passing procedural legislation or passing nonbinding legislation to indicate the will of Congress on an issue, and so on. Indirect/nonlegislative processes involve trying to set the government's agenda, framing the debate regarding a substantive issue, making contacts with foreign officials, and so on. We will discuss each of these in turn.

Direct/Legislative Processes

Direct/legislative processes are the most obvious way MCs make foreign policy. Congress passes bills that make or shape foreign policy, such as authorizing the use of force, legislating economic sanctions, changing immigration laws, changing laws to improve homeland security, dictating import and export policies, and approving or not approving treaties. MCs attend to these matters as political circumstances in the international or domestic environments dictate or as opportunities arise.

Presidents at times take credit for the legislative initiatives that MCs undertake. A good example concerns the Peace Corps, through which U.S. civilians volunteer to help people in other countries, thereby improving the local quality of life while improving the reputation and image of the United States in the process. The idea for the Peace Corps came from Henry Reuss, a Wisconsin Democrat representing Milwaukee who introduced a bill in the House of Representatives to establish a civilian volunteer agency. A journalist told the then presidential candidate John F. Kennedy about Reuss's idea, and Kennedy later proposed it in a campaign speech. After being elected president, Kennedy created the Peace Corps by an executive order, but Reuss and Minnesota Democratic Senator Hubert H. Humphrey got the legislation passed, authorizing the Peace Corps as an ongoing entity with a regular budget.[11] The president got the political credit for the Peace Corps, but Reuss and Humphrey did the heavy lifting that institutionalized it.

Due to constitutional requirements, some governmental matters dictate a significant congressional role. The greatest of these concerns government expenditures of funds. The president proposes a budget each year, but it is the Congress that first authorizes how much money may be spent for each specific purpose each year and then provides the actual money to be spent. Without such budgeted funds, the government literally cannot function. Employees cannot be paid and programs cannot be implemented without funding. Thus, Congress's "power of the purse" is a tremendously significant direct/legislative process, because by appropriating money, Congress makes things happen, and vice versa.

MCs are relentless in using their power of the purse to fund the policies they like and to minimize or end undesired policies by starving them of funds. For example, for years MCs appropriated more money for the National Guard than what presidents requested. National Guard units were based back home, and thus the money was going back to local constituencies in terms of new jobs, new construction projects, better weapons or equipment for those in the Guard, and so on. Keeping the folks back home happy was a good way for MCs to get reelected. Sometimes, MCs just had an idea they wanted to push, like inserting unrequested money into the Intelligence Community's budget to destabilize the government of Iran. On the other hand, cutting off funding was a sure way to kill an initiative. That is how U.S. participation in the Vietnam War ended. In the early 1970s, Congress made it clear to President Richard Nixon that it would cut off funding for the war. Nixon reluctantly heeded the warning and directed negotiators to sign a peace agreement with the North Vietnamese in early 1973, and several months later Congress passed the final version of the legislation cutting off funding for the war, thereby preventing any change of heart by the president. Many such presidential initiatives have been killed by Congress, either by refusing to authorize or fund the initiative or by threatening to do so. Box 7.1 explores this negative power of Congress.

Direct/Nonlegislative Processes

Yet direct/legislative processes are not the only one way MCs influence foreign policy. By pursuing direct/nonlegislative means, MCs influence policy without resorting to legislation. Another example involving President Kennedy illustrates this avenue. One of Kennedy's most iconic moments as president was his "I am a Berliner" speech, made in West Berlin during the 1961 crisis with the Soviet Union. In that speech, he showed solidarity with the beleaguered people of West Berlin and demonstrated to the Soviet Union's leadership that he would not back down in the Cold War. The idea for such a speech, and the general content to include in it, came again from Henry Reuss. Before he went there, Kennedy sought out Reuss for his advice, as a German-American, about what Kennedy should stress while in West Berlin. Reuss told Kennedy what he thought the president should say, and the rest is history.[12]

Beyond consulting or advising activities, another example of direct/nonlegislative processes is congressional hearings. MCs in charge of congressional

BOX 7.1

The Power to Say "No"

In many ways, the easiest power for Congress to utilize is the power to say "No," to prevent the president from getting what he wants. Perhaps just as significant is the congressional ability to threaten to say "No" to the president. As President Barack Obama learned, such negative power can be manifested in a variety of ways.

The list of initiatives Obama delayed acting upon because they would require congressional approval or authorization is fairly lengthy. Despite his repeated references to the idea that the economic embargo of Cuba has been a long-term failure, he has not asked Congress to repeal it. The reason is simple; he does not think he has the votes.

When it comes to new agreements with other countries, Obama has a number of things he wants to achieve. He said he wants the Comprehensive Test Ban Treaty returned to the Senate for its reconsideration. President Clinton signed it, but the Senate rejected it in 1999. Administration insiders say he has been told the votes are not there in the Senate for ratification of it. He wanted a new Climate Change Convention to sign in Copenhagen in 2009, but when he got there, he could agree only informally to very modest future increases in fossil fuel emissions—and to no reductions in emissions—because that was all he thought the Senate would approve. More broadly, anything put in the form of a treaty is particularly difficult, as treaties require a two-thirds vote of the Senate, which means the votes of more than a few Senate Republicans would be needed to pass any treaty proposed by a Democratic president (or vice versa).

Budget battles with Congress are another long-standing point of contention in which presidents generally tend to lose unless their preferences mirror congressional ones. A good example was the effort by Defense Secretary Robert Gates to get the Pentagon to spend less money on big ticket weapons systems needed to fight a major interstate war with a worthy adversary. The chances of such a war seem increasingly remote, but the United States currently has thousands of troops fighting insurgencies, and Gates wanted more money spent on their needs. However, MCs like spending for major war-fighting weapon systems, as that produces more easily visible jobs back in their home districts or states than does spending more for small arms, light weapons, or foreign-language training.

So while presidents are the single-most powerful actors in making U.S. foreign policy, they are far from omnipotent. The typical view from the White House is that Congress either keeps the presidency in handcuffs in terms of what it can and cannot do in foreign policy or it at least tries to do so. Either way, presidents usually see Congress as a formidable obstacle to be surmounted in making U.S. foreign policy.

Source: Based on Stephen Sestanovich, "Hostile Territory," Washington Post, April 24, 2009.

standing committees or their subcommittees often call hearings to set the stage for later policy changes or to pressure the administration regarding current policies. Through the latter half of the 1960s, one of the ways the Democratically controlled Congress kept pressure on President Nixon to end the Vietnam War was to hold hearings on the conduct of the war, what its objectives were, the prospects for victory, and so on. Such hearings became forums in which the arguments for and against continued U.S. involvement in the war could be raised.

Congressional oversight is another type of direct/nonlegislative process. Since they authorize and fund governmental programs and agencies, MCs can periodically investigate those programs and agencies to ensure that they are effectively run and doing what Congress intended. Sometimes such investigations can have embarrassing consequences for the administration. For example, in the late 1960s and early 1970s rumors began to circulate that the Intelligence Community had engaged in a variety of unsavory actions that seemed to contravene traditional U.S. values. Newspaper accounts reported some of what had been rumored, like assassination plots against foreign rulers, support for military regimes with repressive human rights records, and illegal spying activities conducted in the United States against U.S. citizens. Both the House and the Senate created committees to investigate these reports. The Senate committee produced a record of governmental behaviors that shocked many Americans and led its chairman, Frank Church (D-ID), to compare the CIA to a "rogue elephant on a rampage."[13] The committee's final report called for the creation of permanent intelligence committees in Congress to oversee the Intelligence Community, prior notification to those committees of covert operations, publication of the annual total budget for the Intelligence Community, and an end to support for repressive regimes. Most of these changes were later enacted into policy.

Indirect/Legislative Processes

Indirect/legislative processes are available to Congress as well. Sometimes nonbinding legislation sends important signals to the president or other executive branch actors. For instance, in 1997 the Senate put an immediate stop to any serious U.S. consideration of the Kyoto Protocol to the UN Framework Convention on Climate Change, a treaty that would have required the United States to reduce significantly its fossil fuel emissions. A nonbinding "Sense of the Senate" resolution was passed, which opposed the treaty because it exempted developing countries from having to reduce their emissions and would result in harming the U.S. economy. The fact that the resolution passed by a vote of 95-0 indicated that the Kyoto Protocol had *no chance*, as written, to gain Senate approval. To date, the United States still has not joined the Kyoto Protocol.

Procedural legislation is another form of indirect/legislative process. One of the discoveries by congressional investigations in the 1970s was that the Nixon administration had made secret commitments to other governments, often in the form of arms sales. Thus, in 1976 Congress passed the Arms Export Control Act. Since then the act has been amended to keep up with changing times, but it now requires the administration to inform Congress 30 days in advance of any proposed sales of major defense equipment valued at $14 million or more, of defense articles or services valued at $50 million or more, and design and construction services valued at $200 million or more. In this way, Congress has a chance to reject the sales—and the closer ties with that regime—if members so desire.[14]

Trade provides another example. For years Congress mandated that "most favored nation status"—or what is now called **normal trade status**—would be granted to the People's Republic of China only on a year-to-year basis. Thus, Congress created a procedure that allowed MCs to criticize China's economic practices that worked to the detriment of American workers. Such Chinese practices included a currency kept arbitrarily low in value to promote Chinese exports, underpaid workers, poor working conditions, and environmental damage in the name of economic growth. Others broadened the debate to criticize the Chinese communist regime for its repression of Christians, dissidents, practitioners of Falun Gong/Falun Dafa, use of abortion to control population growth, and so on. In the end, China's most favored nation status got approved each year, but many MCs believed the annual outpouring of criticism kept pressure on China and prevented it from pursuing even more reprehensible behaviors.[15]

A final form of indirect/legislative processes involves approving personnel appointments. The Senate is required to approve many top executive branch appointees, like Cabinet secretaries and ambassadors. Most of the time the Senate approves the president's choices for office, but since some of these appointments carry clear policy implications, the Senate will occasionally say "no." In 1989, the Senate rejected the nomination of Senator John Tower (R-TX) as secretary of defense. While many senators cited Tower's personal failings as the reasons for their votes, at least some were concerned that he would have too much influence over his former protégé President George H.W. Bush, who often noted Tower as his mentor. An even more clear-cut example of policy differences came with the refusal of the Senate to consider John Bolton to be the U.S. ambassador to the United Nations (UN) for President George W. Bush, as Bolton was considered by many to be a virtual enemy of the institution in which he would be serving. Rather than totally give up on his nomination, President Bush made Bolton a "recess appointment," which meant he could hold the job on a temporary basis only until that session of Congress ended 17 months later. In this case both sides got a partial victory: The president got Bolton in that role at least for a while, but the Senate prevented Bolton from getting the job for the rest of the president's term of office.

Indirect/Nonlegislative Processes

The final avenue for congressional foreign policy roles involves indirect/nonlegislative processes. A major effort that fits here is agenda setting. Literally, this involves getting the government to deal with the issues Congress wants addressed. NMD provides a good example. The 1995 Republican "Contract with America" called for the establishment of an NMD system, and Republicans in both the House and the Senate pressed the Clinton administration to do more to create a defensive system to protect the United States from missile attack.

Following hundreds of speeches and years of pressure on the reluctant administration, Congress was able to muster the votes to pass the National Missile Defense Act in 1999.

Another example concerns climate change. Despite the opposition of President George W. Bush to significant climate change legislation, in 2006 House Speaker Nancy Pelosi (D-CA) vowed to keep the pressure on by forming the House Select Committee on Energy Independence and Global Warming. Led by Representative Ed Markey (D-MA), the committee held numerous hearings on global climate change and its impacts on the United States. Due to such pressure, before his term ended President Bush was willing to consider legislation that at least set "aspirational" (i.e., nonbinding) goals for reductions in fossil fuel emissions.

However, the record for long-term efforts to set the governmental agenda might go to former Senator William Proxmire (D-WI). Beginning in 1967, Proxmire made a speech on the Senate floor virtually every day the Senate was in session, pressing for the U.S. ratification of the Genocide Convention. When it was finally approved 20 years later, he had given over 3000 floor speeches to ensure that the Senate did not forget about this treaty.[16]

Framing debate is another indirect/nonlegislative process. This refers to casting or "branding" the terms of a debate in ways that help one side over the other. So when Representative Chris Smith (R-NJ) continually cast the most favored nation debate on China in terms of "supporting baby killers," he explicitly linked China's abortion policies to a trade issue. Similarly, congressional supporters of military aid for Colombia continually stressed that the aid is part of a "war on drugs" in the United States. Thus, those who said the aid strengthened a repressive regime guilty of human rights violations then had to protect themselves here at home from charges of being "soft on drugs," and they lost the debate.

A final example of indirect/nonlegislative processes involves contacts with foreign leaders. By meeting foreign leaders and giving them a favorable audience, MCs can push press administrations to do more on certain issues. In the 1980s, the then House Speaker Jim Wright (D-TX) used his contacts with Costa Rican President Oscar Arias to continually press for U.S. support of a Central American Peace Plan. When President Reagan would not meet with Arias to discuss the plan, Wright invited Arias to come speak to Congress about it. Arias went on to win the Nobel Peace Prize for his role in ending the conflict in Central America. More recently, multiple presidents have had difficulty pressing Israeli governments to make concessions in return for peace with the Palestinians. Yet when Israeli leaders come to Washington, they are showered with support by MCs who tell them, as Speaker Pelosi did in 2010, "We in Congress stand by Israel," which undercuts the administration's position.[17]

Obviously, some MCs prefer some of these four processes of congressional activity more than others, whereas some often move back and forth seamlessly between them. Some issues illustrate multiple processes over time as well, as illustrated in Box 7.2. However, the most interesting question is how much impact Congress and its members have had in shaping U.S. foreign policy. We turn to that now.

BOX 7.2

Congressional Opposition to the War in Afghanistan

The power of presidents to make war is widely considered their greatest foreign policy power. By using their commander in chief role to send troops into harm's way, presidents can begin wars at any time. Although Congress has the power to declare war, the last time Congress used that power was during World War II (declaring war against Germany's allies Bulgaria, Hungary, and Romania in 1942). Since then, presidents have expected Congress to back them up with funding to support the troops and, when absolutely necessary politically, authorizations of the use of force. MCs have done so in Korea in 1950, in Vietnam in 1964, in Lebanon in 1982, in Panama in 1989, in Kuwait in 1991, in Somalia in 1992, and in Bosnia in 1995.

However, following the terrorist attacks on New York's World Trade Center and the Pentagon on September 11, 2001, U.S. forces were sent against the Taliban regime in Afghanistan. Initially, this use of force elicited virtually no opposition in Congress for two reasons. First, in the days just after the attack on the United States, President George W. Bush sought a congressional authorization to use force against the terrorists and those who supported them. On September 14, 2001, the authorization passed by a 420-1 vote in the House and a 98-0 vote in the Senate. Second, the war against the Taliban regime that had provided sanctuary to Osama bin Laden seemed justified and was initially successful. That regime fell quickly with very few U.S. casualties.

However, as the prolonged military occupation of Afghanistan prompted significant armed resistance to U.S. forces and the George W. Bush administration chose to go to war against Iraq, congressional opposition to these uses of force began to swell. The opposition grew as these occupations continued year after year, and U.S. casualty counts mounted over time. After the Democrats gained control of both the House and the Senate in the November 2006 elections, they began trying to force the administration to adopt deadlines for the withdrawal of U.S. troops from Iraq, but they were unsuccessful in the face of opposition claims that producing such deadlines would be an advantage to the insurgents fighting U.S. troops. Instead, they had to wait until a new president could be elected, and in Barack Obama they had a candidate who declared that the wrong war being fought in Iraq (wrong in the sense that it was not justified in terms of an Iraqi threat to vital U.S. national interests) had taken military resources from the right war being fought in Afghanistan (right in the sense that it was there that al Qaeda had gained sanctuary and support).

Despite a greater U.S. military effort in Afghanistan after President Obama was inaugurated, the Taliban continued to grow in strength in Afghanistan, U.S. casualty totals continued to climb, and the government of President Hamid Karzai seemed incapable of governing in the countryside outside Kabul or reining in the corruption and drug trafficking that plagued much of the country. Congressional Democrats began pressuring President Obama to get U.S.

forces out of Afghanistan. Some MCs said the war was simply not worth the lives of U.S. troops. Others said the effort was morally justified but militarily unwise. From their point of view, if prior empires like the Greeks, the Persians, the Moghuls, the Sikhs, the British, and the Russians could not control Afghanistan, what made the United States think it could?

President Obama was caught in a dilemma. He had campaigned on fighting the "right war" in Afghanistan and had garnered some hard-won praise for that stance by numerous Republicans in Congress. So he had a lot of political capital invested in staying the course in Afghanistan. On the other hand, pursuing that military option put him on a collision course with a small but vocal and growing number of MCs from his own party, including influential House Speaker Nancy Pelosi (D-CA) and the Congressional Progressive Caucus whose support he needed on other issues. Obama tried to please everyone with a compromise solution. In 2009, he announced a surge in the number of U.S. troops to be sent to

Afghanistan, but he also coupled that announcement with a declaration that the process of removing troops would begin in 2011.

Up to his compromise "surge but begin the withdrawal" announcement, nothing President Obama had said as a candidate or president indicated he would waver from his oft-stated goal of taking the fight to the Taliban and the remnants of al Qaeda in Afghanistan (and even across the border in neighboring Pakistan). Yet congressional opposition to the war in Afghanistan by members of his own party seemingly convinced him to revise his war plans. Thus, the war in Afghanistan demonstrates both direct/legislative processes to authorize the use of force and direct/nonlegislative efforts by MCs to end it. This episode certainly belies the argument that Congress plays no meaningful role in presidential war-making decisions, as does the evidence presented in the book *While Dangers Gather: Congressional Checks on Presidential War Powers* by William G. Howell and Jon C. Pevehouse (Princeton, NJ: Princeton University Press, 2007).

Congressional Foreign Policy Influence

So in the end, how much influence does Congress have over U.S. foreign policy making? The short answer is, *as much as its members desire.* As noted in Chapter 4, Congress has an impressive array of constitutional powers in the realm of foreign policy. Congress can influence almost any aspect of U.S. foreign policy by what it chooses to authorize, to fund, and to mandate the administration to do or by how it chooses to shape the public debate.

Historically, Congress has authorized and funded the basic governmental structures that implement and administer foreign policy—from Cabinet departments like State and Defense and Homeland Security to agencies like the CIA and NSA to presidential advisory bodies like the National Security Council (and staff) and National Economic Council (and staff). Just as Congress can create such entities, it can terminate them as it did with the U.S. Information Agency or submerge them in a larger entity as it did by changing the Arms Control and Disarmament Agency from an independent agency into a subsidiary unit of the State Department, both cases coming at the insistence of one MC—Senator Jesse Helms (R-NC)—in the late 1990s.

Yet on a daily basis, Congress's greatest structural power is its right to appropriate funds for the programs those departments and agencies administer. As noted earlier, if its members so choose, Congress can limit or put conditions on funds for initiatives it questions (such as limiting military assistance to regimes accused of significant human rights violations), deny funds for initiatives it opposes (e.g., supporting the contras in Nicaragua or continuing U.S. participation in the Vietnam War), and provide funds for causes it champions (e.g., NMD or undermining the Iranian regime). If Congress does not provide the administration the funding it requests, it is almost impossible for an administration to continue that foreign policy initiative. In such a case, the president might be able to devote some of his limited discretionary funds to that purpose, but each year the amount of discretionary spending he is allowed is set by MCs, so this is a route presidents would be wise not to abuse. Alternatively, presidents could ask U.S. allies to fund initiatives that Congress rejects, again a course of action presidents prefer to avoid if possible.

Not only can Congress impact the structure of government and what those foreign policy actors do, but it can also help set the basic strategic policy of the United States. In the late 1940s and early 1950s, Congress used economic aid to Spain to push the United States into a relationship with Spain's right-wing regime that President Truman opposed. That push helped facilitate Spain's reincorporation into the Western security alliance which in turn served to encourage the development of a representative democracy in Spain. In the 1960s, Congress chipped away at the policy of containing communist expansion by questioning the Vietnam War, endorsing arms talks with the Soviet Union, and providing support to the communist regime in Yugoslavia. In the 1970s, Congress attacked the U.S. practice of aiding and abetting unsavory dictators and oppressive regimes whose primary value had been that they were reliably anti-communist. In the 1980s, MCs supported a nuclear freeze movement that pushed the Reagan administration closer to arms negotiations with the Soviets, and they also forced the Reagan administration to end its support of the minority white regime in South Africa. In the 1990s, consistent congressional pressures led the Clinton administration to back away from meaningful participation in multilateral approaches to solve global problems like prosecution of war criminals or slowing the rate of global climate change. In the 2000s, Congress banned U.S. participation in the trade of so-called blood diamonds, the revenues from whose sale funded violent militias and other terrorist groups, and it pushed for deadlines to start the de-escalation of military involvement in both Iraq and Afghanistan.

Again, the examples in this chapter show that Congress has substantial power to shape and set U.S. foreign policy when its members choose to do so. However, there are three things presidents can do that Congress cannot equal. First, presidents are the only actors who can claim to speak for the nation as a whole. MCs can legitimately speak only for the citizens of the state or district who elected them. Thus, presidents serve as the face and voice of the United States both at home and abroad. The presidential ability to represent the entire nation gives them a "bully pulpit," in the words of Theodore Roosevelt, to act in the name of the American people.

Second, presidents alone have the sole constitutional ability to grant diplomatic recognition to other regimes, a fact Senator Barry Goldwater (R-AZ) learned when he sued President Jimmy Carter over Carter's decision to end diplomatic recognition of Taiwan and to recognize diplomatically the People's Republic of China (Communist China) instead. The Supreme Court said this constitutional power of the president was clear.

Third, as commander in chief, presidents can send troops into harm's way. Congress can then choose whether to authorize such a use of force, to fund or deny funding for that use of force, to publicly question the reasons behind the use of force, and perhaps to vote on a formal declaration of war again in the future, but those responses typically occur well after the use of force has begun. Thus, presidents have considerable discretion to start wars, and they can create political facts by putting "boots on the ground" or bombs in the air before Congress can react. Once force has been used, presidents may count on a **rally effect**, a short-lived boost in presidential public support that makes many MCs reluctant to take any political actions that open them to the criticism that they do not support the troops or are disloyal in time of war.

Yet even in this instance where presidential policy making influence is highest, it is not without congressional constraints. The most careful study yet done on congressional checks on presidential war powers offers a powerful conclusion that even war-making decisions are never devoid of political considerations that make Congress relevant. A careful analysis of presidential use of force since World War II shows that

- presidents who face Congress controlled by the opposition party send troops into harm's way less frequently than those whose political party controls at least one chamber of Congress;
- the greater the partisan opposition the president faces in Congress, the less likely a crisis is to produce a military response; and
- the greater the partisan opposition the president faces in Congress, the longer presidents wait between the onset of a crisis and an eventual use of force.[18]

The study concludes by saying, "presidents consistently heed the distinctly political threat posed by large, cohesive, and opposing congressional majorities—a threat that is all too often latent, but that when mobilized, materially affects the president's efforts to rally public support for an ongoing deployment and to communicate the nation's foreign policy commitments to both allies and adversaries abroad."[19]

Thus, the degree to which Congresses challenge presidents over foreign policy making in general vary over time, by the type of issues in play, and by the partisan composition of Congress compared to that of the presidency. Across the entire post–World War II period, the frequency of congressional activity in foreign policy making has generally decreased over time but *congressional assertiveness—being willing to question or challenge what the president wants—has increased over time.* From the end of World War II until around 1958, Congress was largely supportive of the president's foreign policy agenda which was dominated by Cold War issues. From 1958 until 1967, Congress became increasingly likely to challenge the president's foreign policy wishes. Some MCs thought presidents were not pressing the Cold War against the Soviets enough, while others began wondering if the Cold War was necessary. From 1968 through the 1980s, Congress was both active in and assertive of its own prerogatives in foreign policy making. Thus, from the height of the Vietnam War to the end of the Cold War, Congress was quite willing to challenge presidential foreign policy initiatives. Since the end of the Cold war until the present, Congress has returned to being less active in foreign policy making but more willing to challenge the president when it decides to act.[20]

Conclusion

In summary, while the role of the president in making U.S. foreign policy should never be underestimated, neither should the congressional role be unnecessarily minimized. Congress routinely sets the legal, financial, or political parameters of what an administration can do in foreign affairs, and at times the basic direction of the ship of state itself.

Glossary Terms

Congressional foreign policy entrepreneurs   those MCs who choose to act on their own foreign policy agendas rather than await administration action on those issues. They are policy innovators.

Normal trade status   previously known as most favored nation status, it means that any state having such status with the United States will get the same, best deal on a trade policy matter that any other state gets from the United States.

Rally effect   the boost in presidential support or popularity by the public during a crisis or emergency, which is usually short lived.

Endnotes

1. See George Crile, *Charlie Wilson's War: The Extraordinary Story of the Largest Covert Operation in History* (New York, NY: Atlantic Monthly Press, 2003); also these facts were confirmed in an interview Ralph Carter conducted with Charlie Wilson on September 3, 2008, at the TCU campus in Fort Worth, TX.
2. For more on congressional foreign policy entrepreneurs, see Ralph G. Carter and James M. Scott, *Choosing to Lead: Understanding Congressional Foreign Policy Entrepreneurs* (Durham, NC: Duke University Press, 2009).
3. Interview with the author, Fort Worth, TX, November 20, 2001.
4. Interview with the author, Fort Worth, TX, November 20, 2001.
5. Nancy Pelosi, "Pelosi Remarks at Congressional Ceremony Commemorating the 60th Anniversary of the Korean War," PRNewswire-USNewswire/, June 24, 2010,

available online at http://www.prnewswire.com/news-releases/pelosi-remarks-at
-congressional-ceremony-commemorating-the-60th-anniversary-of-the-korean
-war-97084504.html.

6. Carter and Scott, *Choosing to Lead*.
7. Carter and Scott, *Choosing to Lead*.
8. See Richard F. Fenno, *Congressmen in Committees* (Boston, MA: Little, Brown, & Co., 1973).
9. For more on these policy cue-givers, see John W. Kingdon, *Congressmen's Voting Decisions* (3rd ed.) (Ann Arbor, MI: University of Michigan Press, 1989).
10. For more on these four avenues, see Carter and Scott, *Choosing to Lead*.
11. For more on this, see Henry S. Reuss, *When Government Was Good: Memories of a Life in Politics* (Madison, WI: University of Wisconsin Press, 1999).
12. Reuss, *When Government Was Good*.
13. Loch K. Johnson, *A Season of Inquiry: The Senate Intelligence Investigation* (Lexington, KY: University Press of Kentucky, 1985, p. 57).
14. Richard F. Grimmitt, "Arms Sales: Congressional Review Process," Congressional Research Service Report for Congress, January 8, 2010, RL31675.
15. See Steven W. Hook and Franklin Barr Lebo, "U.S.-China Trade Relations: Privatizing Foreign Policy," in Ralph G. Carter (ed.), *Contemporary Cases in U.S. Foreign Policy: From Terrorism to Trade* (5th ed.) (Washington, DC: CQ Press, 2014).
16. For more on these efforts, see Carter and Scott, *Choosing to Lead*.
17. Matti Friedman and Matthew Lee, "Pelosi Welcomes Netanyahu: 'We in Congress Stand by Israel,' " *The Huffington Post*, March 23, 2010, available online at http://www.huffingtonpost.com/2010/03/23/pelosi-welcomes-netanyahu_n_510229.html.
18. William G. Howell and Jon C. Pevehouse, *While Dangers Gather: Congressional Checks on Presidential War Powers* (Princeton, NJ: Princeton University Press, 2007).
19. Howell and Pevehouse, *While Dangers Gather*, p. 222.
20. James M. Scott and Ralph G. Carter, "Acting on the Hill: Congressional Assertiveness in U.S. Foreign Policy," *Congress & the Presidency* 29 (2002), 151–169.

CHAPTER 8

Pluralist Policy Processes and Societal Actors

This rally against the role played by AIPAC—the American Israel Public Affairs Committee—demonstrates the degree of influence an interest group can be seen as having in U.S. foreign policy.

Source: Alex Wong/Getty Images News/Getty Images

LEARNING OBJECTIVES

- Explain how a pluralist policy process differs from governmental policy processes.

- Name the different types of domestic foreign policy–making actors.

- Identify the ways political culture and public attitudes

and opinion can influence policy makers.

- Assess which governmental policy makers may be most open to domestic foreign policy influences.

Introduction

In a democracy, the consideration of the public's needs and wants takes on considerable importance. Yet, who comprises the public and what shapes their thinking about foreign policy? These are important questions; the answers are not always self-evident. Moreover, since members of the public are by definition not government officials themselves, they must find ways to influence those officials who can directly make the decisions that shape foreign policy. The way the public engages in foreign policy making is through pluralist policy processes. We first focus on the nature of such processes and then on the types of actors that rely on these processes for a voice in foreign policy making. Then we can examine the types of inputs that motivate those actors and what such actors convey into the policy process, and finally we will examine how societal actors impact foreign policy making and the effects they have on policy—with a particular interest in the types of issues that lend themselves most to public inputs.

Pluralist Policy Processes

Prior to this point, we have discussed how government officials use their formal and informal powers to make U.S. foreign policy. But the United States is a democracy, which raises the question of how the public's views are considered in policy making. An idealized vision of democratic foreign policy making is easily described. Knowing that they are affected by foreign policy (in terms of the external events, threats, and opportunities facing the country), in an ideal world members of the U.S. public would care about these matters, think about these matters, and convey their thoughts to their elected officials who then heed the public's input in foreign policy making to do what contributes to the greater good. The question becomes, to what extent does that really happen?

Most observers would say "not often." There are several reasons why this ideal version of public participation is rarely met. First, most Americans are not that informed about foreign policy. Only around a quarter of the U.S. public actually keeps up with foreign policy news and events on a consistent basis.[1] Most Americans are too busy focusing on their own lives, interests, and responsibilities to take the time needed to educate themselves on foreign policy issues.

Second, if Americans did take the time to educate themselves on foreign policy issues, the process of communicating their ideas to elected officials is not easy. If they want to go beyond contacting the White House (via phone, fax, e-mail, Facebook, Twitter, etc.), citizens must identify at least one or more of the three members of Congress (MCs) who represent them—the two senators and the one representative. They may also decide to contact even more MCs to make sure their message gets out. Then they must determine how best to contact these officials—again, by phone, fax, e-mail, Facebook, Twitter, the officials' websites, and so on. All this takes time and some perseverance. Some will prefer to communicate face-to-face with elected representatives, which means getting appointments either in Washington or when the official is back home in the state or district. Anyone who has sought personal meetings with MCs will tell you that it usually takes weeks or even months to get on their schedule, if you can get on it at all. None of this is easy or quick, and relatively few Americans go to such efforts.

So how do public sentiments get communicated to policy makers? The answer lies in the **pluralist policy process**. Starting in the 1950s, observers began talking about how individuals got their interests and sentiments expressed to relevant policy makers *through the actions of organized groups to which these individuals belonged.*

While it takes a lot of effort for individuals to go through the steps mentioned to influence their elected representatives, group membership can make that process easier. By joining a group that shares interests, group members can pool their resources—for example through group dues—and sponsor the effort of a few of their members (or professional **lobbyists** hired for this purpose) to communicate the group's wishes to policy makers. Thus, governmental policy is shaped through the competition of these groups in gaining the ears of government officials to persuade the officials to act as the groups prefer. If groups are effective in getting their message to the targeted policy makers and are taken seriously by policy makers, then policy makers will take the groups' views into consideration when making foreign policy.[2] Consider this a form of mediated democracy, in which the groups serve as the agents for their members who are their principals.[3] So the essence of pluralist policy processes is that groups compete for the attention of policy makers, so that their interests get represented when decisions are made, and *there is a presumption that no particular group dominates foreign policy decision making all the time.* This last point means that pluralism is the opposite of **elitism**, the idea that a small group regularly dominates foreign policy making. So if no one group dominates foreign policy making, what types of groups get involved in this competition for influence? We turn to that next.

Societal Actors

Four sets of societal actors routinely get involved in influencing foreign policy. One type—interest groups—comes immediately to mind after our discussion of pluralist policy processes. However, think tanks, the mass media, and individual opinion leaders also play important roles. These are illustrated in Figure 8.1, but as you look at it, remember that these multiple interest groups, think tanks, media outlets, and individual opinion leaders also interact with each other as they are trying to influence governmental policy makers. Let's discuss each of these types of actors in turn.

Interest Groups

When citizens come together around a common interest, they can influence policy makers based on their numbers as potential voters, the amounts of campaign contributions they can provide, their ability to get the ear of policy makers, or even their ability to get their members elected or appointed to foreign policy-making roles. A good example of several of these methods can be seen in the activities of the **Cuban American National Foundation (CANF)**.

Created in 1981 by Jorge Mas Canosa and others, with the assistance of President Ronald Reagan's first National Security Adviser Richard Allen, CANF quickly became the dominant political voice of the Cuban-American community. Mas was a Cuban exile who participated in the failed 1961 U.S.-sponsored Bay of Pigs invasion that sought to overthrow Fidel Castro's communist regime in Cuba. Thereafter, he built a personal fortune through a family-run engineering firm in Miami and reportedly maintained close ties with former colleagues-in-arms in the CIA. He established personal relationships with virtually all the leading elected officials in Florida and called on them often to press for their support of anti-Castro policies. Mas also used his friendship with Jeb

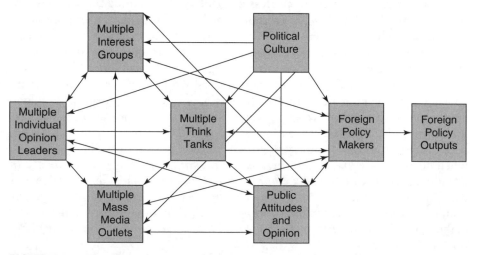

FIGURE 8.1 The Pluralist Policy Process

Bush, the son of the then Vice President George H.W. Bush, to help gain access to officials in the Reagan White House. As far as the Reagan administration was concerned, CANF became *the* voice of the Cuban-American community, and the Reagan administration embraced CANF's uncompromising anti-Castro stance as part of the Reagan Doctrine's emphasis on rolling back prior communist advances.[4]

Starting in the early 1980s, CANF pushed for a variety of anti-Castro initiatives. One involved U.S.-sponsored anti-Castro broadcasts into Cuba. The Reagan administration got behind the idea, as did local Florida officials. As a result, Congress approved the funding and U.S.-sponsored Radio Marti began broadcasting into Cuba in 1985 and, with the help of Senator Lawton Chiles (D-FL), TV Marti began broadcasting in 1990. CANF also owned its own radio station in Miami, broadcasting anti-Castro–themed messages to the local Cuban-American population to keep them mobilized and on message. Another successful foreign policy initiative backed by CANF was the granting of automatic asylum status for any Cuban exile arriving in the United States.[5]

In 1992, two friends of CANF, Senator Bob Graham (D-FL) and Representative Robert Torricelli (D-NJ), sponsored the Cuban Democracy Act that tightened the existing U.S. economic embargo against Cuba in a variety of ways, most importantly by applying it to the foreign subsidiaries of U.S.-based corporations and penalizing foreign corporations that did business in Cuba. However, it also exempted shipments to Cuba of food and medical supplies from the embargo. Many Cubans were suffering after the fall of the Soviet Union, because the Soviets had previously subsidized the Cuban economy. In an election year, the Cuban Democracy Act passed quickly, and when President George H.W. Bush signed the bill into law in Miami, CANF rewarded his reelection campaign with a $550,000 contribution.[6]

Following the 1992 election of Bill Clinton as president, Miami media sources reported that the president-elect planned to nominate Mario Baeza, a Cuban-American attorney working at a prestigious New York law firm, to be the new assistant secretary of state for inter-American affairs. CANF protested the appointment to Senator Graham, Representative Torricelli, and Senator Bill Bradley (D-NJ). The three MCs alerted Clinton to the fact that CANF opposed the nomination of anyone who was not endorsed by CANF, and Baeza subsequently did not get the nomination. Clinton's willingness to help CANF may have been influenced by the fact that when he needed help earlier that year as a presidential candidate, CANF stepped up. In April 1992 when Clinton's presidential campaign was in dire need of additional cash, CANF came through. In a visit to Florida, Clinton attended two fund-raisers sponsored by CANF that raised $275,000 which helped keep his campaign alive.[7]

Any interest group that is well funded and well organized like CANF has the potential for influence. However, CANF's influence was magnified by the residential locations of many of its members. Many of them live in Florida where CANF is based. Large numbers of CANF members also live in New Jersey and New York. These states have large numbers of Electoral College votes, so any organization that can promise to deliver or withhold significant numbers of voters in such states becomes very important to anyone who hopes to win the presidency.

The example of CANF shows the variety of ways in which interest groups can influence foreign policy through pluralist processes. They can gain the ear of elected officials, promote the sponsorship of desired legislation, and use both their voting strength and campaign dollars to help get those friendly to the group's aims elected to office. They can also withhold their help from anyone who has previously benefitted from their votes or campaign contributions and who has subsequently displeased them, or they can direct campaign assistance to those who run against unfriendly elected officials. They can also seek to get their members or similarly motivated individuals appointed to foreign policy–making positions in presidential administrations or elected to Congress. Finally, they can use their contacts in the media to get their message out to the local or national community.

CANF also provides another lesson in terms of interest group influence. Just as a group can rise in influence quickly, it can decline quickly as well. CANF's close identification with the charismatic Jorge Mas Canosa meant that the group was weakened following the death of Mr. Mas in 1997. Infighting among top members led to a number of them splitting off in 2001 to form a new group, the Cuban Liberty Council. At this point, it is unclear that either CANF or the Cuban Liberty Council possesses the kind of foreign policy influence CANF could claim in the 1980s and 1990s. For a more recent example of such interest group influence, see Box 8.1.

In a democracy where all have the legal right to petition their government for the redress of grievances, well-organized and well-funded interest groups may be important players in shaping U.S. foreign policy. They become even more influential when they informally form alliances with bureaucratic agencies and MCs who share their interests. When you get a bureaucratic agency that wants to implement a program, an interest group or set of interest groups that want to benefit from that program, and MCs who want to authorize and fund it, this combination is called a **subgovernment** or iron triangle, and it can be very difficult to oppose it over the long term.[8]

An interesting example comes in the area of agricultural sales. U.S. agribusinesses continually desire new markets for their products, a desire shared by the MCs who represent farming constituencies and bureaucrats at the Department of Agriculture's Foreign Agricultural Service (FAS) who want to promote U.S. agricultural sales. As suggested by the CANF example, an underserved market for U.S. food products can be found just 95 miles south of Key West, Florida. Beginning in the early 1960s, U.S. companies were barred from doing business with Fidel Castro's communist regime in Cuba. Yet Cuba has to import food, and over time watching other countries sell food to Cuba became painful to the U.S. agribusiness industry. Led by agribusiness giants like ADM (Archer Daniels Midland), U.S. food producers began asking MCs and officials at the USDA's FAS why these corporations had to stand idly by and watch their international competition make profits by selling food to Cuba. Consistent pressure from groups like ADM and the officials at FAS led the largely Republican

BOX 8.1

Nuclear Proliferation, U.S. Law, and the Power of Organized Interests

An international set of rules known as the nuclear nonproliferation regime exists to control the spread of nuclear weapons, because these weapons are seen by the international community as inherently destabilizing world peace and order. According to the regime, nuclear "haves" are not to provide nuclear weapons to nuclear "have-nots," and nuclear "have-nots" are not to seek nuclear weapons. The United States is one of the original signatories of the Nuclear Nonproliferation Treaty on which this regime is based and has consistently supported nonproliferation efforts in the past. Now comes the curious case of India.

As one of the few states never to sign the Nonproliferation Treaty, India was legally free to test nuclear weapons, which it did successfully in 1998. However, under the terms of the U.S. Arms Export Control Act of 1976, such a nuclear test triggered automatic economic sanctions by the United States against India. Yet the continuing rise of China as an economic and military power, and the rise of India as the world's largest democracy and a potential counterweight to China in Asia, put the U.S. policy of penalizing India as a nuclear proliferator in question. What was more important: upholding U.S. law and the nonproliferation regime or reaching out to improve U.S.-Indian relations for the strategic and economic advantages such a move offered in Asia? There were compelling arguments on both sides of the debate.

The relatively new India lobby stepped in to tip the balance of this debate. Indian-Americans are one of the fastest growing ethnic groups in the U.S. population, they are found in virtually all the major metropolitan areas of the country, and they have a median family income almost twice the national average. Perhaps not surprisingly, the House of Representatives India Caucus comprises about a quarter of the House membership, and the Friends of India Caucus comprises about 20% of the Senate. Multiple Indian-American interest groups now exist, such as the U.S.-India Business Council, the Confederation of Indian Industry, and the Indian-American Republican Council. To coordinate these and other efforts, there is also a **U.S.-India Political Action Committee (USINPAC)** modeled on the example of the highly influential AIPAC. After 1998, these interest groups pushed to get U.S. sanctions reversed and to promote a close working relationship between the United States and India on nuclear technology matters—despite India's prior nuclear weapons test and failure to sign the Nonproliferation Treaty.

Most of the sanctions against India were waived by President Bill Clinton before he left office and by President George W. Bush in his first year in office. However, the crowning achievement of the India lobby's efforts was the 2005 U.S.-Indian nuclear cooperation agreement, which covered a wide range of activities related to the civilian use of nuclear power but not related to nuclear weaponry. In essence, India would be able to have its cake and eat it too; it could get the benefits of access to U.S. nuclear technology and nuclear fuel for civilian use, protected by the rules of the nuclear nonproliferation regime, but the nuclear nonproliferation regime would not apply to India's nuclear weapons program.

The agreement on U.S.-Indian cooperation needed authorizing legislation in the form of two bills—one exempting India from the Arms Export Control Act and the other approving the nuclear cooperation agreement itself. A number of Indian-American groups led by USINPAC swarmed Capitol Hill, pressing their case, as did the highly regarded professional lobbying firm they hired—Barbour, Griffith, and Rogers (the BGR Group, which was formed by three former White House aides from the Reagan and George H.W. Bush administrations) and Lockheed Martin Corporation (the largest U.S. defense contractor). Also pressing for the agreement were representatives of General Electric and Westinghouse, two of the major U.S. manufacturers of nuclear power reactors. After an intensive lobbying effort, the legislation passed overwhelmingly in both the House and the Senate.

So what do you think is the best course of action in a case like this? Should long-standing U.S. and international law regarding the proliferation of nuclear weapons be upheld, or should strategic and domestic considerations—reaching out to an emerging economic and military power that can serve as a counterbalance to China in Asia as well as helping U.S. corporations—override legal principles?

Sources: Zachary Fillingham, "Privatized Foreign Policy: The India Lobby," *Geopolitical Monitor Situation Reports*, October 30, 2009; Jason A. Kirk, "Indian-Americans and the U.S.–India Nuclear Agreement: Consolidation of an Ethnic Lobby?" *Foreign Policy Analysis* 4 (2008), 275-300; Dianne E. Rennack, "India and Pakistan: U.S. Economic Sanctions," Congressional Research Service Report for Congress, February 3, 2003. Gerald Felix Warburg, "Nonproliferation Policy Crossroads: The U.S.-India Nuclear Cooperation Agreement," in Ralph G. Carter (ed.) *Contemporary Cases in U.S. Foreign Policy: From Terrorism to Trade*, 5th ed. Washington, DC: CQ Press, forthcoming 2014.

representatives and senators from areas like the Great Plains and Midwest to question why the Cuba embargo should apply to *humanitarian* goods like food sales. If Cuba was going to buy food from someone anyway, why should U.S. food producers be denied a chance at this market? The Trade Sanctions Reform and Export Enhancement Act of 2000 was the result, which allowed food and other humanitarian aid to be exempted from economic sanctions.[9]

In 2001, ADM became the first U.S. company to sign a contract with the Cuban government since the embargo began.[10] Since then, U.S. food sales to Cuba have averaged $350 million per year, with a high of $700 million in 2008 just before the beginning of the Great Recession.[11] In this case, the combined efforts of big business, consistent pressure from the FAS, and the large number of farm state MCs were able to overcome the active resistance of the CANF, which as just noted had been weakened by the death of Mr. Mas in 1997.[12] More generally, business-backed interest groups typically triumph over ideologically based interest groups when their positions come into direct conflict, and interest groups that are components of a subgovernment generally prevail over interest groups that are acting without such strong congressional and bureaucratic support. But interest groups are not the only types of groups active in shaping U.S. foreign policy. Think tanks often play key roles as well.

Think Tanks

Privately funded research organizations, commonly referred to as **think tanks**, are another societal source of foreign policy input. For years, entities like the Council on Foreign Relations, the Business Roundtable, the Brookings Institution, and the Center for Strategic and International Studies have studied problems and issued reports, and their representatives have testified before Congress and gone out into local communities to try to educate the public and policy makers on their preferred foreign policy positions. In extreme cases, think tanks can have profound influences, as shown in Box 8.2.

BOX 8.2

The Project for the New American Century and the War in Iraq

Possibly the most controversial think tank influencing U.S. foreign policy in the last half century was the **Project for the New American Century (PNAC)**. Founded in 1997 by William Kristol (editor of the *Weekly Standard* and former chief of staff for Vice President Dan Quayle) and Robert Kagan (a senior associate at the Carnegie Endowment for International Peace and a writer for the *Weekly Standard* and the *Washington Post*), it brought together a group of neoconservatives who believed the 21st century represented a unique opportunity. Since the United States was no longer opposed by a superpower like the Soviet Union, PNAC members felt the United States should use its power to spread its values abroad, in short, to do good.[13]

All think tanks benefit from getting their members placed in policy-making positions, but PNAC was extremely successful in that regard. A number of the original signers of its statement of principles went on to important policy-making posts in the George W. Bush administration. They included presidential Special Assistants Elliott Abrams and Zalmay Khalizad (who also later became ambassador to Iraq, ambassador to Afghanistan, and ambassador to the UN) as well as Vice President Dick Cheney and his Chief of Staff Lewis ("Scooter") Libby and Deputy Assistant for National Security Affairs Aaron Friedberg. Those found in the Defense Department included Secretary Donald Rumsfeld, Deputy Secretary Paul Wolfowitz, and Assistant Secretary Peter Rodman. Those in the State Department included Undersecretary Paula Dobriansky and State Department Counselor Eliot Cohen. Even presidential brother Jeb Bush was an original signatory of PNAC's statement of principles.[14] Thus, members of PNAC were well placed to press their views on U.S. foreign policy.

One of their foremost views advocated the overthrow of the Iraqi regime of

Saddam Hussein. In 1998, they wrote an open letter to President Clinton calling for the removal of Saddam Hussein's regime from power in Iraq, noting that the costs of leaving him in power and accepting the risks of his regime acquiring weapons of mass destruction were greater than the costs of removing him from power by any means necessary. In addition to Rumsfeld, Wolfowitz, Rodman, Abrams, Khalizad, and Dobriansky, other signatories to that letter who would become officials in the George W. Bush administration included Richard Armitage (deputy secretary of state), Jeffrey Bergner (assistant secretary of state), John Bolton (U.S. ambassador to the UN), Robert Zoellick (U.S. trade representative and deputy secretary of state), and Richard Perle (chair, Defense Policy Board Advisory Committee).[15] A similar open letter was also written to House Speaker Newt Gingrich (R-GA) and Senate Majority Leader Trent Lott (R-MS).[16]

Given that PNAC members were so open in calling for the removal of Saddam Hussein from power and that they later assumed high-level positions in George W. Bush administration, it seems hardly surprising that the Bush administration would undertake the overthrow of that regime. Admittedly, President Bush could have overruled all these voices had he disagreed with their policy preferences, but he did not disagree. Bush had his own reasons for wanting Saddam Hussein removed from power, as he once noted in remarks in Houston ("after all, this is the man who tried to kill my dad").[17] Still, he brought these individuals into his administration in high positions knowing what their preferences were, and their policy

preferences seemed to reinforce—not challenge—his own.

Given how publicly the PNAC was associated with the war in Iraq and how that war did not go according to PNAC's predictions—never finding the weapons of mass destruction thought to be there, the resulting breakdown of societal order following the U.S. invasion, the long military occupation and difficult insurgency campaign that resulted, the challenges of rebuilding Iraq with insufficient planning, and so on—the Project for the New American Century did not survive. By December 2006, it had essentially shut down and all that remained was the website and one employee.[18] In 2009, a new think tank was established: The **Foreign Policy Initiative (FPI)**. Two of its four original directors were William Kristol and Robert Kagan.[19]

So what do you think? Should any one think tank have its fingerprints all over a policy issue as important as going to war, or is the apparent influence of this group simply the result of a series of personnel appointments that presidents have every right to make?

Sources: The Project for The New American Century website, available at: http://www .newamericancentury.org/; Statement of Principles, The Project for The New American Century, June 3, 1997, available at: http://www .newamericancentury.org/statementofprinciples .htm; Letter to President Clinton on Iraq, January 26, 1998, available at: http://www .newamericancentury.org/iraqclintonletter.htm; Letter to Gingrich and Lott on Iraq, available at: http://www.newamericancentury.org/iraqletter 1998.htm; CNN Saturday Edition, October 12, 2002, available at: http://transcripts.cnn .com/TRANSCRIPTS/0210/12/tt.00.html; Paul Reynolds, "End of the Neo-Con Dream: The Neo-Conservative Dream Faded in 2006", BBC News, December 21, 2006, available at: http://news.bbc .co.uk/2/hi/middle_east/6189793.stm; Directors and Staff, The Foreign Policy Initiative, available at: http://www.foreignpolicyi.org/about/staff.

The number of think tanks has proliferated over time; however, focusing on just one can help illustrate the ways these entities can influence foreign policy. The **Washington Institute for Near East Policy (WINEP)** was created in 1985 to promote U.S. national interests in the Middle East and, according to its critics, to ensure that U.S. Mideast policy remained solidly pro-Israeli. It made a splash in 1988 when it issued a report calling for the United States to resist growing international pressures to push for a comprehensive peace agreement between Israel and the Palestinians at that time, instead calling for the United States to wait to do so until local "conditions have ripened."[20] The incoming George H.W. Bush administration embraced the report and its recommendation, which is not surprising since six members of the WINEP study group who prepared the report went to work for the Bush administration. Lawrence Eagleburger became deputy secretary of state (and later served briefly as secretary of state), Dennis Ross headed the State Department's Policy Planning Bureau, Francis Fukuyama and John Hannah went to work for Ross at the Policy Planning Bureau, Richard Haass became the Middle East expert on the National Security Council Staff, and Harvey Sicherman became a speech writer for Secretary of State James Baker.[21]

The two main founders of WINEP came to it from the **American Israel Public Affairs Committee (AIPAC)**, the leading voice for the pro-Israel lobby in the United States. The founding president and chairman of WINEP was Barbi Weinberg, a former AIPAC vice president.[22] WINEP's founding director was Martin Indyk, previously a research director at AIPAC. During the 1991 Palestinian–Israeli peace talks in Madrid, Indyk was there as an expert commentator for CNN.[23] During the subsequent Clinton administration, Indyk served as special assistant to the president and senior director for Near East and South Asia at the National Security Council, twice as the U.S. ambassador to Israel, and as assistant secretary of state for near eastern affairs.[24] Under Secretary of State Hillary Rodham Clinton, he served as the Obama administration's special envoy to the Israeli–Palestinian peace talks.

Individuals like Eagleburger, Ross, Fukuyama, Hannah, Haass, Sicherman, and Indyk are not the only people associated with WINEP to serve in policy-making positions. WINEP's board of advisors has included five former secretaries of state (Warren Christopher, Alexander Haig, Henry Kissinger, George Schultz, and Eagleburger), a national security adviser (Robert McFarlane), a director of central intelligence (James Woolsey), an ambassador to Israel (Samuel Lewis), a senior diplomat of ambassadorial rank (Max Kampelman), and a secretary of the air force (James Roche).[25] Thus, another obvious way of having influence in the policy-making process is to have one's own people or other sympathizers in policy-making positions. WINEP has been quite successful in that regard.

Think tanks are research organizations, so an important means of influence is their ability to conduct research on policy-relevant topics. WINEP lists its country research areas as Egypt, Iran, Iraq, Israel, Jordan, Lebanon, the Persian Gulf states, Syria, Turkey, the region of North Africa, and the Palestinian people. Its other research programs include Arab and Islamic politics, democracy and reform in the region, the intersection of energy and economics and geopolitics, military and security issues, the peace process, the proliferation of weapons of mass destruction, and terrorism, in addition to basic U.S. foreign policy positions.[26]

Once a think tank has research findings or policy views it believes could improve policy making, it must get those out before the policy makers and the public. WINEP provides a number of experts who try to guide policy makers whenever possible. Such advising often occurs in private meetings with administration officials. On the other hand, some of it occurs in public before congressional committees. In 2010, WINEP researchers testified in person or provided written testimony:

- About U.S. policy toward the Iran reform movement before the House Foreign Affairs Committee
- About the Middle East peace process before the Senate Foreign Relations Committee
- About efforts to combat money laundering that could be financing terrorism before the Subcommittee on Oversight and Investigations of the House Financial Services Committee
- About disrupting the international financing of terrorist groups before the Subcommittee on Crime and Drugs of the Senate Judiciary Committee
- About new directions in the U.S.-Turkish relationship before the House Foreign Affairs Committee[27]

Think tanks also try to educate the public as well as government officials, particularly the **attentive public** that pays attention to foreign affairs and might also try to influence policy makers. To do so, WINEP publishes and sells books, presidential study group reports, monographs, conference proceedings, military research papers, special studies, policy papers, and research notes that are available through its website. Its policy experts also reach out to the public through media appearances. In just one month, for example (September 2010), WINEP experts appeared in the following press outlets:[28]

- ABC Radio
- Agence France-Presse
- Al-Arabiya
- Al-Jazeera
- *Atlantic Monthly* (twice)
- BBC (twice)
- Canada's CBC
- Canada's CTV
- CBS
- *Chicago Tribune*
- China's Xinhua
- *Christian Science Monitor*
- ForeignPolicy.com
- Fox News (twice)
- Israel's *Haaretz* (twice)
- Israel's *Jerusalem Post*
- *New York Times* (twice)

- PBS
- Politico.com (twice)
- Radio Free Europe/Radio Liberty
- *USA Today*

Older audiences may be reached via print outlets or through radio and television, whereas younger audiences may be reached through new media outlets. WINEP can be followed on Twitter, it has a Facebook page, it provides podcasts and videos via YouTube, and it provides RSS feeds as well.[29]

By being able to influence policy by getting its members or friends positioned in governmental office, by providing multiple means of advising policy makers, and by getting their message out to the public, WINEP and think tanks like it can be a force in helping shape U.S. foreign policy. It seems little wonder that some observers feel that think tanks are the crucial linchpin in the policy-making process in the United States.[30] But again, they are not the only influential societal actors shaping foreign policy. There is also the mass media to be considered.

The Mass Media

You might think of the mass media like a public utility; it is there to serve the greater good. However, the United States mass media also acts much like an interest group by what and how it chooses to cover. Here, the mass media includes news organizations such as the major national newspapers, wire services, television and radio networks, and Internet sites. At times it can also include the entertainment media such as movies or television programs that bear on specific foreign policy–related topics.

For the news media, the challenge is choosing what news to cover. There are far more news events than can be included in the typical daily newspaper, television or radio broadcast, or Internet websites. So what should be covered? Let's use an example to illustrate the dynamic of news coverage.

The Middle East is one of the regions of the world best covered by U.S. news media outlets. Mideast news stories routinely appear on the front page of the *New York Times* and often lead the international news segments of network broadcast news. Still, what someone chooses to cover makes a difference. Consider, for example, the government of Iran. Due to past history, Iran looms large among U.S. foreign policy concerns. During the Eisenhower administration, the CIA played an important role in overthrowing a democratically elected regime there in 1953 and putting Iran's young monarch—Shah Mohammad Reza Shah Pahlavi—in control of an oil-rich country in a strategic location. Over the years, U.S. support for the Shah continued even as his regime became increasingly corrupt and developed a reputation for widespread human rights abuses. Following Iran's 1979 Islamic Revolution, Iranian students stormed the U.S. embassy in Tehran and held 52 American diplomats hostage for over a year. Until the recent 2013 diplomatic breakthrough in which Iran agreed to reduce its nuclear fuel enrichment program and allow international inspections of its nuclear facilities in return for a limited lifting of some economic sanctions by the United

States and EU, Iran's Islamic leaders and elected officials routinely referred to the United States as "the Great Satan."

Given all the earlier discussion, it is not surprising that the U.S. news media watches Iranian events closely. For example, the presidential election there in 2009 was well covered, as a reform movement in Iran coalesced around the candidacy of Mir Hossein Mousavi who was thought to have a real chance of defeating President Mahmoud Ahmadinejad if the elections were conducted in a free and fair manner. However in a multicandidate election, official election results named Ahmadinejad the winner without even a runoff, and all three major opposition candidates rejected the results as rigged. Thousands of Iranians took to the streets to protest what many saw as the "stealing" of an election, and Iranian security forces used lethal force to break up the demonstrations. The Iranian government acknowledged several dozen deaths, but protesters claimed hundreds had been killed by the police and militia forces. All this was well covered in the U.S. media. When U.S. media outlets were prevented from filming demonstrations, they often turned to the demonstrators themselves, who had taken pictures and videos on their cell phones. Those were then shown on network news outlets in the United States. In particular, their photos and video of the shooting death of a young woman named Neda brought a human face to the suffering of the protesters.

Individually, President Ahmadinejad was also well covered in the U.S. news media. Like other world leaders, he came to the United States every fall to attend the opening session of the UN General Assembly. His speeches were typically included in the daily U.S. news, due to his tendency of making controversial statements. In the past he questioned whether the Holocaust really occurred during World War II and, in 2010, he asserted that the 9/11 attacks on the World Trade Center and Pentagon were the work of the United States itself—so as to have a justification to wage war on Islam. As is the case virtually every year, news coverage then showed other diplomats getting up and walking out of the room rather than listening to his heated rhetoric.

Based on this news coverage, many Americans know that Iran has long had a controversial regime that may be pursuing the development of nuclear weapons. Many think its former leader said "crazy" things, even if they cannot remember his name, and they may think he stole an election. Not surprisingly, they may perceive Iran to be a very anti-American place. While that impression may be somewhat moderated by the diplomatic breakthrough mentioned earlier, what many Americans may not know is that Iran represents a civilization that is 3500 years old, that its citizens are highly nationalistic, that Iran's president is not the most powerful official in the country, and that its young people—who make up the majority of its population—tend to be pro-Western if not actually pro-American in their personal attitudes. Because of the way news is covered, many Americans know a fair amount about Iran's government, but that does not mean what they know about Iran or Iranians is totally accurate.

U.S. policy toward Iran has come under challenge from at least one think tank. The **New America Foundation** has an Iran Project directed by Flynt Leverett, who resigned his position as the Mideast expert on the National

Security Council staff due to policy disagreements with the George W. Bush administration. Leverett thinks that the Obama administration's approach to Iran—like Bush's—is unnecessarily hostile and that U.S. interests in the entire region would be advanced by improved relations with the Iranian regime. He has used the New America website and its podcasts to launch two blogs about Iran—www.RaceForIran.com and www.GoingToTehran.com—to advance these ideas. Although some of Leverett's articles and op-ed columns have appeared in outlets such as the *New York Times* and Politico.com, to date other mass media outlets that reach far more Americans have not carried his message that Iran is a major regional player in the Middle East whose interests should be taken seriously by U.S. foreign policy makers. It seems the image of a "crazy" Iranian president and a rabidly anti-American Iranian religious leadership dominates the mainstream news, but the 2013 diplomatic breakthrough on Iran's nuclear program may soften that image.

Another way that the mass media may influence policy making is through films—both documentary and entertainment. Any film that informs and educates the public about a foreign policy–related issue can impact policy makers or those who have their ear. A good documentary example is *An Inconvenient Truth*, the Oscar-winning film about former Vice President Al Gore's effort to get people to take global climate change seriously. Based on viewing this film, many Americans now accept the premise that global climate change is occurring, it is impacted by human activity, and it should be on the foreign and domestic policy-making agenda.

There are far more examples of entertainment films that have impacted the public about foreign policy issues and the way the United States engages others beyond its borders. A number of films were made after the U.S. withdrawal from the Vietnam War, and most of them presented negative portrayals of engaging in counterinsurgency warfare or intervening in other people's civil wars. Movies such as *Platoon*, *Apocalypse Now*, and *Full Metal Jacket* made Americans question not only their country's foreign policy but also about their country's military. Then movies like *First Blood* (a.k.a. Rambo), *Top Gun*, and *An Officer and a Gentleman* made many Americans feel better about their military and its role in society. Today's generation of college students may know something of Somalia and the U.S. role there due to the film *Blackhawk Down*. They also may know about the Rwandan genocide from the film *Hotel Rwanda*, and about the war in Iraq from films such as *The Hurt Locker* and *The Green Zone*. Those interested in the world of intelligence and covert operations might have been attracted to films such as *The Good Shepherd*, *Syriana*, *Zero Dark Thirty*, or the four films in the *Bourne* series.

Finally, television also has an informative role for many Americans. A few years ago, many Americans got their ideas of the modern presidency from the television series *The West Wing*. More recently, viewers might assume the world of U.S. counterterrorism operations resembled that of the series *24*, while others might have seen the counterterrorism operations as more realistically portrayed in *N.C.I.S.—Naval Criminal Investigative Service*, its spinoff—*N.C.I.S. Los Angeles*, or in Showtime's *Homeland*. In short, a number of different mass media outlets provide some information on the external challenges and opportunities that U.S. foreign policy makers must address. But individual opinion leaders also try to shape foreign policy, and thus they must be considered an important societal actor as well.

Individual Opinion Leaders

Select individuals can influence public opinion in ways that shape policy. Celebrities can at times leverage their fame to bring attention to an issue. Actor George Clooney is a good example. While he has pushed a number of issues, two in particular stand out. The first was the relief effort for the survivors of the January 2010 earthquake in Haiti. Within 10 days of the earthquake, Clooney had lined up over 100 entertainment celebrities to appear on the telethon "Hope for Haiti Now" a two-hour program that was shown simultaneously and commercial-free on more than 25 commercial television networks in the United States and around the world. The global audience for the program was estimated at 640 million, and more than $50 million was raised for Haitian relief.[31] Clooney's efforts added public weight behind the efforts of the U.S. government to respond to the Haitian catastrophe.

However, Clooney is probably even better known for his long-term efforts to bring peace to Sudan. Initially, his efforts were to stop the genocide in the Darfur region of western Sudan. To that end, he appeared at a "Save Darfur" rally in Washington, DC, in 2005 and spent 10 days in Chad and Sudan in 2006. There he learned firsthand about the events in Darfur and made a television documentary ("A Journey to Darfur") about the conflict.[32] That same year he appeared before the UN Security Council with Nobel Peace Prize Winner Elie Wiesel to ask for UN intervention to stop the genocide, and he and fellow actor Don Cheadle went to Egypt and China to ask their governments to put more pressure on Sudan to stop the genocide.[33] In 2007, it was reported that he and his co-stars from the film *Ocean's 13* had contributed $750,000 to help the victims of the Sudanese genocide.[34] Further, Not on Our Watch—a group he co-founded with Brad Pitt, Matt Damon, Don Cheadle, Jerry Weintraub and David Pressman—raised over $9 million for Sudanese relief. For his efforts, he was appointed by the UN as a "Messenger of Peace in 2008."[35]

In 2010, Clooney turned his attention to the vote in Sudan to separate the country by allowing the southern portion to become independent. He traveled to southern Sudan with Ann Curry of the NBC *Today Show* where he talked to the people about the 2011 vote on splitting the country. Fearing the violence that might result from the vote, he returned to the United States and tried to spread the message that a diplomatic intervention prior to the vote could save countless lives. He appeared on the *Today Show*, he spoke at a meeting of the Council on Foreign Relations, and he briefed President Obama at the White House.[36] In short, many Americans—particularly those who follow celebrities and so-called soft news but not hard news —know something about Sudan and the events there because of the efforts of George Clooney and his colleagues.

However, one does not have to be a celebrity to have potential foreign policy influence. Greg Mortenson was a mountain climber who was aided by Pakistani villagers when he fell ill and got lost. He repaid them and others by building schools in very remote areas of both Pakistan and Afghanistan, and he has been sought out to give briefings at the Pentagon to military commanders involved in counterinsurgency operations on how to win the hearts and minds of Pakistanis and Afghans.[37] Another example is Armand Hammer, an American businessman who lived in the Soviet Union from 1921 until 1930. Because he had known Vladimir Lenin and Josef Stalin personally during those years, he came to know other later Soviet leaders as well. During the Cold War, he served as an informal adviser to multiple U.S. presidents regarding what the Soviet leaders might be thinking.[38] As these examples suggest, anyone who can get the ear of significant foreign policy makers has a chance to influence foreign policy, but the more important question is, what ideas do such societal actors introduce into the pluralist policy process? What motivates them to get involved? This is our next topic for discussion.

Motivating Inputs

Two very broad sets of societal motivations provide inputs that help shape U.S. foreign policy making. They are the impacts of political culture and of public attitudes and opinion. We discuss each of these next.

Political Culture

Political culture is another way of saying that most people in a country share an identifiable set of values or beliefs. One element of U.S. political culture is the belief in **American exceptionalism**, an idea actually older than the United States itself. As noted in Chapter 3, American exceptionalism holds that *the United States is not only different from other countries, it is better than other countries*. This idea originated with the first European colonists who came to the New World and marveled at the temperate climate and abundant resources. Luckily from the colonists' perspective, the indigenous Native Americans were relatively few in number and often friendly. Those who were unfriendly could not withstand the numbers of colonists who kept arriving or the firearms that those colonists brought with them.

In a nutshell, the colonists' perspective was that such a wonderful land available for their use must be a gift from God, and thus they must be very special people to deserve such a divine gift. Given their material success in this New World, they took it for granted that what worked for them here would also work elsewhere, and so they took it as a God-given obligation to share what they had learned with others.

Many Americans still feel they have an obligation to lead and help others in the world by sharing their values and wisdom. As Secretary of State Hillary Rodham Clinton told the Council on Foreign Relations in 2010:

The world is counting on us .... After years of war and uncertainty, people are wondering what the future holds, at home and abroad. So let me say it clearly: The United States can, must, and will lead in this new century.[39]

As it leads, the values the United States wants to share with others generally come from **liberalism**. As suggested in Chapter 2, traditional liberalism holds that the most important thing in society is the freedom and liberty of each individual, and thus while governments are necessary to do the things individuals cannot easily do for themselves, governments should be kept as small as possible so as not to trample on individual liberties. Since liberalism values the individual so much, democracy is the preferred form of government, as democracy gives free individuals a means by which they can directly participate in choosing who governs them. Finally, liberalism also believes that free-market capitalism is the best economic system, as it enables free individuals to pursue whatever activity they desire to make a living, with the corresponding opportunities to succeed or fail. These values also shape U.S. policy preferences. U.S. foreign policy proposals that do not fit within the parameters of American exceptionalism, individual rights, limited government, democracy, and capitalism become very hard to defend in the public sphere. But political culture is largely static. It set boundaries of acceptable policies. Public attitudes and opinions also play important roles.

Public Attitudes and Opinion

In a democracy, what the public thinks matters. Such public inputs can be either broad attitudes that do not quickly change or the public's opinion on specific issues at a given point in time which may change more quickly.

For broad public attitudes to be relatively stable over time, they must be based on fundamental concerns. While some will talk about Americans being liberal or conservative, the meaning of those labels is hard to pin down. "Liberal" compared to what? "Conservative" compared to what? A more precise way to capture fundamental attitudes about foreign policy is to ask two more specific questions: How do you feel about the use of military power (thus militant internationalism), and how do you feel about cooperating with others (thus cooperative internationalism)?

As Figure 8.2 shows, dichotomies on these two fundamental dimensions create four major attitudinal orientations to foreign policy: *internationalists* who support both cooperative and militant internationalism, *accommodationists* who support cooperative internationalism but oppose militant internationalism, *hardliners* who oppose cooperative internationalism but support militant internationalism, and *isolationists* who oppose both cooperative and militant internationalism.[40] Although U.S. leaders tend to be overrepresented in the internationalist and accommodationist categories and are rarely found in the isolationist category, the distribution of the public's attitudes is far more equal across all four of these attitudinal categories. A reasonable number of Americans fall into each one, with the smallest category being isolationists who generally still account for 18–20% of the public.[41] Thus, while not as

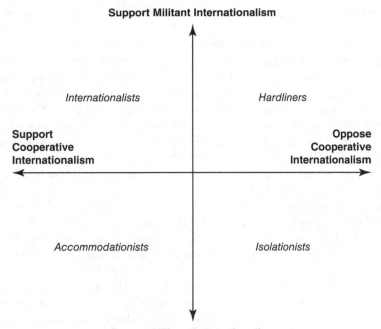

FIGURE 8.2 Foreign Policy Attitudinal Clusters

internationally oriented as its leaders, typically around 80% of Americans favor some form of international engagement. They just disagree on the nature of that engagement; should it emphasize cooperation, the use of force, or both? These attitudes tend to be reasonably stable over time and when they change, they generally change in incremental stages and in response to changes in the external policy environment.

In contrast to such broader attitudes, what Americans think on specific, short-term issues is called **public opinion**. Appointed officials may choose to ignore it, but elected officials normally give it at least some consideration when dealing with foreign policy problems and options. Our policy-making questions center around two concerns: whose opinions are considered and how much weight they are given.

Public opinion polls are a good starting point for measuring what the mass public thinks. For the president, the polls that matter most are national polls, which the national news media and polling organizations conduct regularly, as well as state-wide polls in key Electoral College states thought necessary for a first-term president to carry to win reelection. If those polls do not ask the questions presidents desire, they can commission their own private polls to get that better sense of what the public thinks. For members of the House and the Senate on the other hand, the polls that matter most are those that measure what the people think in their districts and states, respectively. If the local news media or university researchers back home do not conduct the polls MCs desire, those elected officials may commission their own private polls just as presidents do.

Yet general public opinion—whether local, state, or national—may not be what matters most for elected officials. Elected officials may care most about the opinions of those who consistently vote for them—their political base—or those who contribute money to their political campaigns. In the past, keeping track of these key audiences involved not only trips back home but fairly constant monitoring of phone calls, letters, visitors to the office, letters to the editor or editorial opinion columns in the newspapers back home, and so on. With the rise of electronic media, now elected officials monitor the opinions of those who care most about certain issues by tracking their incoming e-mail messages as well as messages posted on their websites and Facebook pages. Many MCs also still travel home on a frequent basis—some virtually every weekend—to keep in touch with what their constituents think.

Not only are elected officials at times clearly responsive to public opinion, but they also actively try to shape it in preferred directions. If successful, they can then cite the resulting public opinion as justification for their policy position. So, for example, if MCs oppose deeper U.S. military engagement in Yemen in the fight against religious extremism, then they may talk up the issue every chance they get with local opinion leaders back home—such as university audiences, the editorial staffs of the local newspapers, local "talk radio" hosts, civil society organizations like Rotary or Kiwanis Clubs or groups like the American Association of University Women, and meetings of their local political party organizations. Then if their public responds, they can say that the public wants what they want, thereby justifying their political stance on the issue.

The most interesting question when considering public attitudes and public opinion is not whether such inputs matter. In a democracy, they do. The more interesting questions are how much they matter and should they matter. For the former, how much public opinion and public attitudes matter varies considerably by issue. Americans care a lot about certain foreign policy issues, particularly issues they see impacting them directly, like homeland security concerns or whether they lose their jobs to foreign competitors. They appear to care less about those issues they do not see impacting them as directly, such as global climate change or poverty in North Korea. For issues that many in the public do not care about, the task for groups and individuals that do care about them is to make those issues meaningful to other Americans. That often means putting a human face on them. So, for example, promoting economic development in Pakistan may not move many Americans to action, but providing schools for Pakistani girls has resonated with many in the United States.[42]

But *should* public attitudes and public opinion play a role in foreign policy making? This may seem like an odd question in a democracy. However, since the days of philosophers like Aristotle and Plato, some have questioned trusting the public with important decisions. In the 19th century, France's Alexis de Tocqueville questioned whether democracy was the best form of government for conducting foreign affairs since the mass public was largely ignorant.

Public opinion polls in the 20th century continued to demonstrate considerable public ignorance about foreign affairs. As recently as the 1990s, 20% of American adults could not name a European country. Fourteen percent of American adults could not find the United States on a blank map.[43] In a 1994 study, adults in eight countries were sampled on four current events questions. In terms of their average correct scores, Germans were placed first, Italians second, French third, British fourth, Canadians fifth, Spanish sixth, Americans seventh, and Mexicans eighth.[44] Finally in another study from that decade, 41% of Americans thought the U.S. foreign aid program constituted the largest single item in the federal budget, at about 15% of the total federal budget. When asked how much it should be, a majority said 5%. They were probably surprised to learn that foreign aid spending actually represented only 1% of the federal budget.[45]

As noted by the **Almond–Lippmann consensus**, such public ignorance was cited for years as a reason for officials to ignore public opinion when making foreign policy decisions.[46] Yet, do such facts—that many in the public do not know where countries are on the map or who the Kurds are or how much the foreign aid budget may be—mean the public has no sense when it comes to foreign policy? Some would say "no" to this question. The lack of factual knowledge of international affairs does not necessarily preclude the public from having a reasoned point of view regarding the major foreign policy issues of the day. The question thus can be rephrased: If the public has such points of view on the issues facing the country, are their views reasonable guides to policy makers? More careful studies suggest that they are.

Whether looking at narrower issues such as use of force decisions or broader aspects of foreign policy, studies have shown that over time public opinion is rational, prudent, and purposive regarding such issues. Contrary to the Almond–Lippmann consensus, public opinion regarding the use of force seems neither volatile nor unstructured. Instead, it seems purposive and rational, moving in reasonable directions based on international events and the inputs of the media and experts. Further, public opinion can provide a check against risky choices. Over time public opinion tends to move foreign policy away from extremist positions and back to the center of the policy spectrum, thereby possibly lessening the chances of major foreign policy mistakes.[47] Put normatively, policy proposals that do not pass the public's "common sense" test may not deserve to be pursued or need to be better explained to the public by policy makers and opinion leaders.

The pluralist policy process is composed of all these societal actors and motivating factors. This process is depicted in Figure 8.1. We next turn to the means by which such societal actors influence foreign policy.

Influencing Foreign Policy

As indicated by the specific illustrations discussed earlier, the U.S. government's foreign policy–making system is unusually open to societal influences, and there are a variety of ways societal actors influence U.S. foreign policy. As noted earlier, public attitudes and political culture set broad parameters of acceptable options and choices for foreign policy makers. Public opinion also pushes policy makers in certain directions on specific foreign policy issues. If that direction is not what those policy makers desire, they can try to redirect public opinion more in line with their own preferences. Sometimes they are successful in shaping public opinion, and sometimes the effort does not work.

Interest groups, think tanks, the mass media, and individual opinion leaders also try to shape foreign policy options by framing the debate in certain ways. Interest groups like AIPAC and think tanks like WINEP stress the fact that Israel is the oldest democratic regime in the Middle East, thereby emphasizing the idea that U.S. and Israeli interests in the region will tend to converge. The mass media's coverage of an issue can help put that matter on the government's agenda, and how that issue is covered can shape how the matter is seen by the public and by elites. For example, a Clinton administration official once said that his position on the Kosovo conflict crystallized when his daughter asked how the United States could stand idly by and allow Kosovar's men to be killed and women to be raped. The daughter got her information by watching television news. Individuals who have the ear of governmental policy makers or who can bring media attention to foreign policy issues can also influence foreign policy, whether they are presidential confidants like Armand Hammer or celebrities like George Clooney. Finally, interest groups, think tanks, and individual opinion leaders take stands on specific issues and convey those to policy makers in every way they can—publicly, privately, in person or through the media, and through campaign assistance or opposition.

Conclusion

In short, domestic preferences often shape U.S. foreign policy. When public opinion, interest groups, think tanks, and individual opinion leaders give mixed signals regarding an issue, foreign policy makers are freer to pursue the policies of their choice. However, when domestic inputs to policy making tend to coalesce around a common view regarding an issue, it becomes harder and harder for foreign policy makers to ignore that view, and in a democracy, that should be expected. As George Washington Plunkitt of New York's Tammany Hall political machine once remarked, going as an individual to City Hall to get something changed is not likely to be successful. However, if you go and say you represent 50 voters who care as you do, your message is more likely to be heard by someone who has some power.[48] The same thing can happen in the realm of foreign policy making. The presence of societal pressures does not guarantee that policy makers will do what these domestic actors want. However, policy makers—and particularly elected ones—will take what societal actors want into consideration when making their foreign policy choices, and the degree to which policy makers do so depends on the importance of the specific societal actors to them and/or the degree to which those actors' preferences coalesce around a common viewpoint.

Glossary Terms

Almond–Lippmann consensus   the ideas that public opinion was too volatile and lacking in underlying knowledge structure to be useful to foreign policy makers and hence it had little impact on foreign policy making in a democracy. The name was based on the works of Gabriel Almond and Walter Lippmann.

American exceptionalism   the idea that the United States is not only different from other societies but also better than other societies.

American Israel Public Affairs Committee (AIPAC)   the leading interest group representing the pro-Israeli lobby in the United States.

Attentive public   the 20–25% of the public that pays regular attention to foreign affairs.

Cuban American National Foundation (CANF)   the leading interest group representing anti-Castro Cuban-Americans, very influential in the latter 20th century.

Elitism   the idea that a small group dominates foreign policy making.

Foreign Policy Initiative (FPI)   a think tank founded in 2009 that may be a follow-on to the Project for the New American Century. Two of its four original directors were William Kristol and Robert Kagan.

Liberalism   the dominant ideology on which the United States was founded, which stresses individual freedoms and limited government, a democracy, and a capitalist economy.

Lobbyists   those individuals who represent a group and who contact government officials to try to influence the decisions those officials make so the decisions reflect the group's policy wishes.

New American Foundation   a privately-funded, nonpartisan think tank to promote broader policy considerations. Its Iran Project questions some of the assumptions of U.S. policy toward Iran.

Pluralist policy process   the idea that the public gets its sentiments injected into the foreign policy-making process through membership in organized groups, and these organized groups then compete to get their preferences enacted into policy.

Project for the New American Century (PNAC)   a think tank founded in 1997, which advocated the use of American power to advance the spread of American ideals in the world; particularly associated with the 2003 U.S. invasion of Iraq.

Public opinion   what Americans think about specific issues.

Subgovernment   the combination of bureaucratic agencies, interest groups, and members of Congress who develop relationships over time and who share policy goals and reinforce each other's efforts to achieve them; sometimes referred to as iron triangles.

Think tanks   privately funded research organizations.

U.S.-India Political Action Committee (USINPAC)   the leading foreign policy arm of the India lobby, modeled after the American Israel Public Affairs Committee.

Washington Institute for Near East Policy (WINEP)   a privately funded research center or think tank dedicated to identifying U.S. national interests in the Middle East.

Endnotes

1. Gabriel Almond, *The American People and Foreign Policy* (New York, NY: Praeger, 1965); Ralph B. Levering, *The Public and American Foreign Policy, 1918–1978* (New York, NY: William Morrow, 1978).

2. These observers of the pluralist policy process included, for example, David B. Truman, *The Governmental Process* (New York, NY: Knopf, 1951) and Robert Dahl, *Who Governs?* (New Haven, CT: Yale University Press, 1961) and *Pluralist Democracy in America: Conflict and Consent* (Chicago, IL: Rand McNally, 1967).

3. For more on agents and principals, see James D. Fearon, "Signalling Foreign Policy Interests: Tying Hands versus Sinking Costs," *Journal of Conflict Resolution* 41 (1997), 68–90, and Walter Carlsnaes, "The Agency-Structure Problem in Foreign Policy Analysis," *International Studies Quarterly* 36 (1992), 245–270.

4. The Cuban American National Foundation website, available online at http://www.canf.org/; Jane Franklin, "The Cuba Obsession," *The Progressive*, July 1993, available online at http://andromeda.rutgers.edu/~hbf/canf.htm. For more on the Reagan Doctrine, see James M. Scott, *Deciding to Intervene: The Reagan Doctrine and American Foreign Policy* (Durham, NC: Duke University Press, 1996).

5. Franklin, "The Cuba Obsession."

6. Franklin, "The Cuba Obsession."

7. Franklin, "The Cuba Obsession."

8. Gordon Adams, *The Iron Triangle: The Politics of Defense Contracting* (Piscataway, NJ: Transaction Publishers, 1981).

9. FAS Online, available online at http://www.fas.usda.gov/itp/cuba/cuba-faq.html.

10. ADM History, available online at http://www.adm.com/en-US/company/history/Pages/2000-present.aspx.

11. Anya Landau French, "Boost Agricultural Trade with Cuba," *Atlanta Journal-Constitution*, June 3, 2010, available online at http://www.newamerica.net/publications/articles/2010/boost_agricultural_trade_with_cuba_32679.

12. CNN, "Few in Cuba Mourn Mas Canosa's Death," November 24, 1997, available online at http://www.cnn.com/WORLD/9711/24/cuba.mas.canosa/.

13. Project for the New American Century, available online at http://www.sourcewatch.org/index.php?title=Project_for_the_New_American_Century.

14. The Project for the New American Century, available online at http://www.informationclearinghouse.info/article1665.htm.

15. The Project for the New American Century, available online at http://www.informationclearinghouse.info/article1665.htm.

16. The Project for the New American Century, available online at http://www.informationclearinghouse.info/article1665.htm.

17. CNN Saturday Edition, October 12, 2002, available online at http://transcripts.cnn.com/TRANSCRIPTS/0210/12/tt.00.html.

18. Paul Reynolds, "End of the Neo-Con Dream: The Neo-Conservative Dream Faded in 2006," *BBC News*, December 21, 2006, available online at http://news.bbc.co.uk/2/hi/middle_east/6189793.stm.

19. Directors and Staff, The Foreign Policy Initiative, available online at http://www.foreignpolicyi.org/about/staff.

20. Quoted in Joel Beinin, "Money, Media, and Policy Consensus: The Washington Institute for Near East Policy," *Middle East Report* 180 (1993), 11.

21. Beinin, "Money, Media, and Policy Consensus," 10–15.

22. Mark H. Milstein, "Washington Institute for Near East Policy: An AIPAC 'Image Problem,' " *Washington Report on Middle East Affairs* (July 1991), 30.

23. Beinin, "Money, Media, and Policy Consensus."

24. "Brookings Experts: Vice President and Director Martin S. Indyk," available online at http://www.brookings.edu/experts/i/indykm.aspx.

25. Washington Institute for Near East Policy website, available online at http://www.washingtoninstitute.org/templateC11.php?CID=133&newActiveSubNav=Board%20of%20Advisors&activeSubNavLink=templateC11.php%3FCID%3D133&newActiveNav=aboutUs.

26. Washington Institute for Near East Policy website, available online at http://www.washingtoninstitute.org/templateI01.php.

27. Washington Institute for Near East Policy website, available online at http://www.washingtoninstitute.org/templateS03.php?contentType=Congressional_Testimony&subType1=eveType&subType2=Congressional+Testimony&year=2010.

28. Washington Institute for Near East Policy website, available online at http://www.washingtoninstitute.org/templateS03.php?contentType=InTheMedia&author=&SID=&year=&subType1=&subType2=&SortOrder=SortDateDESC&recordsPerPage=10&R=0.

29. Washington Institute for Near East Policy website, available online at http://www.washingtoninstitute.org/templateI01.php.

30. See Thomas R. Dye, *Who's Running America: The Bush Restoration* (7th ed.) (Upper Saddle River, NJ: Prentice Hall, 2002).

31. Alan Duke, "Telethon Tries to Raise 'Hope for Haiti,' " CNN Entertainment, January 22, 2010, available online at http://articles.cnn.com/2010-01-22/entertainment/haiti.telethon_1_haitian-people-telethon-donations?_s=PM:SHOWBIZ; Gil Kaufman, "Jay-Z, Justin Timberlake, Bono To Headline MTV's 'Hope For Haiti' Telethon: Bruce Springsteen, Coldplay, Alicia Keys and Christina Aguilera will also perform at the show, airing live Friday at 8 p.m. ET," MTV.com, January 19, 2010, available online at http://www.mtv.com/news/articles/1630013/20100119/jay_z.jhtml.

32. Ishmael Beah, "George Clooney—The Time 100," *Time*, May 3, 2007, available online at http://www.time.com/time/specials/2007/time100/article/0,28804,1595326_1615754_1615880,00.html.

33. Leyla Linton, "Clooney Urges UN Action on Darfur," *Washington Post*, September 15, 2006, available online at http://www.washingtonpost.com/wp-dyn/content/article/2006/09/15/AR2006091500507.html; Roger Friedman, "George Clooney's Secret Mission," *Fox News*, December 12, 2006, available online at http://www.foxnews.com/story/0,2933,235977,00.html#2.

34. "George Clooney's Sudan Help," *Monsters and Critics*, June 8, 2007, available online at http://www.monstersandcritics.com/people/news/article_1315091.php/George_Clooneys_Sudan_help.

35. "UN Gives Actor Clooney Peace Role," BBC News, February 1, 2008, available at http://news.bbc.co.uk/2/hi/entertainment/7220701.stm.

36. "Actor George Clooney Brings Hollywood Star Power to Sudan Issue," Voice of America News, October 13, 2010, available online at http://www.voanews.com/english/news/africa/Actor-George-Clooney-Brings-Hollywood-Star-Power-to-Sudan-Issue-104891414.html.

37. Greg Mortenson, *Stones into Schools: Promoting Peace with Education in Afghanistan and Pakistan* (New York, NY: Penguin, 2010).

38. Armand Hammer, *Hammer* (New York, NY: Perigree Trade, 1988).

39. Mark Landler, "In a Speech on Policy, Clinton Revives a Theme of American Power," *New York Times*, September 9, 2010, A6.

40. See Eugene R. Wittkopf, *Faces of Internationalism: Public Opinion and American Foreign Policy* (Durham, NC: Duke University Press, 1990), especially Chapter 2.

41. Eugene R. Wittkopf, "What Americans Really Think about Foreign Policy," *The Washington Quarterly* 19 (1996), 91–106.

42. For more on this, see Greg Mortenson and David Oliver Relin, *Three Cups of Tea: One Man's Mission to Promote Peace...One School at a Time* (New York, NY: Penguin, 2007).

43. *U.S. News and World Report*, May 29, 1995, p. 20.

44. *Time*, March 28, 1994, p. 22.

45. Barbara Crossette, "Foreign Aid Budget: Quick, How Much? Wrong," *New York Times*, February 27, 1995, p. A6.

46. Ole R. Holsti, "Public Opinion and Foreign Policy: Challenges to the Almond–Lippmann Consensus," *International Studies Quarterly* 36 (1992), 439–466.

47. See Bruce W. Jentleson, "The Pretty Prudent Public: Post Post-Vietnam American Opinion on the Use of Military Force," *International Studies Quarterly* 36 (1992), 49–73; Bruce W. Jentleson and Rebecca L. Britton, "Still Pretty Prudent: Post-Cold War American Public Opinion on the Use of Military Force," *Journal of Conflict Resolution* 42 (1998), 395–417; and Benjamin I. Page and Robert Y. Shapiro, *The Rational Public: Fifty Years of Trends in Americans' Policy Preferences* (Chicago, IL: University of Chicago Press, 1992).

48. William L. Riordan, *Plunkitt of Tammany Hall* (Lawrence, KS: Digireads.com /Neeland Media LLC, 2010, originally published 1905).

CHAPTER 9

Pluralist Policy Processes and International Actors

Two days after the 9/11 attacks, Saudi Prince Bandar bin Sultan (shown here with the president at Bush's Texas ranch) met with Vice President Dick Cheney, National Security Adviser Condoleezza Rice, and President George W. Bush in the White House; just hours later members of Osama bin Laden's family were quietly flown out of the United States and back to Saudi Arabia.
Source: Eric Draper UPI Photo Service/Newscom

LEARNING OBJECTIVES

- Illustrate the types of international organizations, nongovernmental organizations, and foreign individuals who may shape U.S. foreign policy.

- Describe the circumstances that can allow foreign individuals to play roles in the U.S. foreign policy–making process.

- Interpret the roles played by these various international actors when viewed through the lenses of realism, liberalism, idealism, and constructivism.

- Evaluate the openness of the U.S. foreign policy–making system in light of traditional notions of national sovereignty.

Introduction

An oft-heard phrase during the Cold War years was: "politics stops at the water's edge." That sounds good, but it was rarely true then and, as the preceding chapters have demonstrated, it is certainly not true now. While many domestic actors—government officials, bureaucratic components of the administration, members of Congress (MCs), occasionally the courts, public opinion, think tanks, the media, domestic groups, individual opinion leaders, and so on—vie for influence in shaping U.S. foreign policy, others outside the United States also seek to shape the contours of U.S. foreign policy. Using similar pluralist processes, they seek to take advantage of a policy-making system that is very open to influence—even external influence. These external actors may include international organizations, nongovernmental organizations (NGOs), or individuals representing their states, other international groups, or themselves. Each of these types of external actors deserves consideration, and we begin with international organizations.

International Organizations

Contrary to the picture some in the media portray, international organizations figure prominently in U.S. foreign policy. Often they provide the stimulus to which foreign policy makers respond. Examples can be found in the early 1990s UN (United Nations) effort to lead a humanitarian intervention to safeguard the delivery of relief supplies to refugee camps in Somalia. That well-intentioned effort resulted in the United States being pulled largely against its will into a civil war. In 2011, U.S. allies within the North Atlantic Treaty Organization (NATO) pressed for a collective response to safeguard the Libyan people demonstrating against the repressive Qaddafi regime. Libya's government went to war against its own people, and Libyan refugees fled the violence by illegally entering Italy. The decision was made to use U.S. military assets largely to take out Libyan air defense and communications links so other NATO forces could carry out more robust attacks in defense of the Libyan rebels.

A nonmilitary example comes from the UN's creation of the **Intergovernmental Panel on Climate Change (IPCC)**. After reviewing the mounting evidence demonstrating both global climate change and the impact of human activity on the rate of that change, the IPCC recommended mandatory reductions in fossil fuel emissions—which were sought at UN-sponsored meetings in Kyoto in 1997, Copenhagen in 2009, Durban in 2011, and Warsaw in 2013. So far, the United States has refused to accept mandatory reductions in its fossil fuel emissions. This refusal is based either on fairness issues (developed countries are forced to cut their emissions but developing countries who also pollute have so far been exempted from such mandatory restrictions) or on the expected negative economic impact on the United States that would result from a slowdown of its fossil fuel–based economy. However, the U.S. refusal to agree to mandatory emission cuts put it on a collision course with many friends and allies who agreed to make such cuts at Kyoto in 1997.[1]

A more recent example involves air travel to Europe. In 2011, the European Union (EU) issued a rule, to begin on January 1, 2012, that foreign airlines flying to and from EU countries would have to pay a carbon tax on their fossil fuel emissions as part of the EU's Emissions Trading System, a "cap and trade" system designed to reduce emissions. U.S. and other airlines opposed the measure, saying it violated previous international agreements governing the international civilian airline industry. If put into place, this system would force the airlines to pass along millions of dollars in extra costs to the flying public; think of how baggage fees would go up then! Almost certainly the number of passenger-miles flown on U.S.-European routes would decline at least somewhat, and U.S. airlines would lose that corresponding revenue. Backed up by Canada and China, the United States challenged the new rules, saying such matters should be decided by the International Civil Aviation Organization, but the European Court of Justice declared the new rules to be legal. Secretary of State Clinton vowed an appropriate U.S. response if the rules went into effect, which they did on January 1, 2012, as planned.[2] The result was an anti-tax uprising by more than a dozen non-EU states—including the United States. Faced with this opposition, the EU backed down in 2012 but proposed the plan again in late 2013. The opponents of the tax are seeking alternatives to the carbon tax, perhaps in the form of UN-negotiated fossil fuel reduction targets for airline companies.

Just as international organizations can create the need for a foreign policy output, they can also be the means through which the United States tries to accomplish its foreign policy goals. For example, the UN's **International Atomic Energy Agency (IAEA)** is the means by which the members of the international system monitor the nuclear programs of other countries. The Nuclear Nonproliferation Treaty and the IAEA have combined to create the **nuclear nonproliferation regime** that governs the acceptable uses of nuclear technologies. These rules and expectations can be used to promote U.S. foreign policy initiatives toward both those who seek to develop nuclear weapons outside the framework of the agreed rules (e.g., North Korea and Iran) and those who seek to develop nuclear energy for peaceful uses within those rules (e.g., Brazil and Japan).

The use of such international organizations as means to achieve U.S. foreign policy goals is not restricted to just the national security arena. Following the Asian financial crisis of 1997, the **Group of 20 (G-20)** was formed to bring together representatives of the 20 largest developed and developing markets for financial planning and policy coordination.[3] The forum has been particularly important in coordinating responses to the Great Recession of 2008–2010, where the Bush and Obama administrations had mixed success in persuading the other members to agree to their preferred economic policy responses to the recession. The United States was able to get others to coordinate their policies and somewhat increase their own economic stimulus packages to spur economic recovery, but those other nations (primarily led by the EU) were unsuccessful in their efforts to get the United States to tighten regulations on the operations of the financial and banking sectors of the economy.

Such mixed success in economic initiatives is also illustrated by U.S. interactions with the **World Trade Organization (WTO)**, as discussed in Box 9.1. However active international organizations are in trying to shape U.S. foreign policy, NGOs are arguably even more frequent participants in the U.S. foreign policy–making process. We examine NGOs next.

BOX 9.1

What's Fair? The WTO and U.S. Tax Laws

For decades U.S. corporations have faced a distinct disadvantage compared to their European rivals. U.S. corporations are required to pay taxes on *all* their income, whether earned within the territorial confines of the United States or earned abroad. To the contrary, most European states have territory-based income tax laws, so their corporations pay income tax only on the income they earn at home, not the income they earn abroad. Thus, the playing field is not level for all corporations. For example, U.S.-based Boeing is taxed on more of its earnings than its major European competitor Airbus, thereby giving Airbus a comparative economic advantage in the cutthroat competition for global sales of civilian airliners. In this highly competitive industry like many others,

every advantage or disadvantage—no matter how large or small—matters.

In 1971, the Nixon administration and Congress sought to provide much-needed relief to U.S. corporations by creating a new category of tax entities: Domestic International Sales Corporations (DISCs). U.S. businesses could create DISCs to handle their foreign activities, and their earnings abroad were then not subject to U.S. income tax. Thus the inequity between European and American taxation seemed solved. However, in both 1976 and 1981 the **General Agreement on Tariffs and Trade (GATT)** ruled that the DISCs represented an export subsidy and thus were illegal under GATT rules. To accommodate those GATT rulings, in 1984 Congress replaced DISCs with new entities called Foreign Sales Corporations (FSCs), but their purpose was the same. GATT still opposed these FSCs, but since GATT had no power to enforce its rulings, GATT dropped the matter.

The 1995 creation of the WTO as GATT's replacement dramatically changed things, since the WTO had the power to authorize economic sanctions on those who violated its rules. Not waiting very long, in 1997 the EU filed a formal complaint against the FSCs. Two years later the WTO ruled that the FSCs were an illegal trade subsidy just like the DISCs, the United States then appealed that decision, and the U.S. appeal was rejected in 2000. Before that year was over, Congress passed a law creating a new corporate tax break; extraterritorial income (ETI)—the income made on exports or operations by U.S. firms operating outside the United States—would be treated the same as had the income of FSCs. Just two months after the creation of the new ETI tax break, the EU filed a formal complaint against it. In 2001 the WTO ruled that the ETI tax break was an illegal export subsidy just as the other U.S. efforts had been, and a year later, the WTO authorized the EU to impose retaliatory tariff increases that would cost U.S. businesses an additional $4 billion per year.

From 2001 to 2004, MCs struggled to find a legislative language they could agree on that put U.S. and European corporations on a relatively level-playing field when it came to the income taxes they owed their home government. Pressure on Congress escalated in March 2004 when the EU began imposing retaliatory tariffs on U.S. goods. To create maximum pressure in the political arena, the EU specifically picked products made in states with lots of Electoral College votes (e.g., California, Florida, Pennsylvania, and Ohio) or with lots of Republican MCs (e.g., North and South Carolina, Mississippi, Kentucky, and Maine) since Congress was controlled by the Republican Party at that time (who says Europeans don't understand U.S. politics!).

With the U.S. business community pressing for protection from these retaliatory tariffs, Congress quickly increased the pace of its legislative efforts. Just three weeks before the November 2004 general elections, the American Jobs Creation Act was passed, which phased out the ETI tax breaks over time. Politically, the cost of killing the ETI tax breaks was steep. Avoiding the $4 billion per year WTO penalty by removing the $58 billion in ETI tax breaks required a 633-page bill that granted nearly $150 billion in domestic tax breaks for U.S. businesses. To pick up the needed votes in Congress, there were domestic benefits for a diverse array of organized interests: tax breaks for the movie industry, the horse and dog track gambling industry, manufacturers of hunting and fishing equipment, shipbuilders, restaurant owners, ethanol producers, owners of NASCAR tracks, tobacco producers, the railroad industry, and those who lived in states without state income taxes. Critics called the bill another instance of corporate welfare on a grand scale and the triumph of special interests, but the bill's author defended it by saying, *when a bill has to pass*, you do whatever is necessary to round up sufficient votes.

After all the controversy accompanying the bill's passage, the EU was still not pleased, because the ETI tax breaks were to be phased out not immediately, but over time. So, yet another EU complaint was filed with the WTO; the

WTO ruled that the extended phase-out periods also amounted to illegal trade subsidies, and it threatened to authorize new retaliatory tariffs as punishments. In 2006, Congress passed legislation ending U.S. tax breaks on the income corporations derived from exports and overseas operations for good. So after only 35 years, the United States was in full compliance with international law regarding export subsidies. Was the result fair? What do you think?

Source: Based on Wendy J. Schiller and Ralph G. Carter, "The World Trade Organization and Tax Subsidies for Exports: Equal Competition or Corporate Welfare?" in Ralph G. Carter (ed.), Contemporary Cases in U.S. Foreign Policy: From Terrorism to Trade (3rd ed.)(Washington, DC: CQ Press, 2008), pp. 335–355.

Nongovernmental Organizations

International NGOs frequently play important roles in U.S. foreign policy making. They are particularly active regarding an array of humanitarian issues. For example, NGOs often get involved in monitoring human rights situations and generating political pressures on human rights abusers. The case of the Chinese democracy activist **Liu Xiaobo** provides a good example.

A professor and literary critic, Liu was an outspoken critic of the Chinese government's brutal responses to the 1989 Tiananmen Square democracy protests in Beijing, protests in which Liu participated. After being imprisoned by the Chinese government for two years for his role at Tiananmen, in 1996 he was sentenced to three more years at a "reeducation through labor" camp for publicly calling for a multiparty system in China and for the Chinese government to negotiate its differences with the Dalai Lama and Tibetans. In 2008, Liu co-authored Charter 08, a document that called for political reform, the end of the one-party system, and protection of human rights. Liu was immediately detained and put under a six-month house arrest, during which time the Chinese government searched his home, seized computers, and interrogated his associates. Liu was then arrested in 2009 on charges of subverting state power. He received an 11-year prison sentence.[4]

As a prisoner of conscience, Liu came to the attention of a wide array of human rights groups such as **Amnesty International** and **International PEN**. Over a number of years, their public and private pressures led State Department officials to publicly bring up the issue of Liu's release from detention 16 times over a two-year period.[5] The publicity generated by all such NGOs and national governments such as the United States led the Nobel committee to name Liu the 2010 recipient of the Nobel Peace Prize. As this is written, Liu remains in prison.

The role of NGOs in cases such as Liu's is not uncommon. Human rights, humanitarian, and environmental/ecological NGOs put pressures on the U.S. government to intervene in many cases. Sometimes the United States does so—most commonly when there is no other countervailing national security or economic issue at risk or when international NGOs are able to mobilize politically powerful domestic U.S. NGOs to take up the effort. However, when such countervailing pressures or like-minded domestic groups are not present, international NGOs are often disappointed in the U.S. responses to their appeals. Yet no matter how important traditional NGOs are in impacting U.S. foreign policy, international businesses are arguably even more important.[6]

Multinational corporations operating or based in the United States have long swung considerable weight in Washington, DC. In 1953, the Central Intelligence Agency (CIA) overthrew the popularly elected government of Iranian Prime Minister Mohammad Mossadegh primarily due to the urging of the British government acting on behalf of the Anglo-Iranian Oil Company, a British oil firm whose assets had been nationalized by Mossadegh's government. For their part, U.S.-based multinational oil corporations hoped to get a slice of the Iranian oil pie with a new, more pro-U.S. regime in charge. In 1954, the United Fruit Company used its ties to Secretary of State John Foster Dulles and CIA Director Allen Dulles (both brothers were former lawyers whose law firm had represented United Fruit) to persuade the U.S. government to overthrow the Guatemalan government of the popularly elected President Jacobo Arbenz. The Arbenz government had angered United Fruit by nationalizing some of its land holdings in Guatemala and then using United Fruit's own estimates of the real estate's value for tax purposes (which were set at unrealistically low levels) to determine the compensation the corporation deserved.

While the leaders of some international corporations can take their case directly to the White House or halls of Congress, for many international firms, hiring lobbyists to get their cases heard by U.S. policy makers is standard operating procedure. One of the most prominent lobbying firms in the United States is the law firm of Akin Gump Strauss Hauer and Feld, better known simply as Akin Gump. Some of the foreign clients keeping Akin Gump on retainer in 2011 included firms based in Britain (Apollo Advisors), Belgium (Anheuser-Busch InBev, Delhaize Group), Canada (Barrick Gold), China (Lenovo), France (Vivendi), Germany (Siemens AG, Volkswagen), Ireland (Covidien), Japan (Bridgestone), Netherlands (Royal Dutch Shell), and New Zealand (LanzaTech).[7] If lobbyists like the attorneys employed by Akin Gump are successful in stressing how advancing their client's corporate interests intersect with short- or long-term U.S. interests, they can help set government agendas, shape policy options under consideration by policy makers, and possibly set the parameters of acceptable U.S. responses to policy issues.

At times, international firms may use the appeal of campaign contributions to wield influence, but they must do so very carefully so as not to run afoul of U.S. campaign finance laws that prohibit foreign nationals or corporations from contributing directly to U.S. political campaigns. In the 1990s Chinese satellite companies wanted to purchase communications satellites from U.S.-based Loral Space & Communications, but as high-technology military items, sales of such satellites were governed by licenses issued by the State Department. The State Department was required by law to consider the national security impacts of such technology transfers before issuing export licenses. Chinese aerospace companies funneled hundreds of thousands of dollars in illegal campaign contributions to the Democratic Party, and their representatives also met with the then Commerce Secretary Ron Brown (which was legal). For his part, Loral Chairman Bernard Schwartz contributed approximately half a million dollars to the Democratic Party. During this sequence of multiple contributions to his political party, President Clinton issued a waiver to allow the purchase of four Loral satellites by the Chinese. Then the administration later transferred the authority to issue satellite export licenses from the State Department to the Commerce Department, whose mission is to promote U.S. business at home and abroad and is not required to protect national security. The sales of such satellites thus got considerably easier.[8]

As suggested earlier, the way such multinational corporations have influence in the foreign policy arena is by getting their points of view before relevant government officials. One measure of success over time would certainly be when such persuasion and lobbying efforts are sufficiently effective that officials come to anticipate the reactions of multinational corporations and proactively try to accommodate them in their policy proposals.

Another way multinational corporations can influence policy making is through public appeals to shape public and elite attitudes about the issues important to them. Oftentimes multinational corporations will take out full-page newspaper advertisements in national papers like the *New York Times*, *Washington Post*, or *Wall Street Journal* to raise an issue, stress a policy response, or just try to create a more positive image for themselves that might work to their advantage with policy makers at a later date. Another means is to take out advertisements on television programs that elites and the attentive public often watch, such as the Sunday morning news programs on major television networks such as ABC, CBS, NBC, CNN, and Fox News. However, they are not the only actors who use such methods. Foreign individuals representing many different actors do so as well, and we examine them next.

Individuals

A variety of individuals from outside the United States also get involved in shaping U.S. foreign policy. Not surprisingly, many are heads of their respective governments. As noted previously in this work, Costa Rican President Oscar Arias met repeatedly in the 1980s with House Speaker Jim Wright and other House Democrats to build support for a Central American peace plan, particularly after it became clear that President Ronald Reagan would not meet with him. Given Arias's ability to sway MCs of both parties to his point of view, the Reagan administration ultimately realized it had little chance to stop the negotiated peace settlement in Central America and so ended its active opposition to the plan. The resulting peace agreement won Arias the Nobel Peace Prize.

More recent examples come to mind as well. In the 2000s, British Prime Minister Tony Blair was a willing partner to George W. Bush in the war in Iraq. When other European leaders criticized the war, Blair not only contributed British forces to the effort but also constantly encouraged Bush to stay the course and be strong in the face of his critics. More recently, in 2009 Chinese leader Hu Jintao met with President Obama; later that year Obama became the first sitting U.S. president to refuse to meet with the Dalai Lama while the leader of Tibetan Buddhists was in the United States. It seems highly likely that the Chinese government's position—that the Dalai Lama is the treasonous leader of a Chinese separatist movement—was reaffirmed to Obama, and Obama's subsequent decision may have been influenced by either the over one $1 trillion in U.S. debt owned by the Chinese or the important U.S.-Chinese trade relationship. In another example, a 2010 State Department cable indicated that Iraqi Prime Minister Nouri al-Maliki said he was in negotiation with Chevron to develop an oil field that spanned the Iraqi–Iranian border and sought the State Department's guidance on how to avoid existing U.S. economic sanctions on Iran.[9] Thus, it seems clear that leaders of foreign governments press the U.S. government, directly or through intermediaries, to advance their own state interests.

One of the best at "working" the U.S. foreign policy system is undoubtedly Israeli Prime Minister Benjamin Netanyahu. Having lived in the United States as a teenager and with both his undergraduate and master's degrees from MIT, Netanyahu understands U.S. politics and culture well. As prime minister, he never hesitated in going to the White House to ask for what Israel wanted from the United States. Sometimes presidents did what he wanted, but often they did not. When he was unsuccessful in the White House, he routinely went straight to Capitol Hill to ask Congress, where he often got a much more favorable response. Both elected party leaders in Congress—including Republican House Speakers Newt Gingrich and John Boehner and Democratic House Speaker Nancy Pelosi—and rank-and-file MCs alike often publicly profess their support for Israel and its policy stances in the Mideast. Their unwavering support for Israel compromises the efforts of U.S. administrations to use diplomatic pressures or threats of economic retaliation to force Israel to stop constructing Israeli settlements in the occupied territory of the West Bank, to push Israeli officials into meaningful peace negotiations with the Palestinians, or to back away from other policy initiatives the United States opposes.

Oddly enough, the unwavering pro-Israel stance of many MCs has so complicated U.S. outreach to Arabs that in at least one case the Obama administration turned to Netanyahu to serve as a lobbyist. In 2011, both the Obama administration and Netanyahu's Israeli regime favored a $50 million aid package from the United States to the Palestinian Authority (or PA) led by President Mahmoud Abbas. The aid was intended to strengthen the Palestinian Authority's ability to provide needed governmental services to Palestinians in the West Bank and to professionalize further the Palestinian security forces. Both the U.S. and Israeli regimes strongly supported this strengthening of the PA's capabilities to govern effectively as a way to undercut the appeal of the PA's rival, HAMAS. Yet, opposition by Republican MCs to *any* foreign aid to the Palestinian side threatened the aid package. At the request of both President Obama and Secretary of State Clinton, Netanyahu met with dozens of congressional Republicans when they visited Israel in August and urged them not to block the funding, as it was essential to Israel's security. On this issue at least, congressional Republicans trusted Prime Minister Netanyahu more than they trusted President Obama.[10]

Interestingly, as much as Israeli leaders have had significant influence in shaping U.S. policies toward the Mideast, Arab leaders have not been without influence either. As shown in Box 9.2, another individual who has had unusual access to policy makers is Saudi Arabia's Prince Bandar bin Sultan, who was Saudi Arabia's ambassador to the United States from 1983 to 2005 and since then has served as the secretary general of the Saudi National Security Council.

BOX 9.2

How Open to Outside Influence? The Case of Saudi Prince Bandar bin Sultan

Successful diplomats carefully cultivate access to the foreign policy makers of the country where they are stationed. Being able to deliver and receive messages to those wielding power is an important part of their job description. Perhaps, the most successful diplomat in this regard in recent history has been Prince Bandar bin Sultan bin Abdul Aziz of Saudi Arabia.

Prince Bandar's diplomatic career began informally while he was serving as a major in the Royal Saudi Air Force. On a 1978 trip to the United States, he met President Jimmy Carter, who was facing conservative opposition in Congress to his proposed sale of F-15 jets to Saudi Arabia. Carter asked Bandar to go to California to persuade the then California Governor Ronald Reagan—a very influential voice among conservative Republicans—on the benefits of the sale. Bandar succeeded in convincing Reagan to support the sale, and the sale went forward.

President Carter then asked Bandar to persuade Senator James Abourezk (D-SD)—the first Arab-American elected to the Senate—to vote for the Panama Canal Treaties. Upon recognizing young Prince Bandar's access to the Carter

White House, Saudi Crown Prince Fahd began using Bandar as an informal conduit to President Carter. In 1979, Bandar moved to Washington where he earned his master's degree at the Johns Hopkins University School of Advanced International Studies. During that time, he became a friend of (and racquetball partner with) the military assistant to the deputy secretary of defense—a young army officer named Colin Powell.

In 1982, Bandar was named the military attaché to the Saudi Embassy, and when Crown Prince Fahd became King Fahd the next year, Bandar was appointed Saudi ambassador to the United States. Ronald Reagan was now president, and Bandar quickly rekindled their prior positive relationship, to the point that First Lady Nancy Reagan occasionally used Bandar to convey informal messages to members of Reagan's Cabinet! He also became fast friends and a regular luncheon partner with Vice President George H.W. Bush. He and Vice President Bush became so close that Bandar was considered *one of the family*, even earning the nickname "Bandar Bush" from George W. Bush. These relationships clearly paid off when Congress prohibited the Reagan administration from providing direct U.S. aid to the Nicaraguan contras. Bandar assisted the Reagan effort by ensuring that the contras received $32 million from the Saudis.

When George H.W. Bush was elected president, Bandar's access and influence expanded. The seminal event in their relationship was probably the 1990 Iraqi invasion of Kuwait and the Bush administration's subsequent decision to protect Saudi Arabia and to liberate the Kuwaitis. In 1990 when George and Barbara Bush went to Saudi Arabia to celebrate Thanksgiving with U.S. troops there, Bandar's wife Haifa invited the Bush's recently divorced daughter Dorothy and her children to come to the Bandar household in the United States to spend the Thanksgiving holiday with them. The elder Bush was reportedly teary-eyed when he learned of this personal gesture. When Bush ran for reelection in 1992, Bandar stayed over in Houston for the election. Anguished over the possibility of a Bush defeat, Bandar wrote a personal letter to Bush that he had hand-delivered to the Bush home at 4:00 a.m. on election day. In it, he called Bush a winner no matter which way the election results went, a friend for life, and a member of his family.

Even though he had backed George H.W. Bush over Bill Clinton in 1992, Bandar and new President Clinton were already well acquainted. They first met when Clinton was the governor of Arkansas and had asked the Saudis to fund a Center for Middle East Studies at the University of Arkansas. During Clinton's tenure as president, Bandar helped persuade Libyan leader Muammar Qaddafi to turn over the two suspects in the bombing of Pan Am Flight 103 over Lockerbie, Scotland,

for prosecution. At Clinton's behest, Bandar also got involved in other Middle Eastern affairs—trying to arrange a U.S.-Syrian summit conference and helping with negotiations between Israelis and Palestinians in 2000 where he served as a conduit conveying U.S. messages to Palestinian Authority President Yasser Arafat.

In 1997 when George W. Bush began considering his own run for the presidency, he called on old friend Bandar to brief him on a variety of foreign policy issues. Bush told Bandar that while he had his own ideas about domestic policy,

> I don't have the foggiest idea about what I think about international, foreign policy. My dad told me before I make up my mind, go and talk to Bandar. One, he's our friend. *Our* means America, not just the Bush family. Number two, he knows everyone around the world who counts. And number three, he will give you his view on what he sees happening in the world. Maybe he can set up meetings for you with people around the world.[11]

Thus almost a year before George H.W. Bush asked former National Security Council staffer Condoleezza Rice to serve as a foreign policy coach for George W. Bush, Prince Bandar was giving George W. Bush private tutoring on what the leaders of most other important countries were like and the issues that motivated them.

While the al Qaeda attacks on September 11, 2001, were the low point in his time as Saudi ambassador (since most of the 9/11 hijackers were Saudis), Bandar continued to work closely with Bush administration officials. He provided intelligence information on suspected al Qaeda operatives, and he also facilitated the quick and quiet removal of

Osama bin Laden's relatives from the United States. He and George W. Bush were so close that Bush showed Bandar the U.S. plans for the invasion of Iraq even before Secretary of State Colin Powell had seen them. Yet in 2005, Bandar suddenly resigned his position as Saudi ambassador to the United States for personal reasons. Once he returned to Saudi Arabia, he was named the head of the new Saudi National Security Council, primarily tasked with protecting Saudis from home-grown terrorists.

U.S.-Saudi relations have been close for decades. How much of that is due to the intersection of U.S. and Saudi national interests, and how much is that due to the warm, personal relationships of the officials involved? How much influence did Prince Bandar bin Sultan have on U.S. foreign policy? Was he an instrument of U.S. foreign policy or a shaper of it?

Sources: BBC News, Profile: Prince Bandar, available online at: http://news.bbc.co.uk/2/hi /middle_east/4635383.stm; William Simpson, The Prince: The Secret Story of the World's Most Intriguing Royal Prince Bandar bin Sultan (New York: Regan/HarperCollins, 2006); Elsa Walsh, "The Prince," The New Yorker, March 24, 2003, available online at: http://www.saudi -us-relations.org/international-relations/prince -bandar.html; Bob Woodward, State of Denial (New York: Simon & Shuster, 2006).

So while many individuals representing their respective foreign governments have sought to influence and shape U.S. foreign policy, individuals representing other entities have done so as well. Religious leaders have at times prominently pressed U.S. foreign policy makers to change U.S. foreign policy. A good example was Pope John Paul II, the first Polish pope. The leader of the Roman Catholic Church and President Ronald Reagan collaborated in their efforts to weaken the Soviet Union and its hold on Eastern Europe—and particularly on the pope's Polish homeland. In private messages to the president, Pope John Paul II strongly encouraged U.S. pressures on the communist regime in Poland due to its crackdown on the Solidarity movement there, and both President Reagan and White House staffers found the pope's support and encouragement inspirational. In turn, the White House carefully coordinated its actions with those of the pope to put maximum pressure on both the Polish and Soviet governments to liberalize their rule over the people of Poland and Eastern Europe.[12]

In a similar vein, South African Anglican Bishop Desmond Tutu was instrumental in pushing U.S. policy makers to press for the end of apartheid. Unable to bring down South Africa's policy of racial segregation from working within the system from the inside, Tutu sought out U.S. Senator Edward Kennedy (D-MA) and told him: "the world will not pay attention until someone like you comes to South Africa and brings the cameras and spotlights with you."[13] Kennedy thereafter went to South Africa, the cameras followed, and as soon as he returned to Washington, Kennedy introduced and pushed through Congress legislation that became the Comprehensive Anti-Apartheid Act of 1986. When President Ronald Reagan vetoed the bill, Kennedy led the successful effort to override the president's veto.[14]

However, not every foreign individual who tries to shape U.S. foreign policy is well known. Sometimes the individuals who do so are policy experts virtually unknown to the mass public. Agnes Klingshirn of the German aid agency GTZ is such a person. In her view, if the global community really wanted to improve the lives of women and families in developing countries in a meaningful way, someone would invent a cleaner, safer, and more efficient cookstove. In many countries, women and children spend much of their days hunting for firewood to their cookstoves. Moreover, both wood and kerosene cookstoves are highly dangerous; they often explode and always emit toxic fumes that often sicken family members. Three billion people are exposed to these toxic fumes and smoke, and 2 million premature deaths globally are linked to cookstove fumes—or one death every 16 seconds. Klingshirn's ideas found the ear of Secretary of State Hillary Clinton, who announced in September 2010 the formation of a new public–private alliance called the Global Alliance for Clean Cookstoves. The goal of the alliance is to produce and distribute 100 million clean cookstoves by 2020, and the Obama administration's pledge to the effort was almost $51 million over a five-year period.[15] Founding partners in the alliance are the U.S. Departments of State, Health and Human Services, and Energy as well as the U.S. Environmental Protection Agency and the U.S. Agency for International Development. Other founding partners include the governments of Germany, Norway, and Peru, and NGOs like Shell, the Shell Foundation, Morgan Stanley, and the Netherlands Development Organization. A number of UN agencies are the implementing partners.[16] After one year, the United States could point to meaningful progress for the alliance: identifying over 20 country partners, distributing over 2.4 million clean cookstoves thereby improving the indoor air for 14 million people, and raising over $80 million more to support the alliance's work.[17] Beyond those accomplishments is the goodwill such an initiative generates for the United States.

Far more often however, individuals who influence foreign policy from the outside are celebrities who use their fame to focus attention on global problems. Britain's Princess Diana was one obvious example. While the International Campaign to Ban Landmines was already active, public knowledge and awareness of the issue dramatically increased when Princess Diana lent her name and public endorsement to it. President Clinton was very enthusiastic about the effort to ban land mines, but politically he would not go any farther than his military experts would support. He made it clear that he would support the treaty if an exception to the ban was made for the demilitarized zone separating North and South Korea which is strewn with millions of land mines to slow down any future North Korean invasion. When that exception was not forthcoming, he could not commit to the treaty. However, he did issue a Presidential Decision Directive (PDD 64) that would end the U.S. use of land mines elsewhere besides Korea, and the favorable publicity generated by Princess Diana's support made it easier for him to back away from the use of land mines.[18]

An example of a foreign individual who was even more successful in influencing U.S. foreign policy is Paul David Hewson, better known as Bono from the rock band U2. Appalled that millions of Africans died from AIDS when medicines existed that could prolong and improve the quality of their lives, Bono sought a U.S. commitment to do more for African AIDS relief. To accomplish this, he communicated with the George W. Bush White House, met with President Bush personally, and participated with other entertainers in a "Heart of America" tour to raise public awareness about the AIDS crisis in Africa.[19]

Following President Bush's proposal for a $15 billion commitment over five years to combat AIDS in Africa, Bono kept in contact with the president, as he knew Bush would have to press Congress to approve the money. Knowing that many in Congress were skeptical about the benefits of foreign aid programs, Bono also put personal pressure on MCs to ensure that the money was appropriated. Not only did Bono appear on multiple television news programs to get his message across, but he also engaged in personal lobbying on Capitol Hill. He identified specific MCs on the relevant appropriations subcommittees for U.S. foreign aid, met with them personally, and provided them with specific information on the scope of the need in Africa, the benefits the U.S. aid would bring there, and *any relevant connections that might exist with the members' local constituents back home*. Due do his sustained efforts and those of President George W. Bush, Congress came through and appropriated the largest commitment of U.S. economic assistance ever to sub-Saharan Africa.

Shaping Foreign Policy

International actors and other external groups actively engage in U.S. foreign policy making to whatever extent they can to shape favorable outcomes. Representatives of international governmental organizations, NGOs, and foreign states and individual opinion leaders continually make their desires known to U.S. foreign policy makers through appeals via the mass media, personal communications, and face-to-face meetings with top policy makers. They bargain, persuade, cajole, and at times even threaten policy makers in trying to get their way, and they enter into alliances with domestic groups who share their concerns. In a foreign policy–making process very open to outside influence, these external actors engage actively lobby administrative officials such as the president, the vice president, National Security Council members, and other top officials in the White House, relevant Cabinet departments, and the Intelligence Community. They also actively seek out key MCs for their support. It is commonplace for top foreign officials to visit the United States, meet with the president and/or other top administrative officials, and then head to Capitol Hill to visit the offices of the elected party leaders of each congressional chamber, of the Senate Foreign Relations Committee and its key members, of the House Foreign Affairs Committee and its key members, and at times of other committees such as Appropriations, Armed Services, Intelligence, Homeland Security, and Commerce. These foreign actors use many, if not most, of the same techniques to shape U.S. foreign policy, as do the societal actors described in Chapter 8. But how successful are they at influencing policy? We turn to that next.

Influencing Foreign Policy

In an interdependent, globalized world, it is hard to argue that external influences do not matter in the making of U.S. foreign policy. However, determining how much they matter may depend on one's theoretical point of view. As noted in Chapter 3, political realists and neorealists interpret international politics to be primarily the actions of states behaving as unitary actors who make rational choices in reaction to events or opportunities in an international system marked by anarchy. Thus, from this point of view, external influences are very important. They are the impetus for foreign policy in the first place, as states adapt to their external environment. As stimuli, they provide the starting point for foreign policy. Moreover, their subsequent inputs become vital feedback to determine how effective the U.S. governmental output has been and perhaps how it might be improved for the future.

Like realists and neorealists, idealists tend to see international actors as very important to U.S. foreign policy. External events and the actions of international actors and opinion leaders shape the way things are, and idealists then react based on how they think things should be. To the extent they share normative values with other international actors, idealists will view those international actors as legitimate participants in the U.S. foreign policy–making process. They will coordinate their domestic actions with those of external actors with similar views, use the presence of those international actors as leverage to push their preferred policy options, and then seek to engage those international actors to help implement the types of foreign policy outputs they prefer. Thus, when such values about how things should be are shared, domestic and international actors will work hand in glove to achieve their goals.

On the other hand, liberals believe foreign policy is primarily a product of the actions of key subnational actors like elected and appointed officials, political parties, organized interest groups, experts, opinion leaders, the news media, and public opinion. From this theoretical point of view, external factors and actors may be quite important in some cases, but on a day-to-day basis they are normally less important in shaping U.S. foreign policy than domestic factors and the perceptions, needs, and desires of domestic policy makers. From this theoretical standpoint, foreign policy is primarily the product of domestic processes and actors and, once formed, is then projected outward. So liberals may see external actors as notable, but not necessarily determinative, actors in shaping U.S. foreign policy outputs.

However, neoliberals may have a slightly greater appreciation of some external inputs. Neoliberals typically stress the need for creating, and then using, international organizations and other entities to create an international architecture that supports and promotes global cooperation. To the extent that they do so, they must be open to the inputs of representatives of these entities—the international organizations, NGOs, and other groups involved. So neoliberals are quite open to viewing external actors as more significant shapers of U.S. foreign policy.

For constructivists, these external actors have only the importance assigned to them in the minds of domestic policy makers. If U.S. foreign policy makers socially construct a reality in which external actors are thought to be important, then policy makers will act on the basis of that constructed reality, and those foreign actors will vie with domestic factors and actors as influential shapers of U.S. foreign policy. Conversely, if policy makers socially construct a reality that says foreign actors should have little or no say in the formulation of U.S. foreign policy, then such foreign actors will be unsuccessful.

Thus, one could argue that at times the George W. Bush administration, backed up by a Republican-controlled Congress from 2001 to 2005, acted in a realist fashion by stressing the idea that concerns about U.S. sovereignty overrode the inputs of external audiences in making U.S. foreign policy. So international critiques of the U.S. effort to invade Iraq or to oppose mandatory fossil fuel emission reductions, for example, could be ignored as they were seen as illegitimate factors in the decision-making process. Conversely, the election of Barack Obama to the presidency in 2008 ushered in a new group of foreign policy makers who continually reaffirmed to each other that foreign concerns were legitimate. So while the United States did not necessarily have to do what foreign actors wanted, Obama administration officials believed that the views of others deserved a respectful hearing and careful consideration.

Conclusion

There are only a few societies in which foreign influences and the views of external actors seem to matter very little. North Korea—the so-called hermit kingdom—comes to mind, as until recently did Myanmar (also known as Burma) where a military regime long ignored foreign attitudes regarding its policies. However, in most countries, foreign policy makers cannot avoid being influenced to some degree by those outside the country, and that is certainly the case in the United States. The open and fragmented nature of the U.S. foreign policy process provides many opportunities for access by external actors, just as it does for domestic actors. Further, many of those international actors understand well the intricacies of the U.S. foreign policy–making process and know where and when and how to press to get their views considered. In that way, the pluralist process of groups and individuals vying for influence over U.S. foreign policy applies just as much for international actors as for domestic ones.

Glossary Terms

Amnesty International   an international NGO devoted to freeing prisoners of conscience and protecting people from other human rights abuses.

General Agreement on Tariffs and Trade (GATT)   the international organization created after World War II to promote increased global trade through the lowering of trade barrier. GATT"s inability to punish violators of its rules led to the creation in 1995 of its successor - the World Trade Organization (WTO).

Group of 20 (G-20)   the 20 major and emerging markets in the international system. Increasingly the preferred forum by many for global economic cooperation.

Intergovernmental Panel on Climate Change (IPCC)   the international body created by the UN to review the scientific evidence regarding climate change and make recommendations.

International Atomic Energy Agency (IAEA)   the UN agency tasked with promoting the peaceful use of nuclear energy and its related technologies.

International PEN   a British-based NGO composed of writers who push for freedom of expression, one of the oldest human rights organizations in existence.

Liu Xiaobo   Chinese dissident and democracy activist awarded the Nobel Peace Prize in 2010.

Nuclear nonproliferation regime   a set of rules, norms, and procedures that govern the acceptable uses of nuclear technologies.

World Trade Organization (WTO)   the supranational organization that creates the rules for free trade, implements those rules, and adjudicates and enforces those rules.

Endnotes

1. See Rodger A. Payne and Sean Payne, "The Politics of Climate Change: A Consensus for Copenhagen?" in Ralph G. Carter (ed.),*Contemporary Cases in U.S. Foreign Policy: From Terrorism to Trade* (4th ed.) (Washington, DC: CQ Press, 2011), pp. 386–415.
2. "US Rejects European Court Ruling on Airline Emissions," *BBC News*, December 21, 2011, available online at http://www.bbc.co.uk/news/business-16282692.
3. See the G-20 website, available at http://www.g20.org/about_G20.
4. "China: Liu Xiaobo," PEN American Center website, available online at http://www.pen.org/viewmedia.php/prmMID/3029/prmID/172.
5. Liu Xiaobo search on the U.S. Department of State website, "Democracy and Global Affairs" link, available online at http://search.state.gov/search?q=Liu+Xiaobo&site=stategov%7Coig%7Cfpc%7Cbmena%7Cusawc%7Cmepi%7Ctravel%7Cstategov_exchanges%7Ccareers%7Cfoia%7Caiep%7Cpepfar%7Ccspo%7Ccrs%7Cpmdtc%7Cadop%7Cstategov_lang%7Cpitt_summit&client=stategov_frontend&output=xml_no_dtd&proxystylesheet=stategov_frontend&entqr=3&lr=lang_en&oe=UTF-8&ie=utf8&sort=date:D:S:d1&getfields=*&ip=68.177.49.70&access=p&entsp=0&ud=1&num=100.
6. Lawrence R. Jacobs and Benjamin I. Page, "Who Influences U.S. Foreign Policy?" *American Political Science Review* 99 (2005), 107–123.
7. Open Secrets Lobbying Spending Database, available online at http://www.opensecrets.org/lobby/firmsum.php?id=D000000162&year=2011.
8. "Timeline of Clinton China Decisions," *Congressional Record*, June 18, 1998, p. H4760, available online at HYPERLINK "http://www.fas.org/news/china/1998/h980618-prc8.htm" http://www.fas.org/news/china/1998/h980618-prc8.htm.
9. Associated Press, "Wikileaks: Chevron Eyed Oil Deal Involving Iran," *Jerusalem Post*, December 16, 2010, available online at http://www.jpost.com/Headlines/Article.aspx?id=199738.
10. Jennifer Steinhauer and Steven Lee Myers, "House G.O.P. Finds a Growing Bond with Netanyahu," *New York Times*, September 21, 2011, p. A1.
11. Quoted in Bob Woodward, *State of Denial* (New York, NY: Simon & Shuster, 2006), pp. 3-4, emphasis in original.

12. Mark Riebling, "Freedom's Men: The Cold War Team of Pope John Paul II and Ronald Reagan," *National Review Online*, April 4, 2005, available online at http://www.nationalreview.com/articles/214072/freedoms-men/mark-riebling.

13. Adam Clymer, *Edward M. Kennedy: A Biography* (New York, NY: William Morrow, 1999), p. 363.

14. Ralph G. Carter and James M. Scott, *Choosing to Lead: Understanding Congressional Foreign Policy Entrepreneurs* (Durham, NC: Duke University Press, 2009), p. 146.

15. "Global Alliance for Clean Cookstoves: The United States Commitment by the Numbers," Department of State Fact Sheet, September 21, 2010, available online at http://www.state.gov/r/pa/prs/ps/2010/09/147494.htm.

16. "Foreign Policy's Second Annual List of the Top 100 Global Thinkers," available online at http://www.foreignpolicy.com/articles/2010/11/29/the_fp_top_100_global_thinkers?page=0,33; and The Global Alliance for Clean Cookstoves, available online at http://cleancookstoves.org/about-us/partners/.

17. "U.S. Action in Global Alliance for Clean Cookstoves," Department of State Fact Sheet, September 22, 2011, available online at http://geneva.usmission.gov/2011/09/23/clean-cookstoves/.

18. Doug Tuttle, "ICBL Releases New Annual Landmine Report," Center for Defense Information, January 15, 2009, available online at http://www.pogo.org/our-work/straus-military-reform-project/conflict/2009/icbl-releases-new-annual-landmine-report.html.

19. Tom Bonfield, "Rock Star Bono Praises Bush for AIDS Plans," *Cincinnati Enquirer*, July 8, 2003, available online at http://www.washingtonmonthly.com/archives/individual/2005_12/007754.php.

CHAPTER 10

Foreign Policy Outputs

U.S. troops help deliver relief supplies in Africa. Is AFRICOM the new model for implementing U.S. foreign policy outcomes?
Source: Sgt. Ryan S. Scranton/DOD/ZUMA Press/Newscom

LEARNING OBJECTIVES

- Define power in international politics.

- Differentiate between hard power, soft power, and smart power policy outputs.

- Explain when hard power, soft power, or smart power outputs seem most appropriate.

- Predict the mix of hard power, soft power, and smart power outputs in the near term future.

Introduction

We noted in Chapter 1 that foreign policy involves adapting to changes in the external environment. Some changes are welcome; others are not. Some represent challenges to be faced, while others represent opportunities to be seized and exploited. However, the outputs of the foreign policy decision-making process may involve a myriad array of policy instruments. We could try to talk about diplomacy, signaling behaviors, military statecraft, economic statecraft, and so on, but it would be *impossible* to identify every possible foreign policy instrument, behavior, or combination of instruments or behaviors that might be the product of foreign policy processes. Yet there is one commonality here. All such influence attempts involve some use of power.

Power is the ability to get others to do what one wants. The most basic means of doing so involve coercion, payments, and attraction. A useful way to differentiate foreign policy outputs is to identify how they reflect those three means: coercion, payments, and attraction. In the sections to follow, we will examine such means by considering hard power, soft power, and smart power policy outputs.[1]

Hard Power

Hard power involves getting others to do what one wants *when they otherwise prefer not to do so*. Such efforts can be either negative or positive. Negative approaches involve coercion—either threatening to punish another state or society if it does not do what the United States desires or actually going through with that punishment—while positive approaches use some form of payments to reward others for doing what the United States wants. Let's take a closer look at each of these categories of outputs.

Negative Approaches

The most obvious coercive foreign policy output would be the threat or use of military force. Such threats have been used many times. For example, in 1946

President Truman demanded that Soviet forces leave Iran (parts of which Soviet forces had occupied during World War II to protect oil reserves there), and he ordered a U.S. naval task force to move into the eastern Mediterranean Sea, thereby sending a signal that could not be missed. After negotiating a withdrawal agreement with Iran, the Soviet forces departed; after they left the Iranian legislature refused to approve the agreement. In another example from the 1973 October War in the Mideast, when Israeli troops surrounded Egyptian troops in the Sinai desert in violation of a UN-sponsored cease-fire agreement, the Soviets threatened to intervene militarily to save the Egyptian troops. The Nixon administration warned the Soviets not to intervene and conspicuously put U.S. military forces on worldwide alert. The Soviets backed down, and a diplomatic solution to save the Egyptian troops was reached.

Such military threats were not just seen during the Cold War era. When the Chinese made threatening statements and conducted missile tests in the Taiwan Straits prior to the 1996 presidential election in Taiwan in an effort to derail the pro-independence candidate's chances, the Clinton administration sent a naval task force into the contested waters. The Chinese stopped their provocative actions. In 2005–2006, rumors abounded in Washington that plans were under way in the Pentagon for a military strike on Iran to destroy its uranium enrichment program. When specifically asked by reporters about such rumors, President George W. Bush replied that *all* options regarding Iran were on the table for consideration. Perhaps as a result of such threats, Iranian representatives sent personal letters to President Bush inviting him to meet and talk with them at the UN and other international conferences. The tension between the two regimes, which had been building, began to recede somewhat as a result.

Yet threats do not mean much if they are not credible, and to be credible they need to be carried out occasionally. The most obvious form of negative hard policy outputs involves the use of military force, which can result in general wars, limited wars, unconventional wars, and asymmetric conflicts.[2] A **general war** would be one like World War I or World War II involving the United States in a conflict in which the geographic scope of the conflict would not be limited, all the conventional weaponry in the U.S. arsenal would be available for use, and weapons of mass destruction could potentially be used. Given the horrific death and destructions caused by the world wars of the 20th century, the possibility of a general war in the future seems unlikely in the post–Cold War international system.

After the destruction of World War II, **limited wars** have been much more common. These are conflicts that are limited by geographic scope, the amount and types of weaponry used, and the goals for which the war is fought. Typically in these cases, U.S. foreign policy makers would not want a war to expand beyond its current political borders, weapons of mass destruction would not be used, some limits on conventional force would probably be seen, and the goals of the conflict would be restricted. The limits on the use of force could include caps on the number of military personnel committed to the conflict and some types of targets being ruled out of bounds (e.g., targets near heavily populated urban areas or religious shrines). The goals of limited wars are typically to react to a threat or take advantage of an opportunity but generally do not include the total defeat of an enemy society. Both the Korean and Vietnam Wars illustrate this limited war option.

Unconventional wars involving U.S. forces against nonuniformed enemy forces have also become more common since the end of World War II. Much of the fighting in the Vietnam War prior to 1968 was unconventional, in that it involved U.S. uniformed forces fighting against insurgent Viet Cong units who attacked and then melted back into the civilian population. After the initial defeat of the Iraqi uniformed military in 2003, the war continued as informal Iraqi militia forces attacked U.S. troops. All of the fighting in Afghanistan beginning in 2001 was against nonuniformed Taliban and warlord militia forces. So limited wars can be either conventional, unconventional, or both.

Finally, asymmetric conflicts have also marked the post–Cold War and post-9/11 environments. **Asymmetric conflict** pits two forces of vastly different size and apparent power. Thus, the U.S. responses to the 1998 terrorist bombings of U.S. embassies in Kenya and Tanzania as well as the U.S. responses to terrorism after the 9/11 attacks involve asymmetric warfare. Small groups of terrorists—often numbering merely in the dozens—became the focus of the U.S. military.

In pursuing terrorists, U.S. foreign policy makers rely increasingly on covert operations and airstrikes—either manned or unmanned. Each option punishes the enemy target while putting relatively few U.S. military personnel at risk. In 2011, such a covert operation took the life of Osama bin Laden at his compound in Abbottabad, Pakistan. In this case, an operation involving a strike team numbering approximately 70 personnel and multiple helicopters took place in a military town deep inside Pakistan—without detection by the Pakistani military. The result of this policy output not only killed the person most associated with the 9/11 attacks but also sent a clear message to the Pakistani military: "If you don't take out terrorists living in your country, we will."

Airstrikes are a very popular option for employing hard power as well, whether against terrorists or other enemy targets. The obvious military advantage of airstrikes is that they bring death and destruction while risking the lives of relatively few U.S. military personnel. During the Cold War, the use of U.S. airstrikes against a Soviet ally might risk retaliation; however, after the Soviet Union fragmented, airstrikes became very popular with U.S. foreign policy makers. They were used in the former Yugoslavia in the 1990s, both in a limited way during the 1992–1995 Bosnian Civil War and more heavily during the Kosovo War of 1999. In 2011, airstrikes were the option of choice for North Atlantic Treaty Organization (NATO) members seeking to protect Libyan dissidents from attacks by the Libyan military.

Arguably the most popular form of airstrikes now involves the use of unmanned drone aircraft. Piloted remotely by U.S. personnel often very far away from the battle scene, these aircraft can launch air-to-ground missiles without putting any U.S. military personnel at risk in the attack. Airstrikes launched from unmanned drone aircraft have been widely utilized against a number of targets, including terrorist cells primarily in Afghanistan during the George W. Bush administration and in Afghanistan, Pakistan, and Yemen during the Obama administration. The pace of these attacks picked up significantly during

President Obama's administration, and one such attack killed the "Internet" face of terrorism, U.S.-born Anwar al-Awlaki, in Yemen in 2011.

As the world's greatest military power, the United States will continue to rely on military instruments of policy in the future. An interesting question is whether it relies on the military too much or too often. Has the United States become too militaristic? Have U.S. policy makers and the public fallen in love with the use of force as the ultimate form of statecraft? Box 10.1 examines this question.

BOX 10.1

Is the United States a Militaristic Power?

In a provocative book, retired U.S. Army Colonel Andrew Bacevich calls out the United States, saying its public and leaders have fallen prey to militarism. He sees militarism in the assumption that greatness as a nation is defined in military terms, in a willingness to use force as a first rather than last resort, and in the eagerness to give the military whatever it wants. This 20-year military veteran and West Point graduate makes the argument that it is hard to blame the military for trying to professionalize itself after the debacle of the loss in Vietnam. But that is not the real problem.

In Bacevich's eyes, the real problem began with the willingness of elected political leaders—starting with President Ronald Reagan in the 1980s and continuing through the present—to lavish praise on the military and the men and women who choose to serve in the armed forces. At some point, unrelenting praise created negative side effects. As the all-volunteer force members continued to hear that they represented the best of American values, the gulf between those who chose to volunteer and the public they were vowed to protect grew, until an "us versus them" dynamic developed, which was reinforced by the fact that

military service was routine in some families but unheard of in most others. This gulf was augmented by a post-Vietnam generation of movies that glorified either the military (*Top Gun*) or its fundamental values (*First Blood*, the original movie of the Rambo franchise) or its redemptive qualities (*An Officer and a Gentleman*), leading the public to embrace this militarism as well.

So Americans rarely questioned how much was spent on defense and whether it was really needed. In the post–Cold War era, the United States continued to maintain a global system of overseas bases and spent almost as much on defense as the rest of the world combined—even though the United States had no compelling military rivals. Worse from Bacevich's point of view was the fact that the public did not challenge the George W. Bush administration's decision to go to war with Iraq, a war that Bacevich saw as a war of choice and not of necessity.

In the end, Bacevich offers a series of corrective steps to deal with this problem that he sees as corrosive to the fundamental values of U.S. society. These include using U.S. military force for national defense only, not to try to remake the world in the U.S. image; using force only as a last resort when all other options have failed; limiting

U.S. dependence on foreign resources so the United States will not have to go to war to defend its access to foreign oil; pegging U.S. defense expenditures to what others actually spend on defense; finding ways to encourage more Americans to serve in the military so later more civilians (and elected officials) will be military veterans who know what war looks like before they embrace it as a policy option; and remaking the military academies into graduate schools only, which military officers would attend only after having gone to civilian universities like everyone else.

So what do you think of this argument? Is America in love with its military and war-making, or are current U.S. military policies reasonable and prudent given global geopolitical realities?

Sources: Andrew J. Bacevich, The New American Militarism: How Americans Are Seduced by War. (New York: Oxford University Press, 2005); Matthew Schofield, "Some Fear U.S. Is Developing a Warrior Class," Fort Worth Star-Telegram, January 5, 2013.

While the threat or use of force is the most obvious form of negative hard power, a more common form of negative hard power policy outputs is the threat or use of **economic sanctions.**[3] In these cases, economic means are employed to punish another state. The most common form of sanctions is trade sanctions. These typically involve retaliatory actions for another party's trade behaviors. So in 2009, the Obama administration raised tariffs on imports of Chinese tires for a period of three years after U.S. tire manufacturers complained that Chinese tires were being sold in the United States at less than fair market value. China appealed to the World Trade Organization (WTO), and in 2011, the WTO ruled in favor of the United States.

However, sanctions can also used to seek broader political goals. Comprehensive sanctions involve refusing both to buy another country's goods and to sell U.S. goods to that country. For decades, Cuba represented an obvious example of comprehensive U.S. sanctions. After Fidel Castro's communist regime nationalized foreign-owned properties in 1960, the United States responded with an embargo that by 1962 included prohibiting all U.S. trade with and travel to Cuba. The goal was to bring down the Cuban regime. However, Cuba had the Soviet Union as an ideological patron, and while the Cuban economy was surely hurt by the total embargo, Soviet assistance kept the economy afloat. After the demise of the Soviet Union, the Cuban economy suffered, Fidel Castro stepped down, and his brother Raul allowed limited private property rights to be exercised in Cuba. Perhaps after 50 years, the embargo has begun to show some political results. Another example can be found in Iran. During the Islamic Revolution in Iran in 1979, Iranian students stormed the U.S. embassy in Tehran, holding 52 diplomats hostage for over a year. The United States responded with comprehensive sanctions against Iran.

A major problem with both the Cuban and the Iranian sanctions is that they were unilateral in nature. The United States was sanctioning these regimes, but others were not. So others were available to serve as markets for Cuban and Iranian goods and services and as sources of the imports Cuba and Iran desired. Critics of such unilateral sanctions argue that the only ones who end up suffering as a result are the U.S. businesses that are prevented from buying from or selling to those target countries. The Iranian government only agreed to negotiations regarding its nuclear program once the EU added its economic sanctions to the long-standing unilateral ones by the United States and Iran lost significant oil revenues and access to the global electronic banking network.

When comprehensive sanctions are multilateral in nature and imposed by most trading states in the international system, they are far more significant and can have devastating effects on the target. The classic example is Iraq after the 1991 Persian Gulf War. When the war ended, the Iraqi government agreed to follow all UN Security Council resolutions that would follow. When the UN later demanded that Iraq open its weapons of mass destruction programs up for international inspection, the Saddam Hussein regime at first dragged its feet and then later expelled international weapons inspectors from the country. The UN Security Council then passed comprehensive sanctions against Iraq. While regime leaders continued to live in luxury, Iraqi civilians bore the brunt of the economic pain, as the country's infrastructure deteriorated from a lack of maintenance (thereby collapsing the electric grid and many sanitary water systems), food supplies ran short, and medical supplies virtually ran out. As thousands of Iraqis began to die as a result, the UN chose to allow limited sales of Iraqi oil so the Iraqi government would have the funds to buy food and other humanitarian supplies. Unfortunately, much of this money simply got skimmed by Iraqi officials (and some officials in the UN itself), so the Iraqi people continued to suffer.

The suffering of the Iraqi people led to an effort to find better ways to use economic sanctions. Now U.S. policy makers prefer the use of **targeted** or **smart sanctions**. These are meant to punish the specific individuals who actually make the policies that are contrary to U.S. interests rather than the people of the target country as a whole. Such sanctions can include freezing the international bank accounts of regime leaders and supporters, limiting their ability to travel internationally by denying visas, and restricting electronic money transfers to or from the targeted country. Such actions were taken in the 1990s against Haitian military leaders who had toppled a democratically elected government there (reportedly their wives were particularly annoyed that they could no longer go on shopping trips to Miami). Targeted or smart sanctions were also used to punish specific high officials of the Iranian regime. After the Syrian government essentially went to war against its own citizens following the Arab Spring of 2011, such targeted sanctions have also been applied to specific individuals who comprise part of Syria's governing elite.

Yet as noted at the beginning of the chapter, not all hard power is employed negatively. There are positive ways to get others to do what the United States wants when the target would prefer not to do so, and we turn to those next.

Positive Approaches

Positive inducements in the form of rewards can also often get others to do what the United States wants. Depending on the other party involved, those inducements could involve an array of tangible or intangible rewards. For instance, in 2011 the former military government of Myanmar (or Burma) did what the United States had long requested; it passed electoral reforms and allowed formerly imprisoned Nobel Peace Prize winner Aung San Suu Kyi to participate in electoral politics. In return, the United States did what Myanmar wanted; it sent a high-ranking official—in this case Secretary of State Hillary Clinton—on a highly visible official visit to the country. The Burmese regime hoped that such a visit would help open Myanmar up to additional foreign direct investment which its economy desperately needed. Time will tell if that goal is accomplished.

While there may be many random examples of different ways to reward regimes for doing what the United States desires, two common forms of such rewards come in the form of economic or military assistance. Perhaps the best example of economic aid being used as a reward came in 1979 when President Jimmy Carter promised to take care of Israel and Egypt in terms of economic assistance in return for their signing of a peace treaty. Every administration since then has kept that commitment, making Israel and Egypt the top two recipients of U.S. economic aid almost each year. When he was once criticized for having "purchased" this peace agreement, Carter defended the action by asking, "what's peace worth to you?" After the Egyptian military deposed popularly-elected President Mohammad Morsi in 2013, some foreign aid deliveries to Egypt were suspended by the United States. Time will tell if U.S. aid to Egypt returns to previous levels.

A more recent example came during the George W. Bush administration. In the context of the UN's Millennium Challenge Goals that sought to dramatically improve human security in developing countries (by reducing poverty, improving access to education and health care, etc.), President Bush made clear that regimes that embraced free-market economic principles, governed justly, and invested in their people would get more U.S. economic aid. The result has been an increase in U.S. economic aid to the poorest countries of the world and an insistence that they meet measurable targets in terms of improvement in the lives of their peoples. The Obama administration continued this effort. If U.S. administrations can use economic assistance as leverage to get others to do what the United States wants, is it any wonder that presidents tend to fall in love with foreign aid as a tool once they reach the Oval Office?

However, economic assistance is not the only currency with which others might be rewarded. Military assistance is often used in this way as well. For years, the United States provided military assistance to Saudi Arabia, despite the fact that it shares neither the U.S. commitment to democracy nor a commitment to women's rights. Yet, as long as the Saudis were willing to sell oil to the United States and serve as a bastion of anti-communist and anti-Iranian stability in the region, they would be rewarded with significant U.S. military aid. After the Iraqi invasion of Kuwait in 1990, the Saudis even allowed U.S. forces to be stationed in the Kingdom—a step that seriously offended some religiously conservative Saudi elites like Osama bin Laden.

Source: Jimmy Carter

Closer to home, when the Colombian government committed to take tougher actions against drug smuggling cartels there in the late 1980s, the United States rewarded the Colombians with packages of both military and economic assistance. That military assistance has continued to the present and was significant enough for then-Venezuelan President Hugo Chávez to maintain that it represented a U.S. threat to his regime.

In 2011 the United States rewarded the Ugandan government for its willingness to go after the Lord's Resistance Army, a warlord militia operating in the Great Lakes region of Africa (which includes countries such as Uganda, Rwanda, Burundi, Kenya, and eastern Democratic Congo). Not only did the Lord's Resistance Army threaten to destabilize this part of eastern Africa, but some of its former leaders faced trial on war crimes and crimes against humanity charges before the International Criminal Court. Not only would the United States help by providing military aid to the Ugandans, but U.S. military advisors would be sent to Uganda as well to help with this effort. Time will tell if the long-term result is positive (an increase in the stability of eastern Africa) or negative (the inclusion of the United States in the conflicts that plague the region).

So hard power options can include both negative punishments to coerce others and positive rewards to induce them to meet U.S. desires. Yet what is even better than pushing or pulling others to do what the United States wants is to get others *to want what the United States wants*. Getting others to want what you want is the essence of soft power, and we turn to those options next.

Soft Power

As just stated, **soft power** involves the ability to get others to want what you want. In this case, the United States would not be coercing others to do what it wants. Instead, it would be co-opting others by getting them to also want what the United States wants. There are a variety of ways this can be done, but two major and mutually reinforcing clusters of means can be identified: the advocacy of American values and governmental agenda-setting at the global and regional levels. Each of these clusters deserves some attention. Let's discuss value advocacy first.

Value Advocacy

A fundamental way for others to want what you want is for them to share your values. Thus, one way of using soft power is projecting a set of values that are attractive to most people. Values such as liberty, democracy, and human rights are commitments to empowering individuals and showing them respect, and these are far easier values to "sell" to others than the values of authoritarian regimes, such as "rule through fear" or "do what the government tells you to do!" The United States stakes out its values in its Declaration of Independence, the Constitution, its laws, and in the organization of the government that flows from all of these sources. However for these values to resonate with others, they must be shown to be more than mere words. How can this be done?

Certainly the U.S. government can promote these values in a variety of ways. A traditional way in the past for such value transmission was the creation of a library in many U.S. embassies abroad where foreign citizens could learn more about the United States, its society, and its governance. Unfortunately in the post-9/11 era, security concerns and the need to harden embassies against the threat of terrorist attack have severely eroded the ability of U.S. diplomatic installations abroad to serve this type of role, as foreign nationals face more and more obstacles in just entering these facilities.

Now, that educational role falls largely on entities such as the Voice of America (VOA). Funded by Congress, the VOA broadcasts 1500 hours of programming each week in 43 different languages and in a variety of media outlets. Through the use of radio, television, the Internet, mobile media, and social media, an estimated global audience of over 140 million per week is reached. In order to avoid the temptation to become simply a propaganda outlet of the U.S. government, the entity's charter requires it to broadcast the news accurately and objectively. Although it seeks to effectively communicate U.S. policies and actions, it is also required by law to include responsible, critical discussions about those policies and actions. So VOA broadcasts can become a window to the United States, letting others know who Americans are and what they value.

Beyond the activities of the VOA, presidents, secretaries of state and defense, ambassadors, and other U.S. officials can and do routinely stress U.S. values and try to emulate them through their actions when meeting with foreign audiences. When President Obama addressed a Muslim audience at Cairo University, officials like the Secretary of State Hillary Clinton and U.S. Trade Representative Ron Kirk met with Kenyan economic officials, Ambassador Susan Rice addressed the UN General Assembly or Security Council, or Defense Secretary Leon Panetta met with his counterparts in Egypt and Israel, these officials were both discussing and *modeling* U.S. values by who they were and how they operated. There is another way such values are modeled as well. Did you know the United States at times prefers to send female ambassadors to Middle East states? Do you think the gender of these personnel choices is a coincidence? Are values again being modeled?

Another way the government can advocate its values is through the Fulbright Program. Sponsored by the State Department and funded by Congress, this program provides grants for U.S. students and scholars to study abroad and for foreign students and scholars to study in the United States. Thus, U.S. citizens studying abroad can serve as pseudo-ambassadors, telling others about life in the United States, while foreign citizens can come to the United States and see for themselves how America operates. They often may take those values back to their native lands.

Yet it is not just the government that participates in transmitting American values. The U.S. educational system does as well. The United States is reputed to have the best system of colleges and universities in the world, and thousands of foreign students are welcomed to that system each year. Many of them will later rise to the ranks of elite decision makers in their home societies. As noted in Chapter 9, Israeli Prime Minister Benjamin Netanyahu has two degrees from the Massachusetts Institute of Technology. Liberian President and Nobel Peace Prize recipient Ellen Johnson Sirleaf is a graduate of Harvard's Kennedy School of Government, King Abdullah II of Jordan attended Georgetown University's School of Foreign Service, former UN Secretary General Boutros Boutros-Ghali was a Fulbright Scholar at Columbia University, former Bolivian President Gonzalo Sanchez de Lozada went to the University of Chicago, Prince Bandar bin Sultan of Saudi Arabia went to Johns Hopkins University School of Advanced International Studies, and so on. While these foreign students are studying subjects such as English, business, political science, or engineering, they often also pick up American values to take back home. So too do high school students who come to the United States in exchange programs and live with American families. When those individuals rise to positions of influence in their home countries, American values may get represented there.

Yet perhaps the greatest transmitter of American values is in the private, not the public, sector. It is the media. U.S. news and entertainment programming can be viewed by almost anyone in the world with a satellite dish, a cable connection, an Internet link, or a smartphone. U.S. movies are globally marketed, with many U.S. films routinely selling more tickets outside the United States than inside it. To the extent the media illustrates American values, much of the rest of the world can see and judge them. For many abroad, American values are seductive; they regret that their society does not value and respect individual freedoms and opportunities in the same way the United States does. To the extent such values make others look favorably on the United States and begin to see things as Americans see them, soft power is at work.

To be fair, the opposite can happen too. Learning more about America may make others with very conservative values less favorable to the United States. That happened with Egyptian writer Sayyid Qutb, a member of the Muslim Brotherhood and considered by most to be the inspiration for later al Qaeda leaders like Osama bin Laden and Ayman al-Zawahiri. Qutb spent two years in the United States in the late 1940s and subsequently wrote that he was appalled by the consumerism, superficiality, and moral decay of American political culture.

Besides sharing values, there are other ways to get others to want what you want. One of those involves setting the international agenda, and we turn to that next.

Agenda-Setting

As anyone who has ever presided over a meeting knows, one way to maximize your chances of getting what you want is to set the meeting's agenda. The same holds true in foreign policy. The United States did a masterful job of setting the international agenda for the post–World War II era by supporting the creation of a series of international institutions that, by meeting the needs of others, also met U.S. needs.[4] This was done at the global and at the regional levels.

On the global level, consider institutions such as the World Bank, the International Monetary Fund, and the General Agreement on Tariffs and Trade. These institutions sought to bring order and stability to the global economy after World War II. They established structures to address economic situations ranging from routine economic challenges or opportunities to full-blown crises, as well as the rules by which these structures would operate. Yet it took money to bring these institutions to life, and the United States provided more money to them than anyone else. Moreover, the rules were generally written so that those who contributed the most money to these organizations had the most influence on the decisions they made. This meant the United States could largely shape the decisions being made, as it had more voting shares than any other state. States facing economic challenges got help, and the United States got to steer that help in the directions it preferred—typically toward capitalist, free-market–based solutions. From the U.S. perspective, this was a "win/win" scenario.

After the Cuban Missile Crisis scared the world with the possibility of a nuclear war, the U.S., British, and Soviet governments sought to back away from the nuclear brink of disaster. That effort began with the Nuclear Test Ban Treaty. Moreover, the nuclear weapons powers had no desire to see others gain such weaponry as well, but other countries wanted the benefits and/or status of nuclear power. So in 1964 the United States offered a proposal to the UN that later led to the drafting and signing of the Nonproliferation Treaty and the creation of the nonproliferation regime. Thus, U.S. foreign policy makers found a way to get others to want what they wanted: a world in which there are established rules and procedures that safeguard countries' rights to develop peaceful nuclear power without risking a world filled with nuclear weapons states.

At the regional level as well, agenda-setting can be an important form of soft power. In the Western Hemisphere, the United States has encouraged the development of organizations such as the Organization of American States (OAS), which promotes democracy, human rights, security from harm, economic development, and the rule of law. The fact that the headquarters of the OAS is in Washington, DC, tells us something important. When dealing with regional issues such as economic integration, immigration, or combating narco-trafficking rings, the United States was long able to set agendas so that the question was not whether the countries of the Americas would cooperate, but how they would do so.

To be fair, we should note that U.S. ability to determine the agenda in the Americas has been diminished a bit in recent years by the relative neglect of the region by most U.S. administrations and by the rising and vocal challenge of leaders like Hugo Chávez of Venezuela and Evo Morales of Bolivia. Groups such as the Union of South American Nations seek to coordinate the political and economic policies of the region without the guidance of the United States.

Regional agenda-setting and shaping is not just confined to the Western Hemisphere. In Europe in the 1990s, the United States began articulating a theme within the NATO community. If NATO members (and other Europeans more generally) did not like the United States acting as a military superpower, then what military roles were they willing to step up and take on themselves? Again, meetings became more about "what will you do and how will you do it," and less about "will you do anything?" As a result, NATO undertook combat missions in the former Yugoslavia and later in Afghanistan and then Libya.

When discussing hard and soft power policy outputs, we need to keep in mind that the world is a complicated place, and there are far more than two ways to get things done. Hard and soft power policy outputs can be pursued simultaneously. When combined together, they can be thought of as smart power options. We turn to those now.

Smart Power

When correctly applied, hard power policy options can work, because enough coercive force or sufficient incentives can achieve the desired result. However, such policies may breed resentment on the part of the recipients, since those policies were not something the recipients wanted to do on their own. The targets of hard power policy options may thus interpret their subsequent actions as expedient or necessary actions but not necessarily legitimate ones. **Smart power** represents the combination of both hard and soft power options. Adding soft power elements can make a hard power option easier to accept on the part of the target, because there is some degree of attraction or shared values involved. Sometimes, the addition of soft power elements can make more coercive elements less necessary, as the result may be seen as more legitimate in the eyes of the target.

How might smart power work? Consider religious-based terrorism, for example. One way to deal with it is to try to kill every terrorist identified. That's hard power. But it seems an impossible task. Every terrorist killed has family and friends who may turn to terrorism because the United States killed their loved one. The "whack-a-mole" analogy applies; dealing with the problem here just makes it pop up elsewhere. In addition to taking hard-core terrorists out of action when possible, what if other potential terrorists and their co religionists learned that the United States did not hate their religion and was not at war with it, that members of their own religion openly practice their faith in the United States, or that their holy texts did not support the taking of innocent lives? Would the number of potential terrorists drop? For those whose terrorism is rooted in economic misery and lack of opportunity, what if the economy in their society grew, more jobs were available, and the quality of their lives materially improved? Would they turn to terrorism then?

Although the term was not in vogue then, a good example of smart power policy options at work can be found in the U.S. expulsion of Iraqi forces from Kuwait in 1991. Certainly, hard power options were used. Over half a million U.S. troops were moved to the Kuwait Theater of Operations, and the subsequent invasion routed the Iraqi troops in Kuwait and drove them in disarray out of the country. However, what made that operation so politically successful was the other policy options that were also employed. Every major step taken by the United States was approved in advance by the UN Security Council, so the actions were seen as legitimate in world eyes. After the initial Iraqi invasion of Kuwait in 1990, Secretary of State James Baker and other U.S. diplomats traveled extensively throughout the region as well as the world, lining up support from other countries. The fact that more than two dozen other countries were willing to contribute military personnel to the effort to liberate Kuwait—including Arab states such as Egypt, Syria, Morocco, Oman, United Arab Emirates, Qatar as well as Saudi Arabia and Kuwait—made it clear that they too felt the Iraqi occupation of Kuwait was illegitimate and should not stand. In short, others wanted what the United States wanted. Had the United States simply gone to war against the Iraqi forces, Iraqi President Saddam Hussein would have been better able to sell his idea that this conflict was between an Arab state and the United States or between him and George Bush, thereby gaining some sympathy from anti-U.S. sentiments in the region.

So while complementing hard power options with soft power options is nothing new, the idea of smart power has recently gained considerable traction in the Obama administration. As the State Department's website says:

> Military force may sometimes be necessary to protect our people and our interests. But diplomacy and development are equally important in creating conditions for a peaceful, stable and prosperous world. That is the essence of smart power—using all the tools at our disposal.[5]

One might expect the State Department to champion smart power approaches to foreign policy problems, but former Secretary of Defense Robert Gates was also a very highly visible and vocal proponent of a greater reliance on smart power policy outputs. During the Obama administration, he testified before Congress that the State Department needed more money, not less, to serve U.S. interests better. He pointed out that the military successes alone could not win the wars in Iraq and Afghanistan; it would also take more diplomatic initiatives, better U.S. outreach to potentially hostile groups, and far more economic aid to accomplish U.S. goals in those countries. That would require more U.S. funding for the State Department. At one point in his congressional testimony, Gates referenced the final scene in the movie *Charlie Wilson's War*, in which the Congress was willing to spend a billion dollars to defeat the Soviets in Afghanistan but not willing to spend a million dollars to build the schools there, which might have prevented the Taliban from coming to power.[6] In another comparison, Gates pointed out that there are more U.S. personnel in *one* aircraft carrier task force than in the entire U.S. diplomatic corps, and he said that if the State Department had more money to conduct more civilian programs, then the Defense Department might be called upon less and would need less money in the long run.

Gates did not just talk up this idea of relying more on smart power; he acted on it. For example, he appointed Navy Admiral James Stavridis to head U.S. European Command, citing his prior successes as head of U.S. military operations in Latin America. In that role, Stavridis combined soft power options (e.g., providing health-care services and sponsoring soccer teams) with hard power options to take on the challenges of combating narco-trafficking and corruption and to create a more favorable image of the United States in the region. In Gates's view, such a cooperative approach was also appropriate for dealing with European allies, who often needed coaxing to act in what he saw as the U.S. and European shared interests.[7] Even more impressive, he supported the creation of a new Africa Command that blended hard and soft power in its mission statement and personnel choices, as Box 10.2 demonstrates. So smart

BOX 10.2

What's So Different about AFRICOM?

For U.S. foreign policy makers, Africa represents a multitude of current and future challenges. A billion people, one-seventh of the world's population, live there, and the population is growing rapidly. Africa's population could double by the middle of the 21st century. Not only is Africa the world's poorest continent, but it is also plagued by poor governance, corruption, and violent conflicts that have killed over 5 million people since the end of the Cold War. Both traditional and nontraditional security challenges abound there. As a result, the United States created a new military unified command in 2007 to deal with protecting U.S. interests in Africa: the United States Africa Command or **AFRICOM**.

From the start, AFRICOM was different. Its mission statement includes explicit reference to promoting good governance and development:

> Africa Command protects and defends the national security interests of the United States by strengthening the defense capabilities of African states and regional organizations and, when directed, conducts military operations, in order to deter and defeat transnational threats and to provide a security environment conducive to good governance and development.

Moreover, AFRICOM is the first U.S. regional military command to include civilian officials from other branches of government. More than 30 people from 13 other government agencies or departments can be found in key leadership, staff, and administrative roles. Four senior foreign service officers are in key leadership positions, including one filling the role of deputy to the commander for civil–military activities—a position just one step removed from the top of the organizational chart. These interagency appointees help AFRICOM provide humanitarian assistance, crisis relief, and long-term economic development and good governance assistance for African states.

What do you think? Is AFRICOM's emphasis on combining hard and soft power options into smart power options the right way to go? If so, are such policy options appropriate just for Africa, or do they resonate elsewhere as well? On the other hand, is the military's role, as President George W. Bush once stated, to fight and win wars?

Sources: "Advanced Questions for General William E. 'Kip' Ward, U.S. Army, Nominee for Commander, U.S. Africa Command," Senate Armed Services Committee, September 2007;

"Population Dynamics of Africa," World Population Awareness, December 17, 2011;

U.S. Africa Command website; available online at: http://www.africom.mil/AboutAFRICOM .asp;

"World Population," Population Reference Bureau, UN Population Division, September 2011.

power policy options seem to be increasingly the "new normal" when it comes to U.S. foreign policy outputs.

Conclusion: The State of the U.S. Foreign Policy Toolbox

As the United States moves deeper into the 21st century, foreign policy challenges that are increasingly global and transnational in nature will call for a variety of foreign policy outputs. Hard power outputs—the ability to get others to do what you want—will always have a role. The power to coerce—through the threat or use of force—or to reward—through incentives like foreign aid and other side payments—will be used where appropriate.

However, as someone once said, you cannot nuke global warming. Numerous other foreign policy challenges and opportunities will call for soft power outputs—emphasizing shared values and common concerns so that others want the same things that the United States wants. For example, improving the quality of life elsewhere—through outputs like targeted foreign assistance or democratization assistance—can serve U.S. interests in a variety of ways. Societies can become more stable and less violence-prone. As other societies improve their economies, they have the ability to purchase more U.S. goods and services and have a greater stake in preserving an increasingly beneficial international order.

As the Obama administration stressed, the coupling of hard and soft power policy outputs into smart power approaches seems to be the wave of the future. The United States is not a hegemonic military power that can impose its will on others with impunity. That was evident in the first decade of the 21st century, as the ability to fight two wars at the same time seriously stressed the U.S. military and gave countries such as Iran the breathing room to more actively pursue their national interests at the expense of U.S. interests. When the George W. Bush administration threatened Iran with the use of force over its support for terrorist groups and its nuclear weapons program, Iranian Supreme Leader Ayatollah Sayyid Ali Khamenei called the U.S. bluff, publicly stating that the U.S. military was stretched so thin that it could do nothing to Iran. At the time, he was largely correct. Further, as the United States slowly recovers from the Great Recession of 2008–2010 and faces a "fiscal cliff" of mounting debt, the need to find lower-cost options than the use of military force will be paramount.

Thus, the United States now pursues a range of foreign policy outputs to deal with ongoing issues. The first step is normally soft power—diplomatic outreach and engagement—which tends to be more successful to the degree the United States has been able to share its values with the target state. Should those means prove insufficient, hard power outputs in the form of rewards offered or threats made may be next. Should those fail to suffice, U.S. foreign policy makers have to decide if the issue is significant enough to justify the use of force. If so, in the 21st century, that use of force—to be most effective—will probably be accompanied by other soft power elements to form a smart power response so that the matter is seen as a more legitimate step by the international community.

Glossary Terms

AFRICOM   the Defense Department's U.S. Africa Command, which combines both military roles and humanitarian and development roles in its mission statement and which includes nonmilitary as well as military personnel.

Asymmetric conflict   a conflict featuring two forces of vastly different size and apparent power.

Economic sanctions   economic means to punish a state, such as by refusing to buy its products or sell it what it needs.

General war   a conflict in which all the conventional weaponry in the U.S. arsenal would be available for use, the geographic scope of the conflict would not be limited, and weapons of mass destruction could potentially be used.

Hard power   getting others to do what you want when they otherwise do not want to do so, typically by using coercion or payments.

Limited war   a conflict that is limited by geographic scope, the amount and types of weaponry used, and the goals for which the war is fought.

Smart power   the combination of hard and soft power, in which targets are encouraged to do what they would otherwise choose not to do but are encouraged in such a way that the request seems more legitimate.

Soft power   getting others to want what you want by co-opting rather than coercing them.

Targeted/smart sanctions   sanctions meant to punish the elites who actually make the policies that are contrary to U.S. interests rather than the people of the target country as a whole.

Unconventional war   a conflict in which one side employs uniformed troops and the other side does not.

Endnotes

1. This chapter borrows heavily from the work of Joseph S. Nye, Jr., *The Paradox of American Power: Why the World's Only Superpower Can't Go It Alone* (New York, NY: Oxford University Press, 2002); "Get Smart," *Foreign Affairs* 88 (July, August 2009), 160–163; and his book with Robert O. Keohane, *Power and Interdependence* (4th ed.) (Boston, MA: Longman, 2012).
2. This section draws upon Chapter 5 of James M. Scott, Ralph G. Carter, and A. Cooper Drury, *IR* (Boston, MA: Wadsworth, Cengage, 2014).
3. This section draws upon Chapter 9 of James M. Scott, Ralph G. Carter, and A. Cooper Drury, *IR* (Boston, MA: Wadsworth, Cengage, 2014).
4. For more on this idea, see G. John Ikenberry, *After Victory: Institutions, Strategic Restraint, and the Rebuilding of Order after Major Wars* (Princeton, NJ: Princeton University Press, 2000).
5. "American 'Smart Power': Diplomacy and Development Are the Vanguard," Department of State website, April 28, 2011, available online at http://www.state.gov/r/pa/plrmo/162247.htm.
6. Lisa Daniel, "State Department Needs Iraq Funding," American Forces Press Service, February 17, 2011, available online at http://terrorism-online.blogspot.com/2011/02/state-department-needs-iraq-funding.html.
7. Gordon Lubold, "Pentagon to Show Softer Side to the World," *Christian Science Monitor*, March 25, 2009, available online at http://www.csmonitor.com/USA/Military/2009/0325/p03s03-usmi.html.

CHAPTER 11

The Future of American Foreign Policy Making

Source: KRT/APTN/ AP Images

What represents a greater challenge to U.S. future foreign policy, the military challenge of North Korea and its young leader Kim Jong-un (previous page) or South Korea's rapid rise as an industrial and consumer-oriented power as indicated by UN Secretary-General Ban Ki-moon and rapper Psy?
Source: UN Photo/Eskinder Debebe/Photoshot/Newscom

LEARNING OBJECTIVES

- Define national security inputs, economic security inputs, and human security inputs.

- Evaluate any changes in the degree to which each of these three types of policy inputs may shape U.S. foreign policy in the near term future.

- Assess which policy-making actors may gain relative influence in the near term future and which may lose some influence.

- Predict how U.S. foreign policy–making outputs may change in the future.

Introduction

As someone once said, the one great constant is change. After World War II, expectations that the Allied Powers would continue to cooperate, reflected in the creation and structure of the new United Nations (UN), were dashed by the rise of the new Cold War. The rivalry between the United States and the Soviet Union dwarfed all other foreign policy issues and caused most issues to be perceived through the prism of national security interests. When the Cold War ended, the decade of the 1990s offered the expectation of a new era of peace and cooperation. As Francis Fukuyama suggested, "we're all liberals now."[1] However, long pent-up tribal, clan, and sectarian rivalries exploded in multiple parts of the world. The result was a messy, violent political order, famously characterized as "a clash of civilizations" by Samuel Huntington.[2] Thus, the Clinton administration spent far more time than it anticipated dealing with humanitarian threats and regional security crises. Then came the terrorist attacks of September 11, 2001. Not surprisingly, the George W. Bush administration launched a "war on terror" that again dwarfed most other issues.

The election of Barack Obama promised a change in U.S. foreign policy, and in some stylistic ways, that change was realized. The phrase "war on terror" no longer escaped the lips of U.S. foreign policy makers. Instead, "change" and "engagement" were the mantras of the new administration. Based primarily on a different mind-set by officials of the new administration, many of the challenges—that the previous administration had defined as national security inputs to be met with largely unilateral or only selectively multilateral policy outputs—were now socially constructed as opportunities impacting the international system as a whole. Motivated by liberal and neoliberal interpretations, these challenges were to be met with multilateral responses. Time will tell if the substantive outputs of the Obama administration are that different from those of its immediate predecessors.

So what types of inputs, processes, and outputs can we expect in the early part of the 21st century? Let's consider each in turn.

Policy Inputs

As indicated in Chapter 2, foreign policy makers rely on their understandings of the way the international system works—in other words, the theories that explain behavior—to cut through the noise of the international system and decide which threats and opportunities to respond to and how to respond. Most American administrations are largely made up by realists and neorealists, who try to address national interests expressed in power terms. The George W. Bush administration had its share of such realists and neorealists, but it also had idealists. President Bush, Vice President Cheney, Defense Secretary Rumsfeld, and others were, to varying degrees, idealists who wanted to use American power to impact the world for the better, while relying on U.S. military power to defend the nation against the scourge of terrorism. For their part, the officials at the top of the first Obama term were largely neoliberals. Led by

President Obama, Secretary of State Clinton, and Defense Secretary Gates, they sought to use cooperation as a means to achieve U.S. national interests.

The administration that follows President Obama may or may not reflect such neoliberal impulses. Yet whatever its basic understandings of how the international system works, it surely will face events that, as foreign policy inputs, are understood in terms of security interests: national security, economic security, and human security.[3] Each of these merits discussion.

National Security Inputs

While it is impossible to note all potential national security threats facing the United States, a few bear special mention. First, the national security situation has evolved significantly after the decade marked by the war on terror. While Takfirist terrorism has not ended, it has fundamentally changed. Al Qaeda as a monolithic entity has been defanged—through the drying up of its ability to easily move money across international borders and the targeted killing or capturing of its top leaders and field operatives. Now terrorism is more locally based, whether within the United States by home-grown terrorists or by terrorist cells who have the ability to strike near their own locations—like Al Shabaab in Somalia, al Qaeda in the Arabian Peninsula in Yemen, al Qaeda in the Islamic Maghreb in northwestern Africa, or Boko Haram in Nigeria.

Second, the 2013 Iranian agreement to suspend its enrichment of nuclear fuel, reduce its supply of previously enriched fuel, and allow international inspections of many of its nuclear facilities for a trial period of six months was welcomed by the five permanent members of the UN Security Council, Germany, and many other states in the international system. However, the deal did not reassure the Israelis or other Sunni regimes in the region who continue to insist that the Iranians are developing the missile and nuclear fuel enrichment technologies needed for nuclear weapons. Who would be the targets of such a potential weapon? The Israelis? The Saudis? Further, Iran continues to play an assertive role in the region by supporting the Shi'a or Shi'a-friendly forces elsewhere. These include the Shi'a militia and political party Hezbollah in Lebanon, the Shi'a Iraqi regime led by Prime Minister Nouri al-Maliki, and the Alawite-dominated regime of Bashar al-Assad in Syria (which is still in power at the time of this writing). In short, Iran's role in the region keeps both Israeli and Sunni Muslim populations on edge. Would Israel launch a preventative strike on Iran? Is sectarian war within Islam a looming possibility within the region, with Shi'a Iran and its allies challenging Sunni Saudi Arabia and its allies?

Third, other national security risks plague the Middle East. The events of the Arab Spring of 2011 continue to play out, and depending on the nature of the regimes that take root in Egypt, Libya, Yemen, and, possibly, Syria, more pro-Islamic or anti-Western challenges may rock the region. Will the new pro-military regime in Egypt be any more reform-minded than was the old Mubarak regime? Will the Muslim Brotherhood stage a comeback in Egypt? In short, will Egypt become a friend or an enemy to the United States? Nearby, Turkey continues to flex its regional military muscle. Its pursuit of Kurdish insurgents across the border into Iraq and Syria risks the threat of border clashes that could easily escalate.

Fourth, in 2011 and 2012 the Obama administration began moving more military personnel to Asia, to offset provocative Chinese activities there. Particularly troubling are Chinese efforts to assert their control over the South China Sea and the resources surrounding the Senkaku/Diaoyu Islands jointly claimed by China and Japan as well as the resources surrounding the Spratly Islands, which China, Vietnam, and the Philippines all claim. Further, clashes have occurred between Chinese and Japanese fishing and naval vessels, and in 2013 China proclaimed a controversial sovereign airspace over the contested waters between these two states.

Finally, North Korea cannot be ignored in this list. As a nuclear power with a large standing army, a failed economy, an impoverished and often starved civilian population, and an uncertain leader in young Kim Jong-un who in 2013 had his uncle—the number two man in the regime—executed, the possibilities for national security crises are manifold. Under Kim's father Kim Jong-il, North Korea often undertook provocative actions, such as firing missiles over Japan. What might his relatively inexperienced son do?

Some national security opportunities deserve mention as well. The United States has been relatively successful since the 1990s in getting North Atlantic Treaty Organization (NATO) members to shoulder more military burdens, in places such as Bosnia and Afghanistan. Arguably it was the EU embargo on purchasing Iranian oil and denial of the use of the global electronic banking network that finally pushed Iran to the negotiating table, and European members of NATO might be more willing to work with the United States in deterring any unwise future Iranian military actions. Several NATO states already work with the United States in patrolling the waters of the western Indian Ocean to protect maritime traffic from Somalia-based pirates. So, there are precedents for more cooperation and burden-sharing.

Economic Security Inputs

The effects of the Great Recession of 2008–2010 continue to linger. U.S. economic growth has been sluggish since the recession, and additional steps will be needed to stimulate U.S. economic growth, to coordinate international responses to shared economic problems, and to regulate the practices that led to the recession. Each of these deserves some brief discussion.

The George W. Bush administration reacted to the Great Recession with selective bailouts of large financial institutions and corporate entities and with steps designed to stabilize the credit markets. The Obama administration got two large stimulus packages passed, but neither of them had a transformative effect on the growth of jobs in the country. The prospects of another large stimulus package seem dim, as concerns in Congress about the size of the U.S. deficit prompt efforts to rein in government spending, not to increase it. Consequently, the most likely steps in the future will be to address the underlying fundamentals of the economy (tax policy, monetary policy, regulatory actions, etc.) that will help the private sector revive on its own. Luckily in late 2013, unemployment dropped and the economy seems to be growing at a slow but steady pace.

The threats of countries such as Greece, Italy, and Spain going bankrupt also figure on the U.S. foreign policy agenda. U.S. corporations have heavily invested in Europe, and U.S.-European trade ties are extensive. Anything that hurts the European economy will also hurt the U.S. economy. Anything that hurts the euro as a currency puts additional pressures on the U.S. dollar, at a time when the Chinese have been calling for the replacement of the dollar as the global default currency. As Europe goes, so goes the global economy, and that includes the United States. U.S. administrations may be called upon to help European states more in the coming years, and that may be a hard sell with the voters back home.

European leaders—particularly the Germans and French—have been calling for greater regulation of the practices that led to the Great Recession in the first place. They call for more regulation of the business practices of banks and other financial institutions, and they continue to insist on restrictions of what they see as outrageously large bonuses for successful risk-takers in corporate America. The quest for such huge bonuses, often in the multimillion-dollar range, led to the ill-considered investments that caused the U.S. housing bubble and ultimately destabilized American credit markets. Given the call for smaller government by many in the Republican Party and as long as Republicans control at least one chamber of Congress, greater regulation of the private sector seems unlikely.

Finally, others are rising from the chaos of the Great Recession more quickly than the United States. Compared to the third quarter in 2012, China's annual GDP increased by 7.8% in the third quarter of 2013, while U.S. annual GDP for the same period increased by only 1.8%.[4] For the same time period, South Korea's rising economic might was indicated not only by a 3.3% growth rate in annual GDP but also by the rising visibility of Hyundai and Kia automobiles, Samsung smartphones, and LG appliances in the American marketplace.[5]

Human Security Inputs

Human security involves the ability of people around the world to live their lives with some reasonable expectation that they will have adequate food, shelter, health care, education, income, and safety from violence to ensure a reasonable quality of life for their families. The challenges from this point of view are many. For example, how will sluggish economic growth and widespread societal violence in Mexico impact the United States? Will the violence spread across the border, or has it already done so? Will illegal immigration escalate as the violence between narco-trafficking rings takes its toll on Mexican cities and towns? The same questions can be posed for considerable portions of Central America as well.

However, as the example of AFRICOM suggested in Chapter 10, Africa is the real problem in this regard. Amid grinding poverty, corruption, and intrastate violence, desperate people will do whatever it takes to survive. They will work in dangerous conditions—such as illegal gold and diamond mines where their risk of injury or death is high. Some will sell their family members into slavery or push them into prostitution. Either willingly or unwillingly, others will join criminal groups or militias run by warlords. Some will become refugees and thus someone else's domestic problem.

These situations may well pose national security threats for U.S. interests at home and abroad, as does Al Shabaab in Somalia or al Qaeda in the Islamic Maghreb, for example. Yet they can present opportunities as well. The United States gained great respect in many African societies through its economic assistance to offset the scourge of HIV/AIDS. What other possibilities to create goodwill might be present in places such as Africa?

More broadly, as the global economy slowly lurches out of the Great Recession, many around the world are hurt. However, women in poor societies are hurt more than their male counterparts. Women employed outside the home are often the first fired, they tend to become victims of violence and oppression, and they often lack access to opportunities to change their circumstances. Much needs to be done to protect women's rights, and this creates an opportunity for the United States if its leaders choose to seize it.

Finally, in terms of human security, other transnational issues have risen in importance in recent years as well. Perhaps, the best single example is the issue of global climate change. Despite the presence of some naysayers, the UN and most national governments now accept the premise that human activity is influencing global climate change and producing more intense storms and weather phenomena. Some results linked to global climate change are easy to see. In 2010 alone, thousands of people died in record-setting floods (in Chad, China, Colombia, Italy, Pakistan, and the Philippines), heat waves (in Russia and the United States), and snowstorms (in China, Russia, and the United States).[6] Severe weather is getting more severe, and more people are dying as a result. Dealing with such problems located in the "global commons" will pose real difficulties for U.S. foreign policy makers. Whatever the types of inputs, the policy-making processes of the U.S. government have the task of transforming them into outputs. We turn to those processes next.

Policy-Making Processes

To get a good sense of likely directions for U.S. policy making, we need to think about the types of actors likely to participate meaningfully in U.S. foreign policy making, as well as about the ways policy making works. Let's consider actors first.

Actors

At first glance, the actors who typically make U.S. foreign policy have not changed. The president is still in a favored position to make foreign policy, with the help of personal advisers as well as numerous officials from the White House, National Security Council, the major Cabinet departments, the military, the Intelligence Community, and so on. Congress is still "hard-wired" into the foreign policy process, through such roles as the legislative authorization and appropriations processes, oversight and investigative processes, and senatorial approval of treaties and key personnel appointments. The courts will occasionally venture into the foreign policy realm, as they have regarding the rights of detainees in the war on terror. Elected officials still listen to public opinion and interest groups, and everyone seems to listen to experts, celebrities, and foreign leaders, albeit to varying degrees.

However, changes seem apparent in the weight some actors may have in shaping U.S. foreign policy. In the executive branch under George W. Bush, the national security–related actors took center stage, which did not seem surprising due to the 9/11 terrorist attacks and the resulting U.S. war on terror. However, it now seems clear that sound advice from civilian experts working for the State Department, the National Security Council, and in other parts of the administration was at times overlooked by the White House, and time has also shown that combating terrorism abroad requires all the tools of statecraft—political, diplomatic, economic, and cultural—as well as military and paramilitary tools. In the first two years of the Obama administration, the State Department received the budget authority to increase its numbers of new hires, and the administration's civilian personnel with national security–related responsibilities are generally perceived as now being somewhat more influential than they were in the prior administration.

Beyond needing more civilian help across-the-board, the United States also needs more experts who focus on parts of the world relatively underrepresented among government employees—areas such as Africa, Asia, and the Mideast. Also needed is an expedited clearance procedure so U.S. citizens whose families are relatively recent immigrants from such areas (and who can thus speak languages such as Arabic, Farsi, Dari, Pashto, Punjabi, Urdu, and Somali) can get security clearances more rapidly so they can bring their linguistic and cultural skills to the federal government.

In the current economic setting, the influence of economic officials will probably continue to grow as well. The U.S. trade representative is an increasingly significant foreign policy actor. As globalization more tightly connects national and global economies and as the continuing impacts of the Great Recession of 2008–2010 are felt, actors like the National Economic Council and the Council of Economic Advisers will find more of their time spent on things formerly thought of as foreign policy.

On Capitol Hill, another change can be seen. The assertiveness of members of Congress to challenge the administration's requests has generally increased over time.[7] Congressional assertiveness in foreign policy making dramatically increased during the Vietnam War, increased again after the Cold War ended, and increased again after the 9/11 attacks.[8] Even in the arena long thought to be the president's sole preserve—use of force decisions—the partisan makeup of Congress now plays an important role in shaping whether, and how quickly, an administration will choose to go to war.[9] Thus, any idea that members of Congress will willingly take a backseat to the administration in formulating U.S. foreign policy can probably be safely discarded.

Processes

Within the executive branch, some things stay the same. Presidents and their close advisers have always struggled to keep effective lines of communication open within the administration, so they can know what they need to know and when they need to know it. After all, knowledge is power. For their parts, bureaucracies have generally tried to control the flow of information to increase their relative influence or to attain other bureaucratic goals, as bureaucrats often equate what is good for their agency or department with the broader national interest. Thus, within the executive branch, interagency communication, cooperation, and coordination is a constant challenge, and structural adjustments cannot make this challenge go away.

A good example can be found in the Department of Homeland Security. It was created as a response to the fact that, prior to the 9/11 terrorist attacks, different parts of the executive branch were in possession of different pieces of information about the heightened threat of a terrorist attack or about the 19 future terrorists who were already in the United States. The thought in Congress after 9/11 was that if many of these agencies were lumped together in the same department, they would talk to each other more readily and someone might be able to connect the dots of what we know and see the whole picture of any potential threat. However, since its formation in 2002, the different components of the administration responsible for homeland security still find it difficult to coordinate their efforts or to even communicate with each other. Thus within the administration, more and more time is spent in meetings in an effort to produce a coordinated U.S. response to foreign policy opportunities and challenges, and it takes a considerable investment of effort on the part of White House officials to try to get all relevant administration actors moving in the same direction in support of the president's foreign policy initiatives.

Just as administrations are conflicted by bureaucratic cleavages, Congress is beset by partisan ones. The idea that partisan politics stops at the water's edge has been an outdated assumption since the 1950s.[10] Partisan control of the presidency and Congress matters tremendously. While some exceptions can be found, we can even speak of a Republican or Democratic foreign policy. In recent years, Republican officials in Washington have generally stressed foreign policy themes that emphasize national security goals, a preference for hard over soft power, and a more unilateralist stance on protection of U.S. sovereignty from international, multilateral, or supranational intrusions. Conversely, most Democratic officials in Washington have typically emphasized economic goals, soft or smart power over hard power alone, and greater multilateral engagement and cooperation to achieve U.S. objectives. Thus, perhaps more than ever before, *which party controls the presidency and Congress matters, in terms of both the issues seen as important and the preferred means by which to address those issues.*

Within Congress, party polarization is stronger in the House of Representatives than in the Senate, because centrist Republicans and Democrats have increasingly chosen not to seek reelection or have been defeated in reelection. Thus, as groups, House Republicans have generally become more conservative and House Democrats generally more liberal. As a consequence, presidents not only face difficulty wooing members of the opposition party but also often have difficulty securing the support of their own party members in the House.

Because of their need to do what is best for the country as a whole, presidents often propose more moderate or centrist policies that are neither conservative enough to satisfy House Republicans nor liberal enough to satisfy House Democrats.

Despite the party polarization in the House, the House is still capable of passing highly contentious foreign policy legislation, as all it takes is a simple majority vote. If the majority party in the House speaks with one voice, it can pass bills. Although some centrist Republicans and Democrats can still be found in the Senate, Senate procedures greatly complicate getting things done that require votes. Due to the Senate's cloture rule, 60 votes are normally needed to end debate on any issue, so unless the majority party leaders can identify 60 of the 100 senators willing to vote to end any possible filibuster, they will often avoid even scheduling contentious issues—like passing a budget. Thus, structural gridlock is increasingly frequent in the Senate. In late 2013, Senate Democrats addressed one frustrating facet of this gridlock by changing the number of votes needed to end filibusters on most presidential appointment nominations from 60 to a bare majority of 51.

The impacts of growing partisanship in both chambers have been seen in foreign policy making. The impact of congressional committees has relatively diminished over time as the influence of elected party leaders in each chamber has grown. More and more foreign policy issues get caught in partisan legislative battles, in which neither side wants to give in to the other, and the result is even fewer pieces of legislation passed than before. As suggested earlier, just passing the annual budgets for the foreign policy bureaucracy is increasingly difficult—even though funds have to be appropriated for the government to function. As a consequence (and often well after the new fiscal year has begun on October 1), more and more different issues get lumped together in massive omnibus appropriations bills. The result is that individual budget items get less careful evaluation than before and legislators are forced to vote "yes" or "no" on a huge collection of things just to get the money needed for the few issues that are important to them.

Although it may seem counterintuitive, as Congress is more hamstrung by partisan politics and passing legislation becomes more difficult, the influence of individual members of Congress who care about foreign policy has actually grown. Congressional foreign policy entrepreneurs work with administrations to get their foreign policy agendas advanced, but when administrations do not cooperate, these entrepreneurs find a wide variety of ways to push the issues they care about anyway. Like congressional assertiveness in general, the number of congressional foreign policy entrepreneurs has steadily increased over time.[11] Future presidents will have to contend with multiple members of Congress who are quite willing to tell the administration what it should do and how it should do it, and members of Congress will be more than willing to penalize presidents who fail to go along with their wishes—often by saying "no" to the important items on both the president's foreign and domestic policy agenda. Those entrepreneurs who occupy elected party leader positions in their chamber or sit on the appropriations, armed services, or foreign affairs committees in Congress will be even more able to use their negative power to hinder or kill administration requests if their policy wishes are ignored. Thus, if the president and Congress cannot agree on the broad outlines of U.S. foreign policy, policy gridlock will continue.

Policy Outputs

As we saw in Chapter 10, we can differentiate between hard power, soft power, and smart power policy outputs. Some initial thoughts on each of these can be offered.

Hard Power Outputs

In the second decade following the 9/11 terrorist attacks, U.S. foreign policy priorities are shifting. The emphasis on combating terrorists is changing, as are the means for doing so. War-weariness on the part of the public and the political need to reduce the number of U.S. combat casualties have led to the removal of U.S. troops from Iraq and a gradual withdrawal of U.S. troops in Afghanistan. The result has been a lessening of the number of combat casualties, which then reduces the press coverage devoted to what was previously called a "war on terrorism" and is now more often referred to as the fight against religious extremism. The U.S. counterterrorism efforts of the Obama administration increasingly rely on attacking suspected terrorist sites through the use of clandestine or special operations forces, unmanned drone aircraft, willing allies, or some combination of all these means. Those terrorist sites thought to be of greatest threat are located less in Iraq or even Afghanistan and more often in places such as Pakistan, Yemen, Somalia, and Mali.

Not only did the political need to reduce combat casualties drive a change in military strategy, the rising financial costs of military operations did as well. For example, the Iraq War was the second most costly war in U.S. history, trailing only World War II in inflation-adjusted terms. The direct costs of the war exceeded $800 billion (not the $50–$60 billion the George W. Bush administration predicted), and the indirect costs of medical care and disability compensation costs for wounded veterans over the next 40 years are expected to reach nearly $1 trillion.[12] Given such rising costs and the need to cut nearly $500 billion from the defense budget over the next 10 years, the Pentagon announced a shift in strategy in which the United States would no longer be able to fight two wars at once; instead, its goal would be the simultaneous capability to fight one war and respond to a "military situation" elsewhere. The defense spending cuts announced in early 2012 emphasized reductions in the numbers of personnel in the Army and Marine Corps and a greater reliance on smaller special operations forces, the use of unmanned drone aircraft, and cybersecurity initiatives. So, assuming these budget cuts survive the congressional appropriations process (which seems likely but is not guaranteed), the future hard power options for U.S. foreign policy makers will be fewer than they have been in the past.

Soft Power Outputs

Barring a major shift in thinking in Washington, a greater reliance on soft power policy outputs seems likely. There are several reasons for this shift. First, the Obama administration has already moved in this direction, both because of the desire to differentiate itself from its predecessor the George W. Bush administration and because it saw soft power options such as enhanced diplomatic engagement to be the preferred way to address difficult 21st-century situations.

For example, shortly after assuming office, President Obama made his famous address at Cairo University to reach out to the Islamic world. Obama augmented this effort by appointing Farah Anwar Pandith to the newly created position of special representative to Muslim communities, a post that reports directly to the secretary of state. An American Muslim originally from the predominantly Muslim Kashmir region of India, Representative Pandith previously served in the George W. Bush administration as director of Middle East regional initiatives for the National Security Council and before that as the chief of staff for the Bureau for Asia and the Near East of the U.S. Agency for International Development (USAID).[13] Another step came in early 2012 when administration officials began meeting with representatives of Egypt's Muslim Brotherhood, trying to forge some form of relationship with the organization that won the largest share of seats in Egypt's parliamentary election in late 2011. Such outreach is a reversal of long-standing U.S. policy, which saw the Muslim Brotherhood as an Islamic fundamentalist organization opposed to U.S. interests in the region. The administration seeks to find common ground with Egypt's military now that it has ousted Egypt's Islamist president, Mohammad Morsi.

Second, many of those difficult 21st-century situations are increasingly global in nature. Problems such as global climate change, pandemic diseases, and human rights concerns are extraordinarily difficult to resolve unless there is at least regional, if not global, cooperation. Such cooperation requires all the tools of multilateral diplomacy to be effective. While the UN and its various components will continue to be important forums for diplomatic efforts, groups like the G-8 major industrial powers, the G-20 major market countries, and regional groups such as Asia Pacific Economic Cooperation will increasingly be the locations for negotiation over such regional and global issues.

Third, soft power outputs are attractive after the Great Recession. While these outputs may take considerable time to bear fruit, they often require fewer out-of-pocket expenses than do hard power outputs. As suggested in Chapter 10, the entire U.S. diplomatic corps entails fewer employees than one aircraft carrier task force. A global architecture already exists to reach out to others to deal with mutual problems and challenges; it is the system of U.S. embassies, consulates, and missions. Additional numbers of well-trained diplomats could take better advantage of this existing resource. To paraphrase former British Prime Minister Winston Churchill, to jaw-jaw is better than to war-war.

Smart Power Outputs

In an era in which the United States is not a hegemonic power that can impose any of its desires on the rest of the international system, using every combination of tools in the U.S. foreign policy toolbox just seems to make sense to most observers. Smart power outputs thus appear to be the wave of the future.

For example, consider the problem of improving the quality of lives of women and children in the Great Lakes region of eastern Africa. Informal militias in the region at times forcibly conscript children into their ranks, using death threats against them or their families if they do not comply. These militias (and at times national armies) in Uganda, Kenya, Somalia, Rwanda, Burundi, and eastern Democratic Congo also prey on women, either simply because they can or to humiliate and shame their rivals. To this violence directed against women, add the problems of daily life that these women and children face: finding sufficient water, food, and cooking fuel to meet their needs of their families. The United States is addressing their needs in a variety of ways.

Hard power is used in the form of U.S. military assistance. U.S. military aid helps the Kenyan government's military offensive into Somalia to stop Al Shabaab raids in Kenya and Uganda, and both U.S. military assistance and armed military advisors help the Ugandan government's military campaign against the Lord's Resistance Army that preys on women and children. Unmanned drone aircraft are also now based in eastern Ethiopia and can be used in the Great Lakes region if needed. These efforts help local regimes protect their own citizens.

Soft power is used as well. As noted in Chapter 10, the U.S. State Department, USAID, U.S. Department of Health and Human Services, U.S. Department of Energy, and the U.S. Environmental Protection Agency combined with German, Norwegian, Dutch, and Peruvian governmental agencies and numerous nongovernmental organizations from the United States and abroad in the Global Alliance for Clean Cookstoves. The alliance seeks to stop the shortening of women's and children's lives caused by breathing toxic fumes from cooking fuels. Among its other global locations, this effort to improve women's and children's health is active in Kenya, Rwanda, and Uganda. U.S. economic assistance is also going to address long-standing women's and children's health problems, such as combating malaria and tuberculosis, providing safe drinking water, and assisting with family planning in both Kenya and Rwanda, among other places. Through this combination of hard and soft power, the United States is seeking to improve the lives of millions of women and children in eastern Africa.

Conclusion

"The more things change, the more they stay the same." Both parts of that sentiment apply to U.S. foreign policy making in the 21st century. To some degree, the inputs to policy making have changed. The global context is quite different from the scary days of the Cold War and the heady days of the post–Cold War period of the 1990s. In some ways the United States is more powerful than ever, but it finds itself facing challenges from terrorists who would prey on U.S. citizens and allies, global economic competitors, and those who say its time as the world's leader has come and gone. In terms of foreign policy–making processes, this new environment for foreign policy making will almost certainly require some rebalancing of needs, interests, and means. Yet that rebalancing will be done by the same governmental and political actors and processes by which foreign policy has been made for decades. Can U.S. foreign policy–making structures and entities designed for the Cold War effectively address the challenges of the post-9/11 world? If not, can sufficient agreement be found among the relevant actors to make the institutional or structural changes needed to produce effective policy outcomes for this new environment? As has been the case in the past, people of goodwill can rise to this challenge, but only time will tell.

Endnotes

1. Francis Fukuyama, "The End of History?" *National Interest* 16 (1989), 3–18.
2. Samuel P. Huntington, "The Clash of Civilizations?" *Foreign Affairs* 72 (1993), 22–49.
3. The emphasis on national, economic, and human security is based on the approach illustrated in James M. Scott, Ralph G. Carter, and A. Cooper Drury, *IR* (Boston, MA: Wadsworth, Cengage, 2014).
4. China GDP Annual Growth Rate," available online at http://www.tradingeconomics.com/china/gdp-growth-annual; "United States GDP Annual Growth Rate," available online at http://www.tradingeconomics.com/united-states/gdp-growth-annual.
5. "South Korea GDP Annual Growth Rate," available online at http://www.tradingeconomics.com/south-korea/gdp-growth-annual.
6. Seth Borenstein and Julie Reed Bell, "2010's World Gone Wild: Quakes, Floods, Blizzards," Associated Press, December 26, 2010, available online at http://www.dailynews.com/news/ci_16942651?source=rss.
7. James M. Scott and Ralph G. Carter, "Acting on the Hill: Congressional Assertiveness in U.S. Foreign Policy," *Congress & the Presidency* 29 (2002), 151–179.
8. Ralph G. Carter and James M. Scott, *Choosing to Lead: Understanding Congressional Foreign Policy Entrepreneurs* (Durham, NC: Duke University Press, 2009).
9. William G. Howell and Jon C. Pevehouse, *While Dangers Gather: Congressional Checks on Presidential War Powers* (Princeton, NJ: Princeton University Press, 2007).
10. Ralph G. Carter, "Congressional Foreign Policy Behavior: Persistent Patterns of the Postwar Period," *Presidential Studies Quarterly* 16 (1986), 329–359.
11. Carter and Scott, *Choosing to Lead.*
12. Mike Dorning, "U.S. Will Keep Paying for Iraq War for Years," *Bloomberg News*, January 7, 2012; available online at http://www.star-telegram.com/2012/01/07/3642512/us-will-be-paying-for-iraq-war.html.
13. "Biography: Farah Anwar Pandith," State Department website; available online at http://www.state.gov/r/pa/ei/biog/125492.htm.

INDEX